Queen Mary's Hospital Carshalton

An Iron Age and early Romano-British Settlement

Andrew B. Powell

Queen Mary's Hospital Carshalton

An Iron Age and early Romano-British Settlement

Andrew B. Powell

with contributions by
Phil Andrews, Alistair J. Barclay, Catherine Barnett, Nicholas Cooke
Kirsten Egging Dinwiddy, A. P. Fitzpatrick, Phil Harding, L. Higbee
Lorraine Mepham, Rachael Seager Smith and Sarah F. Wyles

Illustrations by
Will Foster and S. E. James

Wessex Archaeology Occasional Paper
2017

Published 2017 by Wessex Archaeology Ltd
Portway House, Old Sarum Park, Salisbury, SP4 6EB
www.wessexarch.co.uk

British Library Cataloguing in Publication Data
A catalogue record for this book is available from the British Library

ISBN 978-1-874350-94-1

Designed and typeset by Kenneth Lymer
Cover design by Will Foster
Copy-edited by Philippa Bradley
Printed by Lightning Source UK

Front cover
Horse burial in Iron Age pit 3231, and decorated spearhead/ensign from Iron Age pit 3998

Back cover
Top to bottom: site during excavation; dog burial in Romano-British pit 2047; *pars pro toto* deposit in Iron Age pit 3898

Wessex Archaeology Ltd is a company limited by guarantee registered in England, company number 1712772. It is also a Charity registered in England and Wales number 287786, and in Scotland, Scottish Charity number SC042630. Our registered office is at Portway House, Old Sarum Park, Salisbury, Wiltshire, SP4 6EB.

Contents

List of Figures

List of Plates

List of Tables

Acknowledgements

This project was commissioned by CgMs Consulting Ltd, and Wessex Archaeology would like to thank Duncan Hawkins for his assistance throughout. Thanks are also due to John Brown, Jane Sidell and Mark Stevenson of the Greater London Archaeological Advisory Service (GLAAS) who monitored the work on behalf of the Local Planning Authority. Alex Bayliss and Frances Healy provided useful advice and guidance on the radiocarbon dating programme. Nick Truckle provided support and advice throughout the various stages of the project.

The excavations were managed by Sue Farr, and directed by Mike Dinwiddy (2008) and Chloe Hunnisett (2010). The post-excavation assessments were undertaken by Andrew Powell and Chloe Hunnisett, and the post-excavation assessment and analysis was managed by Sue Farr. Alistair Barclay managed the final stages of analysis and the production of the report was coordinated by Philippa Bradley. The project archive will be deposited with the London Archaeological Archive and Research Centre (LAARC) under the Museum of London site code OHH 08.

Abstract

In 2008–10 a programme of archaeological works was undertaken on land formerly occupied by Queen Mary's Hospital, Carshalton, in the London Borough of Sutton, in advance of the site's redevelopment. The site, which lies on the north-facing dip slope of the North Downs overlooking the valley of the River Wandle, lay immediately outside a substantial Late Bronze Age ringwork, which is a Scheduled Monument (LO 163).

The excavations found very little evidence for Late Bronze Age activity, but by the Early/Middle Iron Age an open settlement had been established, represented on the site by a single roundhouse with an adjacent square post-built granary-type structure, and a number of relatively shallow pits, the deepest possibly for storage but others containing large quantities of burnt flint. There was a single neonate burial dating to this period. By the end of the Middle Iron Age part of the settlement area had been bounded by small enclosure ditches, the larger D-shaped enclosure, with a west-facing entrance, to the west, and a smaller sub-square enclosure to the east, and with a possible trackway running along their northern sides.

The eastern enclosure was subsequently twice enlarged, during the Late Iron Age and early Romano-British period, while the western enclosure was also modified, but their overall arrangement remained largely the same during these later periods. No later structures were identified however, and apart from a small number of further neonate burials, almost all the features were pits. These were of varying size and shape, but many of them were of classic storage pit form, a few of them being bell-shaped.

The ditches and pits produced artefactual and environmental evidence of activities relating to farming, settlement, craft/industry, and ritual/religion. The mixed farming economy involved the cultivation of wheat and barley on the surrounding Chalk downland, and the keeping of livestock (sheep, cattle, pig and goat). Dog, cat, horse and domestic fowl were also represented in the bone assemblage, along with a few wild species (deer, fox, hare and corvids – raven and crow/rook). On-site craft/industrial activities included the manufacture of yarns and probably also textiles, and, by the early Romano-British period, metalworking.

The pits of all periods contained very variable deposits, although a relatively common feature in the Late Iron Age and early Romano-British period was the presence of groups of articulated animal bone, comprising partial or complete animals, sometimes in large numbers. A single fill of one early Romano-British pit contained the butchered partial carcasses of 25–30 animals, predominantly sheep/goat but also including two dogs, a perinatal horse, two domestic fowl and a raven. Also of note were a number of dog burials which showed particular care in the arrangements in the animals, presumably for symbolic reasons, occasionally occurring with pots. In addition, one small subrectangular (almost grave-shaped) Late Iron Age pit contained a careful selection of broken or incomplete objects, including large parts of a single pottery vessel, a decorated iron spearhead, a nave hoop (from a wheel axle), and lumps of tar with impressions of twisted vegetable fibres.

While the pits also contained dumps of domestic waste and soil, it is likely that many of these below-ground contexts, used initially for the storage of grain, and therefore central to the community's survival and prosperity, had powerful symbolic associations, relating to ideas of life and death, decay, regeneration and fertility, which may have been transferrable to the animal remains. It seems likely that many of the acts of deposition involved elements of ritualised and religious sacrifice designed to appease and show gratitude to the local deities.

Chapter 1
Introduction

In 2010, an Iron Age to early Romano-British settlement, characterised by a dense cluster of pits and a multi-phased arrangement of enclosure ditches, was excavated on land formerly occupied by Queen Mary's Hospital (latterly known as Orchard Hill), Carshalton, in the London Borough of Sutton (Fig. 1.1), following a smaller excavation in 2008. The combined excavation site, covering 0.6 hectares centred on NGR 527820 162480, lay 50 m north-west of one of the largest and best-known Late Bronze Age ringworks in south-east England, which is a Scheduled Monument (LO 163) (Adkins and Needham 1985) (Fig. 1.2). The excavation was undertaken ahead of the redevelopment of the former hospital site.

Geology and Topography

The site lies on the dip slope of the North Downs overlooking the broad valley of the River Wandle to the north, and slopes down from 99 m OD at the south-east to 94 m OD at the north-west. The underlying geology is a localised cap of Thanet Formation Sand, overlying Upper Chalk (Lewes Nodular Chalk Formation, Seaford Chalk Formation and Newhaven Chalk Formation) (British Geological Survey online viewer).

The excavation area lay within the footprint of the demolished former hospital buildings. Prior to their construction at the start of the 20th century, the ground surface had been landscaped and terraced, and this, combined with the building foundations, had impacted significantly on the archaeological remains (Fig. 2.1). A colluvial layer, consisting of mid-brown silty sand with rounded pebbles, which overlay the natural sand in the southern part of the excavation, appeared to have been previously removed in the northern part.

Archaeological Background

A range of archaeological sites are known on the dip slope of the Chalk downs on which the site is located and the surrounding area, the most prominent of which is the Late Bronze Age ringwork to the immediate south-east of the site. It was first investigated in 1903–4 following the salvaging of finds during the construction of the hospital (Robarts 1905; 1909; 1910), then further excavated in 1937 and 1939 under the auspices of the Surrey Archaeological Society (Lowther 1944–5). During these works a number of sections were excavated across its V-shaped ditch, which was up to 2.1 m deep and 3.6 m wide, and defined an area 150 m in diameter with a possible entrance at the south-west. No traces of a bank survived, but large flints and chalk blocks at one level within the ditch were interpreted as a collapsed bank revetment. Two hearths, presumed to be contemporary with the enclosure, were recorded in its interior, while outside it up to eight burials were recorded to the south, and one or two possible unurned cremation burials to the north.

These excavations produced a large assemblage of predominantly Late Bronze Age finds, mainly from the ditch. This material, which has since been re-assessed (Adkins and Needham 1985), included pottery, comprising a range of post-Deverel-Rimbury plain-ware jars and bowls, and fired clay objects such as perforated clay slabs, loomweights and spindlewhorls. Among the stone objects were saddle querns, whetstones and grinding stones, as well as an amber bead. There was evidence of metalworking in the form of a crucible fragment, a lump of copper and a bronze ingot fragment; a number of other bronze objects were found, including a ring with a suspension loop.

Other sites in Carshalton and the surrounding area include Westcroft Road, 2.4 km to the ENE of the site, where there was evidence for Late Bronze Age/Early Iron Age ritual deposition in pits and a ditch (Proctor 2002), an Iron Age and early Romano-British farmstead 1.4 km to the north at the War Memorial Hospital site (Killock 2012), and a Late Iron Age/early Romano-British site 4 km to the west at Reigate Road, Ewell (Cotton 2001). A possible Roman villa has been identified from wall and foundation trenches 2 km north of the site at West Street, Carshalton, close to the springline north of the downs; the finds suggest that it had been occupied in the 1st and 2nd centuries AD, possibly having developed from an Iron Age farmstead (GLAAS

Figure 1.1 Location of the site, the Roman road network, and other sites mentioned in the text

2002, 5–6; Bird 2004, 106). The Roman villa at Beddington was also established on a site occupied during the Bronze Age and Iron Age (Adkins and Adkins 1983; Howell 2005).

Previous Archaeological Works

There have been a number of phases of archaeological works relating to the redevelopment of the Queen Mary's Hospital site (Fig. 1.2). An evaluation in 1988 (QMH 88) in the eastern part of the site revealed two intercutting prehistoric ditches aligned north–south with large pits at their northern ends, and a large Iron Age pit (Tucker 1988). A watching brief to the west (QMH 90) revealed no archaeological deposits. An excavation south of the Late Bronze Age enclosure in 1993 (OHC 93) revealed a large possible ditch, overlain by hillwash, containing a substantial quantity of Late Bronze Age pottery, perforated clay slabs, burnt flint and worked flint (Bruce and Giorgi 1994). An evaluation in 1995 (QMA 95, not shown on Fig. 1.2) identified three further areas of archaeological potential, the area with the largest concentration of features and artefacts (Late Bronze Age pottery, a loomweight and worked flints) lying immediately north of the enclosure (MoLAS 1995).

In 1999, further evaluation and excavation (QPL 99) was undertaken both inside and to the north of the enclosure. The excavation to the north exposed a

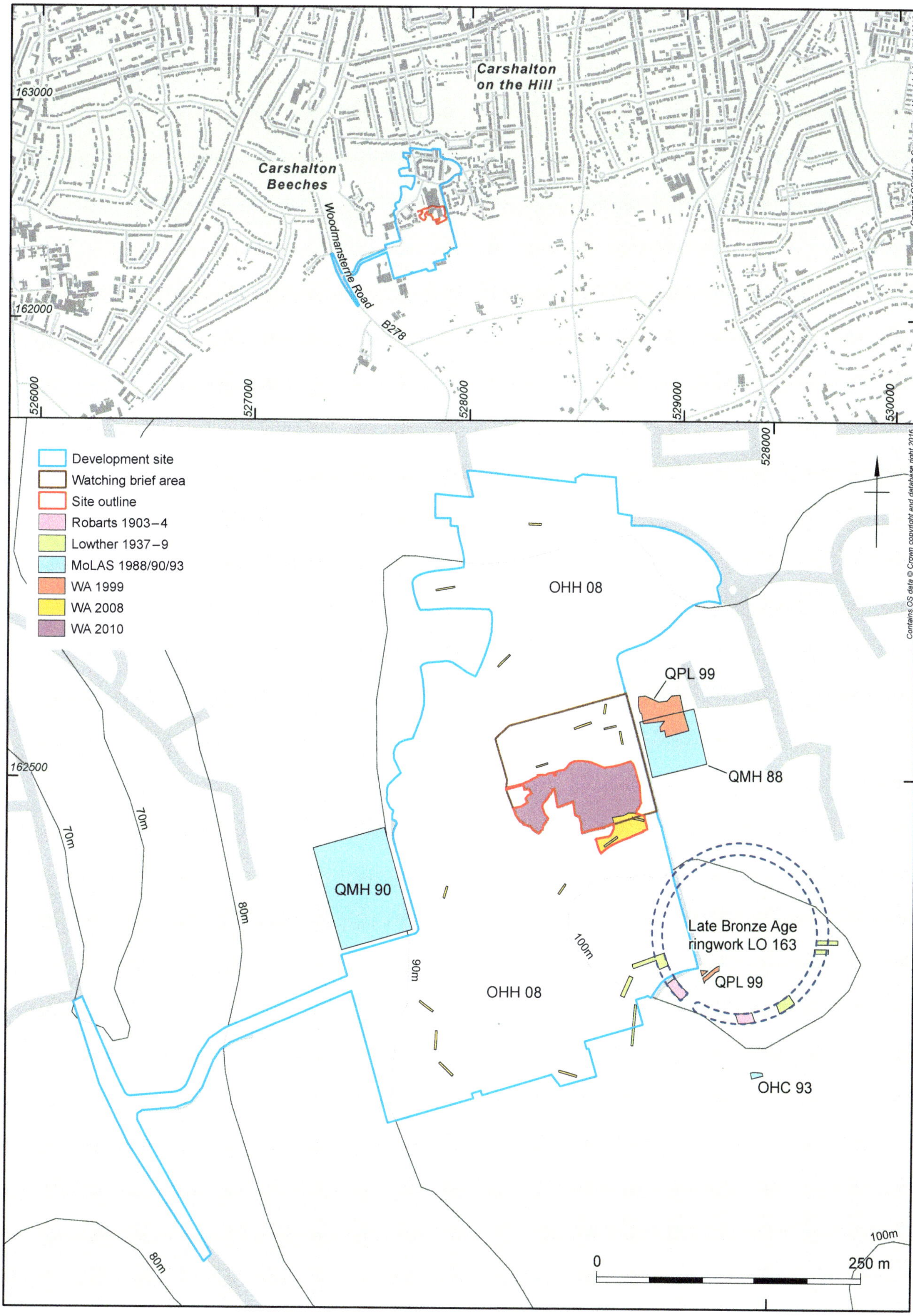

Figure 1.2 Plan showing the development area and excavations around the site

pit containing Late Bronze Age pottery and a perforated fired clay slab, and two large chalk quarries possibly associated with the enclosure, but producing Late Iron Age, Romano-British, Saxon and medieval sherds from their upper fills (Groves and Lovell 2002). Another Late Bronze Age pit was recorded inside the enclosure.

Further evaluation in 2008 (OHH 08) revealed a number of early Romano-British ditches, and a pit containing the remains of a horse's head (Wessex Archaeology 2008); the area around these features was the object of the 2008 excavation (Wessex Archaeology 2009). Following these works an archaeological watching brief was maintained during groundworks over an area of 1.3 hectares, as well as along a pipe trench to the east of the site. This led to the identification of substantial and well-preserved features in the area to the immediate north-west of the 2008 excavation which were then subject to full excavation in 2010 (Wessex Archaeology 2011).

Chapter 2
The Excavation

Phasing

The excavation lay 50–150 m north-west of the previously investigated Late Bronze Age enclosure, but the pottery shows that the excavation site was occupied from the Early Iron Age (800–400 BC) through to the early Romano-British period (AD 43–123/130), possibly without any substantial break. As a result, many features contained sherds of mixed date, reflecting both high levels of residuality and, in some cases, the presence of intrusive material. A significant number of features contained too few sherds to provide reliable dating, and many others contained no datable finds. Some features, however, are well dated, and a number of them have also been subject to radiocarbon dating.

While some of the stratigraphic relationships between the ditches were recorded, others either could not be clearly established due to similarities in their fills, or because they had been destroyed by later disturbance. Nonetheless, their overall arrangement indicates the creation, maintenance and modification of a small complex of adjacent, and in some cases connected enclosures (Fig. 2.1).

Three phases of enclosures were identified (see Figs 2.3, 2.5 and 2.8). The first phase enclosures (Enclosure 1 and 2a) appear to have been constructed around 100 BC, around the end of the Middle Iron Age. At some point during the Late Iron Age, possibly around the turn of the 1st centuries BC and AD, the layout of the enclosures was changed, although their overall form was partly replicated (Enclosures 2b, 3 and 4). A subsequent change, involving less substantial modifications, is dated to the early Romano-British period (Enclosures 2c, 5 and 6). Although elements of the phasing must be considered tentative (with a small number of ditches unaccounted for by this scheme), these are not

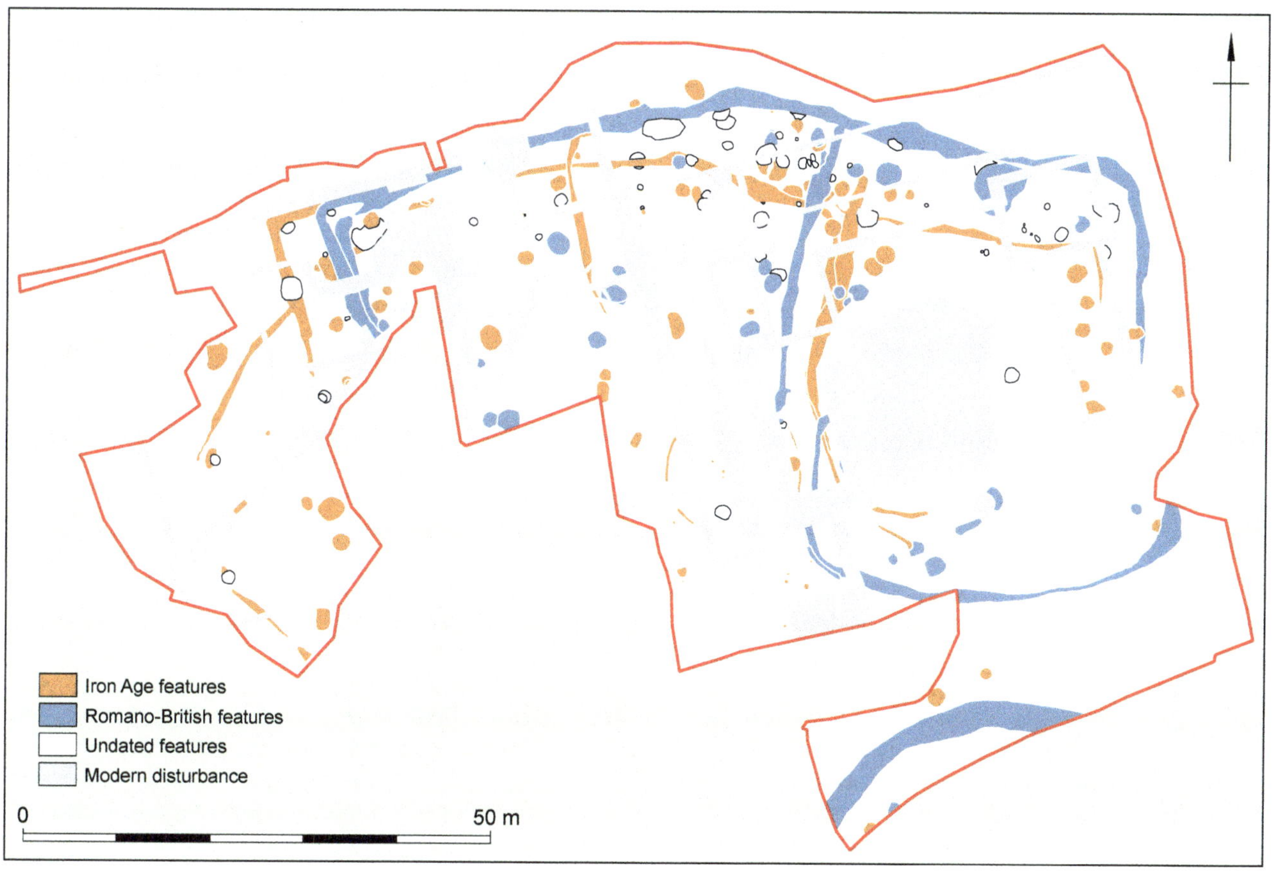

Figure 2.1 The 2008/2010 excavation area, showing all features by period

considered to significantly alter the wider interpretation of the site.

While some of the pottery can be assigned to specific periods (ie, Early, Middle and Late Iron Age and early Romano-British) much of it was insufficiently diagnostic to be assigned to any one period with confidence, or was of forms and fabrics which extend across these periods. As a result, a significant proportion of it is dated as Early/Middle Iron Age, Middle/Late Iron Age or Late Iron Age/early Romano-British. In order to prevent the unnecessary division of features into multiple sub-phases, three broad periods have been employed in this report: Early/Middle Iron Age (*c.* 7th–2nd centuries BC), Late Iron Age (*c.* 1st century BC–AD 43) including also features dated as Iron Age and Middle/Late Iron Age, and early Romano-British (*c.* AD 43–120/130) including features dated as Late Iron Age/early Romano-British.

Presentation of Radiocarbon Results

The radiocarbon measurements have been calculated using the calibration curve of Reimer *et al.* (2013) and the computer program OxCal (v4.2.3; Bronk Ramsey and Lee 2013) and cited in the text at 95% confidence and quoted in the form recommended by Mook (1986), with the end points rounded outwards to 10 years.

A Bayesian approach has been adopted (see Barclay, Chapter 4) for the interpretation of the chronology from this site (Bayliss *et al.* 2007). The ranges quoted in *italics* are posterior density estimates derived from mathematical modelling of given archaeological problems. The ranges in plain type have been calculated according to the maximum intercept method (Stuiver and Reimer 1986). All other ranges are derived from the probability method (Stuiver and Reimer 1993).

Features

The features excavated on the site consisted mainly of pits and enclosure ditches. Structures were rare, comprising one roundhouse, defined by a circular drip-gully and a small number of probably associated postholes, and a small square post-built 'granary-type' structure. No clear hearths, ovens, furnaces or kilns were identified (apart possibly from feature 3317, see below), but there was much evidence of burning in a number of features. Some pits contained pieces of perforated fired clay, of a form often interpreted as loomweight fragments but which could, alternatively, represent some form of oven/kiln furniture; there was also a concentration of iron-working slag in one early Romano-British pit.

Pits

Approximately 100 pits, of all phases, were recorded on the site, in most cases being widely dispersed, their distribution showing little relationship to the layouts of contemporary structures or enclosures. Although survival was affected by the varying levels of truncation and construction across the site, their distribution appears largely random, although there is some evidence of clustering in some periods.

Approximately a quarter of the pits contained either no pottery (or other datable finds) or pottery in too small quantities to provide reliable dating. Others contained generally small quantities of burnt flint, worked flint, animal bone, fired clay and stone, which could be of either prehistoric or Romano-British date. As some of these pre-date Iron Age features, while others postdate Romano-British features, it is likely that a proportion of pits from each period is undated. Other features contained no finds at all.

The pits were of widely varying form and size, and therefore probable function. Most were roughly circular, but a few were noticeably subrectangular in shape. Some of the deeper pits, with steep to vertical sides and largely flat bases, are of a form suited for grain storage. Some of these appear to have been cylindrical (even if later eroded at the top), while a few narrowed towards the top resulting in variants of the bell-shaped pit, which would have been most easily and effectively sealable for storage purposes. A number of shallower, flat-based, vertical-sided pits may have been heavily truncated versions of such storage pits, or they may have had a completely different function; the latter is suggested in some cases by the proximity of both deep and shallow pits.

A number of pits, with less regular profiles, and often concave bases, are of uncertain function. Some may have been quarry pits, for the extraction of either sand/clay or the underlying chalk, for various uses within the settlement, while others may have been dug specifically for deposition purposes, either for the dumping of settlement waste, or for the more formal acts of symbolic and ritual deposition.

While the grain storage pits may be viewed as practical and functional features, their importance to the survival and prosperity of the community may have imbued them with a symbolic significance that required some ritual acknowledgement during the act of placing foodstuffs into storage. While any such acts appear to be archaeologically invisible, a reflection of them may be evident in the subsequent uses to which the pits were put, once the grain had been removed from storage.

The pits had widely variable fill sequences, indicating different modes of deposition. Some fills were the result of natural erosion and silting processes, while others represent deliberate dumps of settlement waste (pottery, fired clay, worked flint, burnt flint and animal bone), or simply backfilling. In many cases, however, there appear also to have been acts of deliberate and formalised deposition with the pits, particularly of animal remains, but also of other cultural materials.

The pits are summarised in Appendix 1, and a selection from each period is described in detail below. These are not a representative sample, but have been chosen to illustrate some of the more distinctive features, and more notable deposits.

Ditches and Gullies

The many ditches and gullies recorded were of varying scale, due in part to the different levels of truncation across the site (principally during the construction of the hospital). However, there was a clear distinction between the generally larger ditches, which defined the various enclosures, and an arrangement of shallower, parallel gullies, running approximately east–west in the north-eastern part of the site; these may reflect the line of a trackway (see below).

Other Features

A number of features (initially recorded as 'pits') cannot be readily categorised, but are nonetheless of potential interest.

Feature 3317

An undated subcircular feature (3317), recorded cutting one the parallel 'trackway' gullies in the north-east corner of the site (Fig. 2.3), may have been some form of oven or dryer. It was 0.7 m wide and less than 0.2 m deep, and had a number of stakeholes in its base, possibly indicating the presence of its superstructure. There was evidence of burning on its south-east side, and its single charcoal-rich fill contained 3.3 kg of burnt flint and 2.5 kg of fired clay (including from one or more perforated object), along with small quantities of worked flint, animal bone and stone, as well as a significant quantity of charred plant remains (hulled wheat and barley grain frags, and chaff) (Wessex Archaeology 2011, 37).

Feature 3676

At 3.7 m deep, this undated 'shaft' was the deepest feature on the site, lying close to its north-east corner (Figs 2.2 and 2.3). Its upper 1.7 m was largely truncated by a very wide early Romano-British pit (3683, see below); their stratigraphic relationship was partly obscured by a modern concrete footing, but the shaft appears to have been up to 2.5 m wide, with vertical sides and a flat base. Due to its depth, it could only be excavated by machine, which may account for the fact that no finds were recorded from its fills; this also hampered the detailed recording of its fills, although these appeared to consist predominantly of naturally derived deposits. The feature was partly cut through a vertical seam of natural sand that had permeated into a wide crack in the underlying chalk, and the erosion of this sand may have hastened the silting process.

It is possible that this shaft was dug as a well, although none of the fills showed signs of having been waterlogged (and the water table was never reached during excavation). Alternatively, it may have had some ritual function, although such an interpretation must remain a matter of speculation in the absence of any evidence of deliberate deposition or other activity. Whether its location had a bearing on the digging of the later pit, which at over 5 m wide was the widest feature on the site, is also unclear.

Early/Middle Iron Age

The earliest phase of the enclosure complex appears to date to the end of Middle Iron Age, ie, *c.* 100 BC (see below), but a significant number of features are dated to the Early and Middle Iron Age, strongly suggesting a period of pre-enclosure settlement (Fig. 2.3). The only two structures recorded on the site, a roundhouse (4246) and an adjacent small sub-square post-built structure (4247) may belong to this phase, as may a few lengths of undated ditch (eg, 3942, 4010 and 4234) which appear to pre-date the identifiable enclosures.

Roundhouse 4246

The roundhouse, which had an internal diameter of 14 m, was represented by three lengths of truncated gully, averaging 0.1 m deep and 0.3 m wide. There were 11 m wide gaps (due largely to modern disturbance) at the north and the south, and a narrower (3 m wide) gap, apparently flanked by gully terminals, at the west, suggesting the probable position of an entrance.

Although much of the interior had been disturbed, there was a small group of three postholes, all of similar size, near its centre. These are likely to be associated with the roundhouse as there were relatively few other postholes recorded across the rest

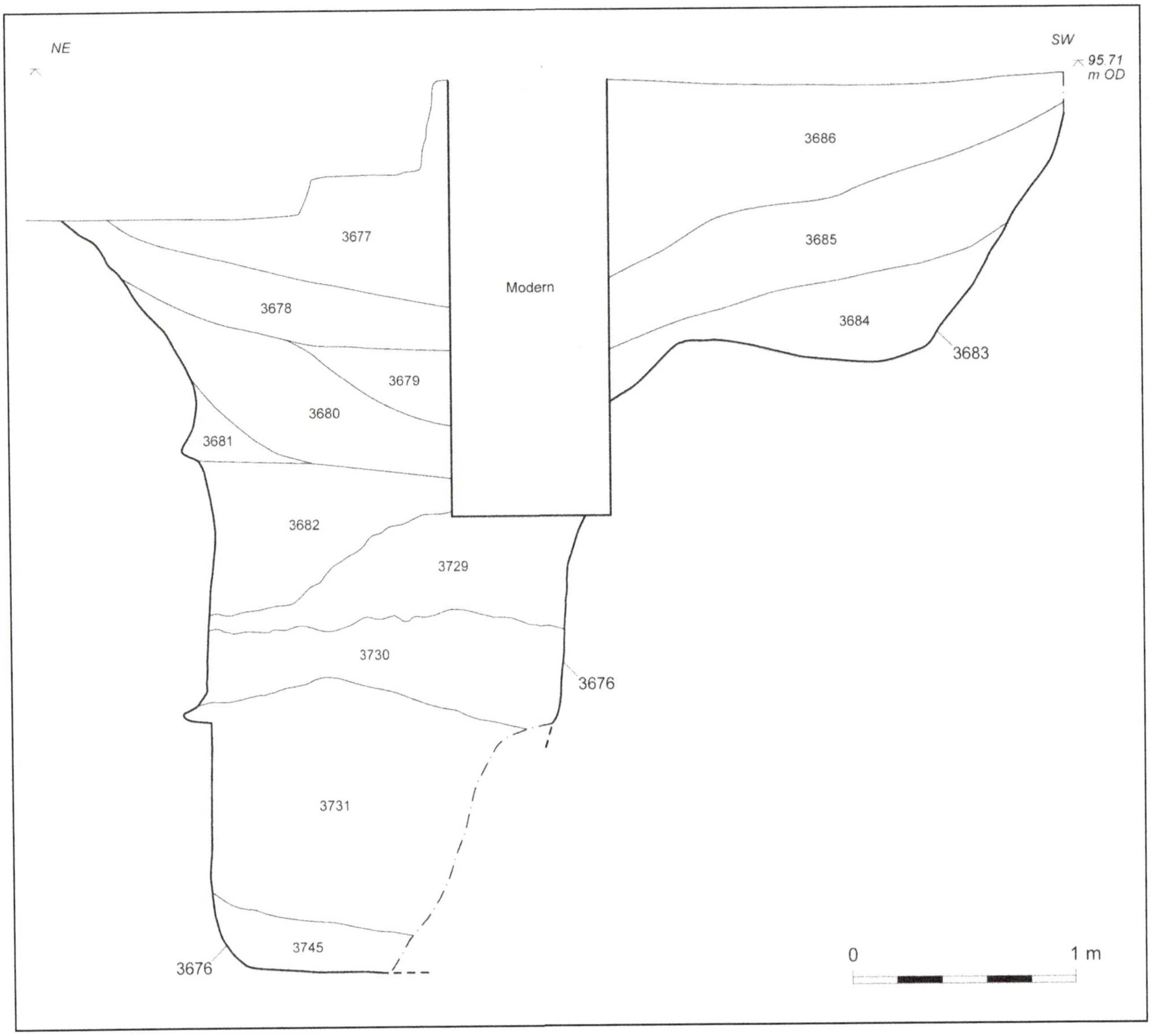

Figure 2.2 West-facing section of shaft 3676 and feature 3683

Plate 2.1 Grave 3052 in ditch 3050, viewed from the north

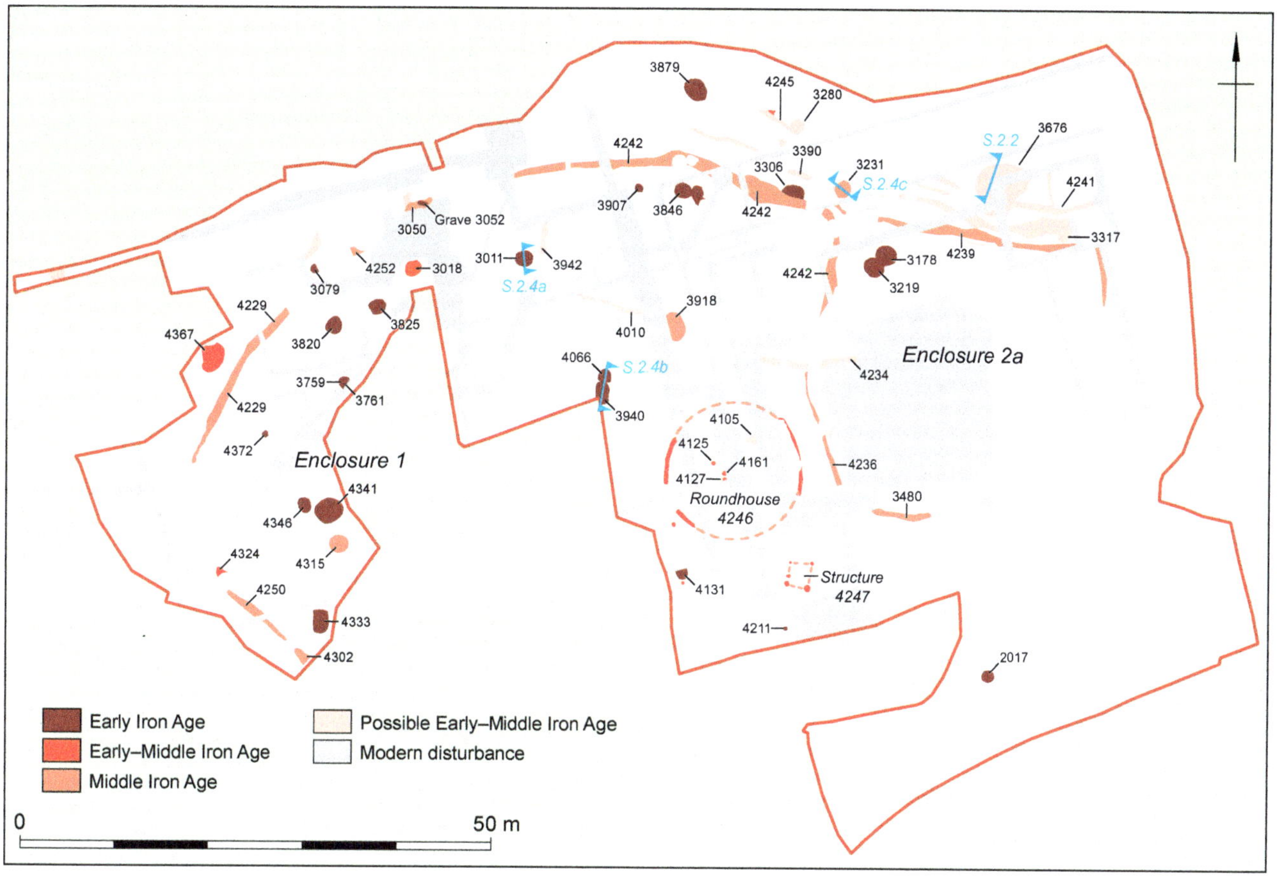

Figure 2.3 Features of the Early/Middle Iron Age phase

of the site. Two of them (4125 and 4127) contained single sherds of Early/Middle Iron Age pottery, whilst the third (4161) contained three Middle Iron Age sherds. Three sherds of Iron Age pottery (one of them Middle/Late Iron Age) were recovered from the roundhouse gully, along with fragments of animal bone and burnt flint. Four pits within the interior, three of them cutting the inner edge of the gully at the east, appear to be later features (Fig. 2.1); one other feature of uncertain character (4105) contained a single Early/Middle Iron Age sherd.

Square Structure 4247

Just outside the roundhouse to the SSE, there was a small sub-square (slightly trapezoidal) arrangement of five truncated postholes, the largest being 0.5 m in diameter. This structure measured up to 2.9 m by 3.2 m, its longer axis aligned NNE–SSW; the fifth posthole lay near the centre of its western side. It was comparable in size and form to many four-post structures, often interpreted as granaries, found on late prehistoric sites. Three sherds of Iron Age pottery were recovered from the posthole fills.

Grave 3052

In the north-west of the site, a small grave (3052) containing the inhumation of a foetus/neonate (3057) was recorded in the base of a short linear feature (3050), possibly part of the Enclosure 1 ditch (Pl. 2.1). It was accompanied by part of an Early Iron Age pottery vessel (ON 54; Fig. 3.1, 1) (19 sherds, 203 g). Whether the grave was cut into the ditch fill (3051), or was cut by the ditch, was unclear due to the heavy disturbance in this area, although the latter is suggested the recovery of a further six Early Iron Age sherds (30 g), two of them in the same fabric as ON 54, from the ditch fill along with a small number of redeposited foetus/neonate bones. The grave also contained an iron pyrites nodule (ON 55), and small quantities of possibly residual animal bone, worked flint, burnt flint and fired clay.

Pits and Postholes

Few postholes were recorded on the site, and most of them were undated, although one (4211) south of the square structure contained Early Iron Age pottery.

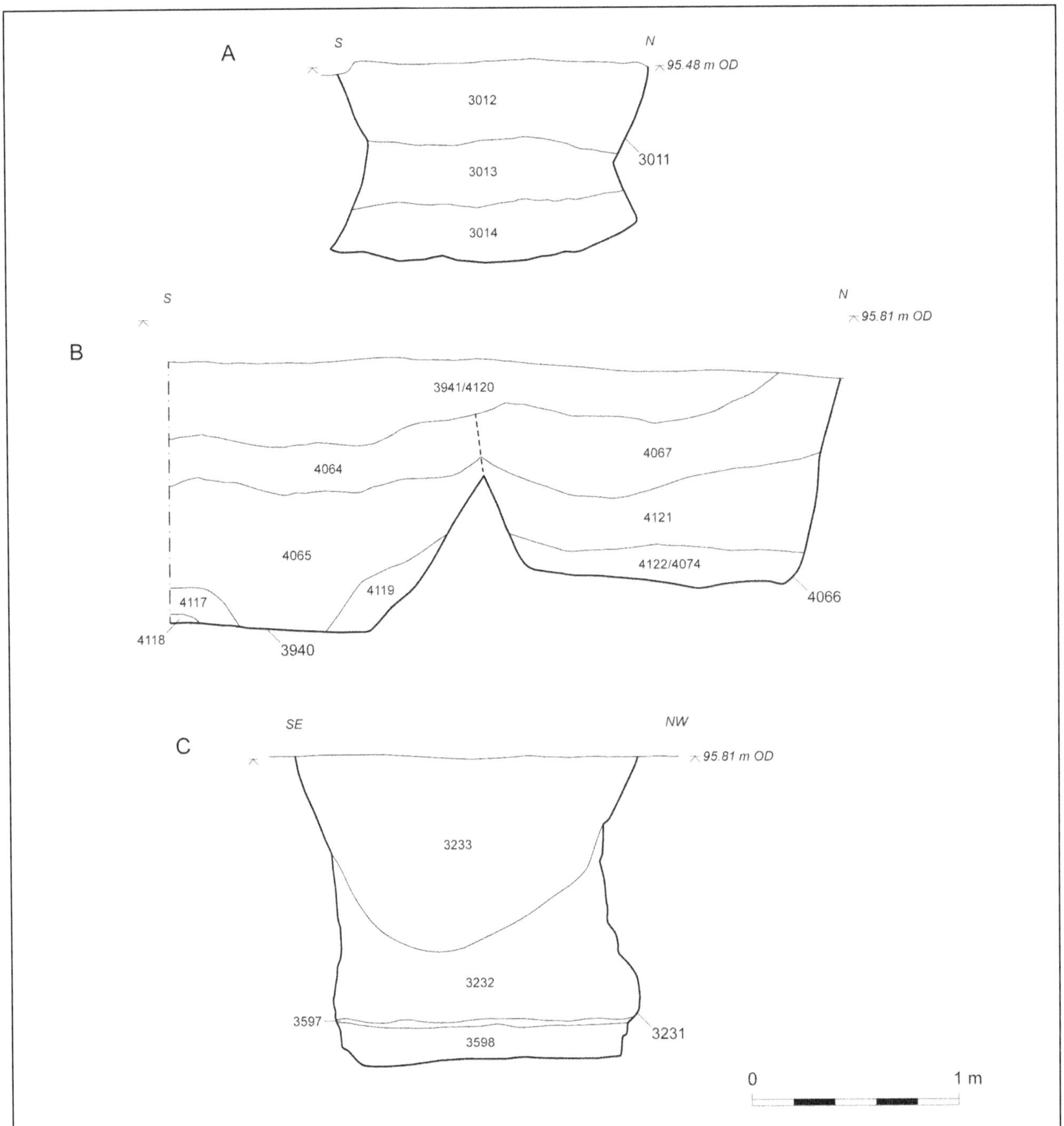

Figure 2.4 Sections of Early Iron Age pits 3011, 3940 and 4066, and Middle Iron Age pit 3231

Given the levels of truncation on the site it is likely many other postholes have not survived.

Approximately 25 pits can be assigned to the Early/Middle Iron Age phase (Fig. 2.3). Most were roughly circular, the largest (4341) being 2.6–3 m wide, but a few (eg, 3940, 4333) were noticeably subrectangular in shape. Of the possible storage pits, the deepest Early Iron Age example (3178) was 2.2 m in diameter and 1.3 m deep; the deepest Middle Iron Age pit (4315) was 2 m wide and 1.6 m deep; other possible storage pits survived to as little as 0.6 m deep.

Most of these pits contained varying quantities of finds suggestive of domestic waste (pottery, fired clay, worked flint, burnt flint and animal bone) but whether any of them had been dug specifically for the purposes of waste disposal cannot be ascertained. There was generally little evidence for any formality in the deposition of this waste material.

Pit 3011

While some Early/Middle Iron Age pits had slightly undercut sides, this was the only one with a profile approaching a clear bell-shape (Fig. 2.4); it was 1 m deep, narrowing from 1.5 m wide at the top (where it may have been eroded) to 1.2 m at approximately mid-depth, then widening to 1.5 m at the base. It contained three fills, the lower two of which had level upper surfaces, possibly indicating that these deposits had been levelled as the pit was being filled. This is a feature noted in a number of the later pits, and in some cases associated with formal deposits (see below).

Pit 3178

This, the deepest Early Iron Age storage pit, was 2.2 m in diameter and 1.3 m deep. Its basal fill (3181), up to 0.15 m thick, contained 14 sherds (145 g) of Early Iron Age pottery. This was overlain by a sequence of largely sterile dumped layers (containing only a piece of fired clay) together filling the lower third of the pit, then a substantial backfill deposit (3180) containing a further 21 sherds (235 g). Both of the layers containing pottery also produced small quantities of animal bone, worked flint and burnt flint, but in neither case was there any evidence of formal deposition, this material being consistent with unstructured dumps of domestic waste.

Pit 3846

The partial, semi-articulated remains of a neonatal lamb (ABG 113), along with a small number of disarticulated horse bones, were found on the base of this Early Iron Age pit, located towards the northern limit of the excavation. It is the earliest example on the site of what appears to have been a deliberately placed deposit. The pit, which was 1.6–1.8 m wide and 0.7 m deep with a slightly concave base and steep–vertical sides, is of uncertain function, although it could potentially have been a truncated storage pit.

Pits 3940 and 4066

This pair of pits, 8 m north-west of the roundhouse, just intercut although their stratigraphic relationship could not be clearly discerned (Fig. 2.4). The southern, subrectangular pit (3940), measuring 2.4 m by 1.4 m, was deeper (1.3) than subcircular pit 4066 (0.9 m), but both had steep sides and flat bases, and similar fill sequences, with primary fills overlain by two possible backfill deposits, suggesting that they may have been broadly contemporary.

Pit 3940 contained Early Iron Age pottery, fired clay and animal bone, while the primary fill (4074) of pit 4066 contained an iron La Tène 1 brooch dated *c.* 450–375 BC (ON 134; Fig. 3.5, 1). The brooch was recovered from above the base (in layer 4074) and does not appear to have been deliberately placed (a small Late Iron Age sherd recorded from the same layer was either intrusive or wrongly assigned to this context). Both pits were sealed by a single thick, charcoal-rich deposit (3941/4120), up to 0.4 m thick, containing much burnt flint (5 kg) and fired clay (almost 1 kg), as well as further Early Iron Age pottery and animal bone.

Plate 2.2 Horse skeleton (ABG 70) in Middle Iron Age pit 3231, viewed from the north

Pit 4333

This pit (like pits 3940 and 4066) was subrectangular, and of similar dimensions (2.5 m by 1.6 m). Although only 0.4 m deep, its profile (with vertical sides and a slightly concave base) suggests it had been truncated. It may have had a similar (albeit unknown) function to pit 3940, and it too contained a significant quantity (4.6 kg) of burnt flint, in addition to some pottery, fired clay and animal bone.

Pit 3231

This pit, which cut an earlier 'trackway' gully, contained clear evidence for formalised deposition, perhaps reflecting a relatively late date in the Middle Iron Age. It was possibly cylindrical in form, although slightly undercut at the base (but far from bell-shaped) and eroded at the top; it was 1.3 m wide at the midpoint and 1.4 m deep (Fig. 2.4). The 0.2 m thick basal layer (3598) contained Middle Iron Age pottery, burnt flint and animal bone, possibly domestic waste but including articulated cattle vertebrae (ABG 80), and the partial remains of an adult sheep (right side only; ABG 244). This was overlain by a thin layer of sterile soil (3597), both these layers appearing to have levelled surfaces. Above them had been laid the partial remains of a juvenile pig (ABG 71) and a neonatal pig (ABG 232) followed by an adult (pony-sized) horse, complete apart from its lower front legs which had been removed and the animal skinned (ABG 70) (Pl. 2.2). These were covered by a thick deposit of soil (3232) containing further pottery (including much of a shell-tempered, proto-bead rim jar of 2nd-century BC date), worked flint and burnt flint. The upper part of

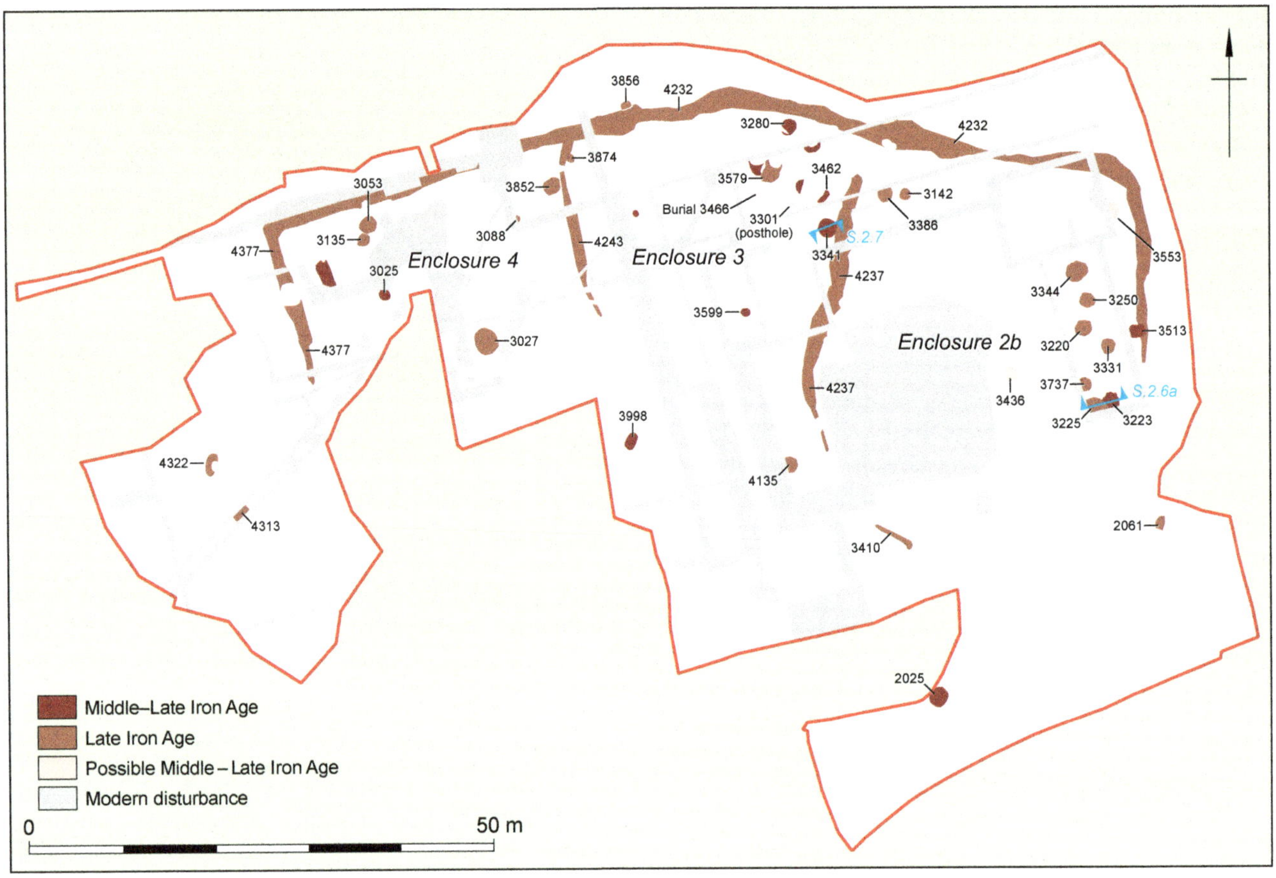

Figure 2.5 Features of the Late Iron Age phase

the pit may have silted up naturally (layer 3233) as the bone deposit decomposed and compacted.

A radiocarbon date of *180–50 cal BC (SUERC-38154, 2115±35 BP at 95% probability)* was obtained on the sheep bones (ABG 244) in the pit's basal layer, which is consistent with Middle Iron Age pottery from this layer. A similar date of *150 cal BC–10 cal AD (SUERC-38142, 2100±35 BP at 95% probability)*, was obtained from the partial horse skeleton (ABG 70) at the base of layer 3232, which also contained predominantly Middle Iron Age pottery, albeit with a few sherds dated Middle/Late Iron Age. While it is possible, given the apparent levelling of the underlying layers, that these latter deposits were made at a later date, the two radiocarbon measurements are statistically consistent, indicating that they belong to the same phase of activity (see Barclay, Chapter 4). From modelling the radiocarbon dates the pit was dug at some point during *135–60 cal BC (at 68% probability modelled as First Dig pit 3231 or 175–50 cal BC at 95% probability)*.

Enclosures 1 and 2a

The first phase of enclosure construction saw the laying out of Enclosures 1 and 2a (Fig. 2.3). To the west, ditches 4250 and 4302 formed part of the south-western side of Enclosure 1, while its northern side was defined by a gently curving ditch (4229), the line of which is continued to the north-east (after a 27 m area of disturbance and other features) by ditch 4242; two short lengths of ditch (4252 and 3050) in this gap may belong to this phase. The eastern section of ditch 4242 turned sharply to the south. These lengths of ditch were up to 0.8 m deep (although considerably less where heavily truncated).

Ditch 4242 cut an Early/Middle Iron Age pit (3306) (and another that was undated) (Fig. 2.3). These early phase enclosure ditches were also cut by one Middle/Late Iron Age pit (3341) and by Late Iron Age ditch 4237 (Fig. 2.5), as well as by early Romano-British ditches 4233 and (possibly) 4230 (Fig. 2.8); other stratigraphic relationships were not established.

The small quantity of pottery recovered from these ditches ranged from Early to Late Iron Age, but the material's contexts suggest a construction date for at least Enclosure 1 of towards the end of the Middle Iron Age, around the end of the 2nd century BC, the enclosure probably continuing in use into the Late Iron Age. This is consistent with a radiocarbon date from a horse bone, from the single fill (3302) in a section of ditch 4242 (cut 3303), of *170–60 cal BC*

(SUERC-38149, 2060±35 BP at 95% probability). A later date, of *100 cal BC–cal AD 80 (SUERC-38151, 2005±35 BP at 95% probability)*, was obtained from a pig bone from the same ditch, but this came from the upper (3490) of three fills (in cut 3493), and therefore when the ditch had largely silted up.

The eastern boundary of Enclosure 1 (formed to the north-west by ditch 4242) appears to have curved towards the east (as ditches 4236 and 3480) forming the western side of Enclosure 2a. The northern side of Enclosure 2a was formed by ditch 4239, which continued eastwards the line of the northern side of Enclosure 1, before itself turning south; ditch 4239, which was up to 0.35 m deep, did not cut any earlier features, but was cut by an undated pit.

This arrangement of ditches suggests that Enclosure 1 was approximately D-shaped, measuring 67 m east–west by at least 53 m north–south, while Enclosure 2a (for which no trace of its south-eastern side was recorded) measured approximately 30 m square. A large area within the interior of Enclosure 2a (and later Enclosures 2b and 2c, see below) had also been destroyed by modern disturbance.

Gullies

To the north-east of the enclosures there were are a series of slightly irregular, roughly parallel gullies, each up to 0.25 m deep (Fig. 2.3). They are of uncertain function, but could possibly indicate the presence of a slightly shifting trackway along the northern side of the Enclosures 1 and 2a, and therefore potentially of the same phase. While one gully (4245) cut a pit (3280) containing four sherds of Middle/Late Iron Age pottery, others were cut by Late Iron Age pits (see Fig. 2.5, and below). The gullies contained small quantities of predominantly Middle/Late Iron Age pottery.

Late Iron Age

Enclosures 2b, 3 and 4

The second phase of enclosure construction saw the substantial modification of the earlier boundaries, but keeping some of their overall layout, with Enclosure 1 being replaced by Enclosures 3 and 4 (Fig. 2.5). The ditches on the western side of Enclosure 2a were recut by ditch 4237, which may have continued further south as ditch 3410. To the north, ditch 4237 extended 4 m north of the early enclosures, cutting across the lines of some of the parallel gullies and stopping 4 m short of a new east–west ditch (4232), leaving an access point between Enclosures 2b and 3. To the east, ditch 4342 formed the northern side, and part of the eastern side, of an enlarged Enclosure 2b, now measuring 32 m east–west by up to 40 m north–south. To the west, it formed the northern side of two small enclosures (Enclosures 3 and 4), defined by ditches 4243 and 4377, both of which were perpendicular to it, towards the south. Enclosure 3 measured 22–30 m east–west by at least 20 m north–south, and Enclosure 4 measured 30 m by 20 m, both appearing to have been open at the south.

Ditch 4237 contained pottery with a range of dates, but predominantly Late Iron Age. This is consistent with a radiocarbon date of *130–1 cal BC (SUERC-38152, 2095±35 BP at 95% probability)* obtained on a pig mandible from its primary fill (3496, in cut 3498). The four sherds from ditches 4243 and 4377 were insufficient to date them.

There were relatively few stratigraphic relationships between these ditches and other securely dated features. Ditch 4237 was cut by two early Romano-British pits (3183 and 3533) (see Fig. 2.8), as well as by pit 3419 which contained early Romano-British pottery in the third of its four fills, but also which produced a radiocarbon date of *90 cal BC–cal AD 50 (SUERC-38150, 2045±35 BP at 95% probability)* from an articulated cattle leg (ABG 77) in its basal fill. Despite its good individual agreement (A:106) with the OxCal model (see Fig. 4.1), this radiocarbon date is inconsistent both with the Romano-British pottery and with the suggested phasing of this ditch, and therefore needs to be treated with caution. To the east, ditch 4232 was cut by Middle/Late Iron Age pit 3513 (Fig. 2.5), although the relationship may not be straightforward (see below).

Pits

As in the Early/Middle Iron Age, the pits in this period appear to have a largely random distribution, both within and outside the areas defined by the enclosure ditches (Fig. 2.5). There were, however, two noticeable clusters – one along the eastern side of Enclosure 2a, in the area devoid of earlier pits, the other in the north-eastern corner of Enclosure 3. Whether these reflect the zoning of activities within the enclosures cannot be determined, given the general lack of other types of features which might indicate other activities.

In this period also the pits varied widely in size and form, although deep steep- to vertical-sided pits suitable for grain storage were significantly more common than in the Early/Middle Iron Age.

Pit 3225

This was potentially the largest pit on the site, and the most southerly of the eastern group in Enclosure 2b. Although only its north-eastern quadrant was excavated (it was truncated to the south and west

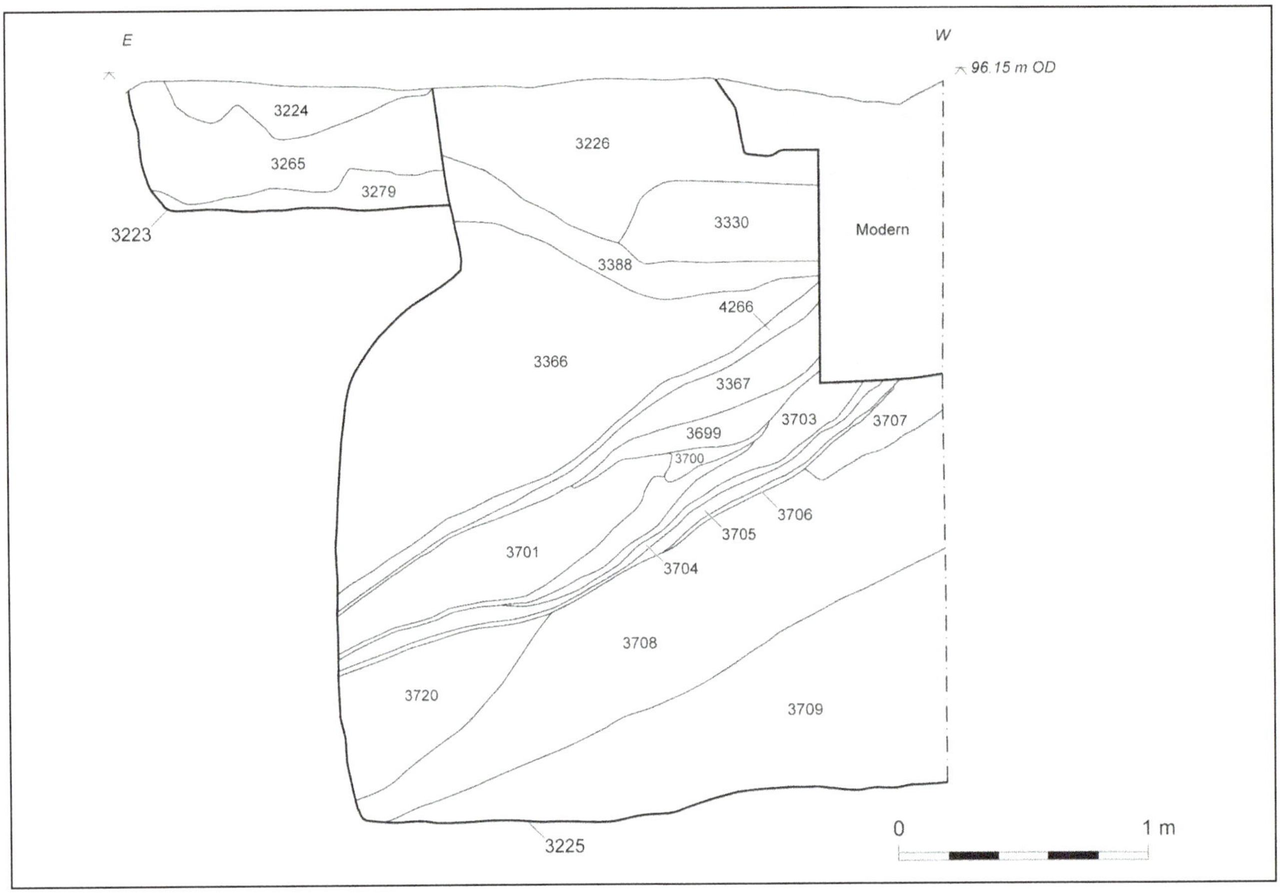

Figure 2.6 Sections of Middle/Late Iron Age pit 3223 and Late Iron Age pit 3225

Plate 2.3 Placed deposit in pit 3088, viewed from the west

by modern wall foundations) its projected line suggests a possible diameter of over 3.5 m, and it was 3 m deep, with steep to vertical sides and a flat base (Fig. 2.6). It contained no evidence of formal or placed deposition.

The nature and contents of the lower fills were not clearly established as these had to be excavated by machine to reveal its full profile. Unlike many of the storage pits, however, much of this pit had been filled in with material clearly dumped from one side (western), including thick deposits of chalky rubble interspersed with thinner lenses of soil and silt. Where these fills, sloping down to the east, were excavated by hand they produced few finds – one piece of worked flint and a small quantity of burnt flint. They were overlain by series of more level deposits, the lowest of which (3366), a thick layer of stone-free soil, contained a single Late Iron Age sherd and small quantities of worked flint, burnt flint and animal bone. All the other pottery from the pit, comprising sherds of both Late Iron Age and Romano-British date, was recovered from the uppermost fill (3226).

Pit 3088

The fact that the sizes of the pits appear to have no correlation to the presence of formally placed deposits is further illustrated by this small pit, 0.7 m wide (cut by a modern foundation) and 0.3 m deep, in Enclosure 4 (Pl. 2.3). Near the centre of the pit was a large flint nodule, on either side of which had been placed a jar, one Late Iron Age, the other dated as Middle/Late Iron Age (Fig. 3.3, 25 and 26). The pit's dark, organic-rich fill also contained fragments of briquetage, worked flint, burnt flint, fired clay, slag, animal bone and charred cereal remains, predominantly grain.

Pit 3025

This relatively small pit, 1.1 m in diameter and 0.3 m deep, also in Enclosure 4, contained an iron object (ON 50; Fig. 3.5, 5) of uncertain nature although it

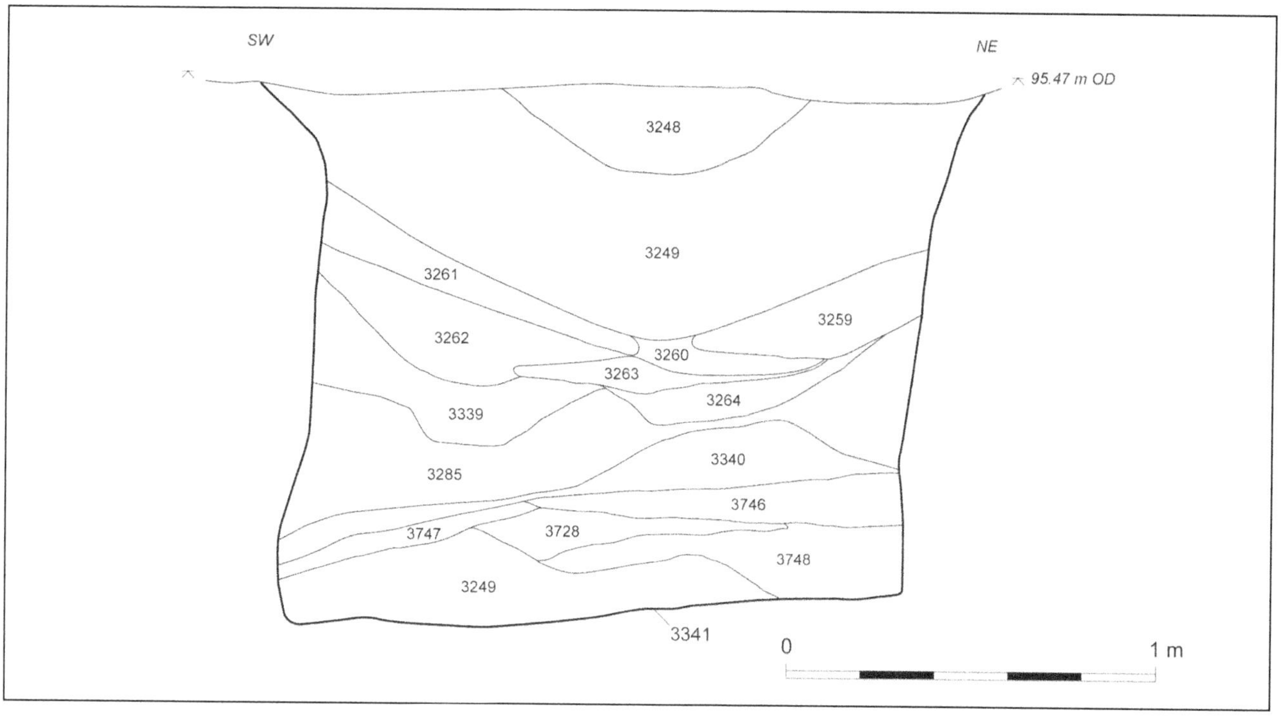

Figure 2.7 Section of Middle/Late Iron Age pit 3341

bears some resemblance to medical instruments (see Fitzpatrick, Chapter 3), along with sherds of Middle/Late Iron Age pottery, burnt flint, animal bone, including a fragment of red deer antler and a possible nail (ON 53). However, in contrast to pit 3088, both metal objects were recovered from within the pit's single fill, rather than on its base, and there was no clear indication that any of the finds had been formally placed.

Pit 3341

This cylindrical pit was 2.0 m wide and 1.4 m deep (Fig. 2.7). It contained 17 fills, representing a sequence of repeated but relatively limited deposition events; 15 of these deposits filled the lower two-thirds of the pit, while just two filled the upper third. What is notable is that five of the lower fills contained one or more animal bone groups, all of which (apart from a raven skeleton – ABG 98 from layer 3728), were of foetuses or neonates: two dog foetuses (ABG 245 from primary fill 3749, and ABG 69 from layer 3285), two pig neonates (ABG 67 from layer 3285, and ABG 64 from layer 3264), and a sheep neonate (ABG 234 from layer 3340). In addition, one deposit (3263) contained disarticulated cattle and horse bones (the latter possibly from a single horse), these apparently representing food refuse that have been collected and deposited together; there was also a radius from a possible donkey. Other finds from the pit also appear to represent general domestic waste – fired clay, worked flint, burnt flint and two chalk spindlewhorls (ONs 93 and 95).

The identification of rodent and amphibian bones in the lowest fills suggests that there were intervals when the pit was left open between deposition events. The fill profiles in section suggest that there may have been some levelling of the deposits when the pit had been filled to a depth of 0.3 m. However, the presence of pig and sheep neonates suggest that all of these deposits may have been made over the course of a single spring (see Higbee, Chapter 3); they may have largely filled the pit, with the subsequent decomposition and compaction leaving a concave hollow in the upper one third. One particularly notable deposit, resting on the base of this hollow, comprised the skeletons of two adult dogs (ABGs 61 and 62) their positions, with their hind legs interlocking, suggesting that they may have been arranged so as to appear to be in the act of mating (Pl. 2.4) (see Discussion, Chapter 5). The hollow appears then to have been deliberately backfilled (3249).

The pottery from the pit had a date range of Early/Middle Iron Age to Late Iron Age/early Romano-British, but the contexts of this material indicate a general Middle–Late Iron Age date for the sequence of fills. Three radiocarbon dates were obtained from the animal bone: of *130–10 cal BC (SUERC-38159, 2085±35 BP at 95% probability)* from layer 3728 near the base, and *100 cal BC–cal AD 10 (SUERC-38342, 2055±30 BP at 95% probability)* on the donkey radius from the deposit of disarticulated bone from layer 3263 near the midpoint, both of which are consistent with the Middle–Late Iron Age pottery. From higher in the pit fill sequence, a radiocarbon date of *60 cal BC–cal AD 60 (SUERC-38144, 2030±35 BP at 95% probability)* was obtained on one of the dog burials. The three dates are statistically consistent, suggesting that they all belong

Plate 2.4 Dog skeletons (ABG 60 and 61) in pit 3341, possibly arranged so as to appear to be mating

Plate 2.5 Placed deposit in Late Iron Age pit 3998, viewed from the east-north-east

to a phase of activity that is close in date. The three dates also appear to be sequential in age, which is consistent with some delay in the pits infilling, as the lower fills compacted, before the burial of the two dogs. From modelling the radiocarbon dates the pit was dug at some point during *115–55 cal BC (at 68% probability modelled as First Dig pit 3341 or 155–40 cal BC at 95% probability)*, supporting the suggestion that it was dug as some point during the late 2nd or early 1st century BC.

Pit 3998

This subrectangular pit (south of Enclosures 3 and 4), measured 1.7 m by 0.9 m, and was 0.4 m deep with vertical sides and a flat base. It contained a small hoard of placed incomplete, possibly broken items, of considerable significance (see Fitzpatrick, Chapter 3).

The basal fill (4115) contained the head of an iron set hammer (ON 135; Fig. 3.5, 2), probably used to work hot metals, along with pottery, worked flint, burnt flint and animal bone. This was overlain by a charcoal-rich layer (4114), containing burnt flint and burnt animal bone, over the surface of which had been placed large pieces from a single Middle/Late Iron Age jar, possibly deliberately broken, on top of which was an iron nave hoop (from a wheel axle) (ON 133; Fig. 3.5, 3) surrounded by organic-rich material (Pl. 2.5). There was also an iron socketed spearhead or ensign/standard with appliqué decoration (ON 132; Fig. 3.5, 4), but insufficient room for the whole of its shaft unless it was deposited broken. In addition, there were lumps of birch tar with impressions of twisted vegetable fibres. The overlying fill (3999) consisted of multiple small dumps of burnt material, including burnt flint (4.7 kg) and fired clay, as well as worked flint, animal bone and crop-processing waste. The distinctive form of this features, the nature and condition of the finds and their apparently deliberate placement and arrangement clearly indicate that this was a deposit of specific ritual significance (see Discussion, Chapter 5).

Pit 3513

This subcircular pit (cut by a modern wall in Enclosure 2b) was at least 1.7 m wide and 1 m deep, with a flat base, undercut on its north-east side. Its four lower fills all extended across its full width, giving the appearance of having been spread evenly as they were deposited; they do not have the profiles of either naturally accumulated fills, or simple dumps of material. The sterile, 0.2 m thick basal fill was sealed by a thin, charcoal-rich spread on which, in the centre of the pit, an almost complete vessel (ON 86) had been placed. The overlying layer (3647) contained further pottery, fragments of briquetage, two water-worn flint pebbles (possibly hammerstones), and small quantities of worked flint, burnt flint and animal bone. Little was recovered from the two overlying fills, but a second almost complete vessel (ON 85, Fig. 3.3, 21), with post-firing perforations in its base, and repaired with birch bark tar adhesive, was recovered from the second from top fill.

Both vessels were of Middle/Late Iron Age (*c.* 2nd–1st century BC) date, but the pit was recorded (in plan) as cutting the fill of an early Romano-British recut (cut 3714) of ditch 4232 on the eastern side of Enclosure 2b/2c (Fig. 2.5). The pit's 0.3 m thick upper fill (3514) contained of 34 sherds of early Romano-British pottery (and only scraps (3 g) of earlier material), so it is possible that, as the pit's lower fills compacted, the resulting hollow filled up during the early Romano-British period, giving it the appearance (in plan) of a later feature.

Pit 3220

The profile of this pit, 0.9 m wide and 0.5 m deep with steep sides and a near-flat base, could indicate that it was the base of a heavily truncated storage pit, but all but one of the other pits in this group (on the east side of Enclosure 2b) are deeper, some substantially so, suggesting that this area (surrounded by modern building foundations) had not been heavily truncated. The pit contained a sequence of six fills, representing clearly distinct deposition events. The basal fill (3266) contained small quantities of Late Iron Age pottery, worked flint, burnt flint and animal bone, consistent with a dump of domestic waste, but an overlying fill (3268), extending across the pit, contained a very different deposit comprising the skull, mandibles and foot bones of an adult sheep (ABG 233). Similarly, the layer above (3222) contained vertebrae and the right hindleg of a neonate pig (ABG 231) along with two semi-complete Late Iron Age (1st century BC) vessels, both with post-firing perforated bases.

Pit 3344

This probable storage pit, 2–2.4 m wide and 1.2 m deep, had irregular near-vertical sides, slightly undercut/eroded at the base (but not in the form of a bell-shaped pit). It contained a sequence of 17 often interleaved fills, many of them apparently dumped from the eastern side. The lower six fills contained no finds, and the finds in the layers above were generally in small quantities – Middle and Late Iron Age pottery, fired clay, worked flint, burnt flint, animal bone and slag. There were no animal bone groups, and none of the finds had the appearance of having been deliberately placed; it appears instead that the pit was used consistently for waste disposal, and then covered with a thick capping layer of chalk rubble.

Burial 3466

A partial neonate burial (3466) was found within Enclosure 3 (Fig. 2.5) (in the uppermost fill of Enclosure 1 ditch 4242, possibly laid flexed on the right side; no grave cut was noted. The bone was radiocarbon dated to *120 cal BC–cal AD 30 (SUERC-39061, 2055±30 BP at 95% probability)*. This indicates that the burial was possibly made at some point during the 1st century BC.

Early Romano-British

Enclosures

The third phase of enclosure construction saw minor changes to the Late Iron Age enclosures, with ditch 4232 continuing to define their northern boundary (Fig. 2.8); there was evidence that it had been recut along the eastern side of the eastern enclosure (now Enclosure 2c). The only coin from the site, a late Roman copy of an 'Urbs Roma' issue of the House of Constantine probably struck between AD 330 and AD 345, was recovered from this ditch, in a section with a single fill.

Enclosure 2c was defined to the west by ditch 4233 (which lay 3–5 m to west of phase 2b ditch 4237), and to the south by ditch 2071. The lines of ditches 2071 and 4233 created a staggered entrance, 4 m wide, on the western side of Enclosure 2c, the earlier gap at its north-west corner now being closed; there may have been a similarly staggered entrance on the eastern side, although the enclosure's circuit here was badly disturbed. The resulting enclosure measured 45 m north–south by 38 m east–west. To the west, Enclosures 3 and 4 appear to have been combined to form a single enclosure (Enclosure 5) defined at the west by ditch 4230 (realigned as ditch 4378). A range of pottery was recovered from these ditches, which together suggest an early Romano-British date for this phase.

Enclosure 6 also appears to belong to this phase. This lay on the southern edge of the site, 10 m south of Enclosure 2c. The regular curve of its ditch (2070) suggests that it may have been circular, in which case it would have an internal diameter of 40 m, and would have extended to within approximately 25 m of the ditch of the Late Bronze ringwork. Sections through the ditch show that its circuit consisted of at least three overlapping cuts, indicating some reworking of the boundary over a relatively short period – all contained predominantly early Romano-British pottery. Other finds included redeposited neonate human bone, animal bone (including articulated cattle vertebrae – ABG 1), worked flint, burnt flint, fired clay, ceramic building material and a small piece of a square-sectioned copper alloy rod of unknown function.

Pits

Pit 3183

This well-preserved bell-shaped pit lay in the north-west corner of Enclosure 2c, cutting the northern end of Late Iron Age ditch 4237 (Fig. 2.8). It was 2 m deep and 2.3 m wide at its flat base, its sides rising vertically for 1 m before narrowing to 1.6 m wide (Fig. 2.9). It contained a sequence of 21 fills, 12 of which contained finds, with a significant proportion of these coming from three charcoal-rich fills (3669, 3197 and 3194).

Above what appears to be a levelled basal fill (3673) there was a series of slightly domed soil fills that were overlain by charcoal-rich deposit 3669 lying mainly against the eastern side of the pit. Among the pottery from layer 3669 were four early Romano-British sherds (providing a relatively secure early Romano-British date for the infilling of the pit). There were also at least 88 hobnails, in two groups

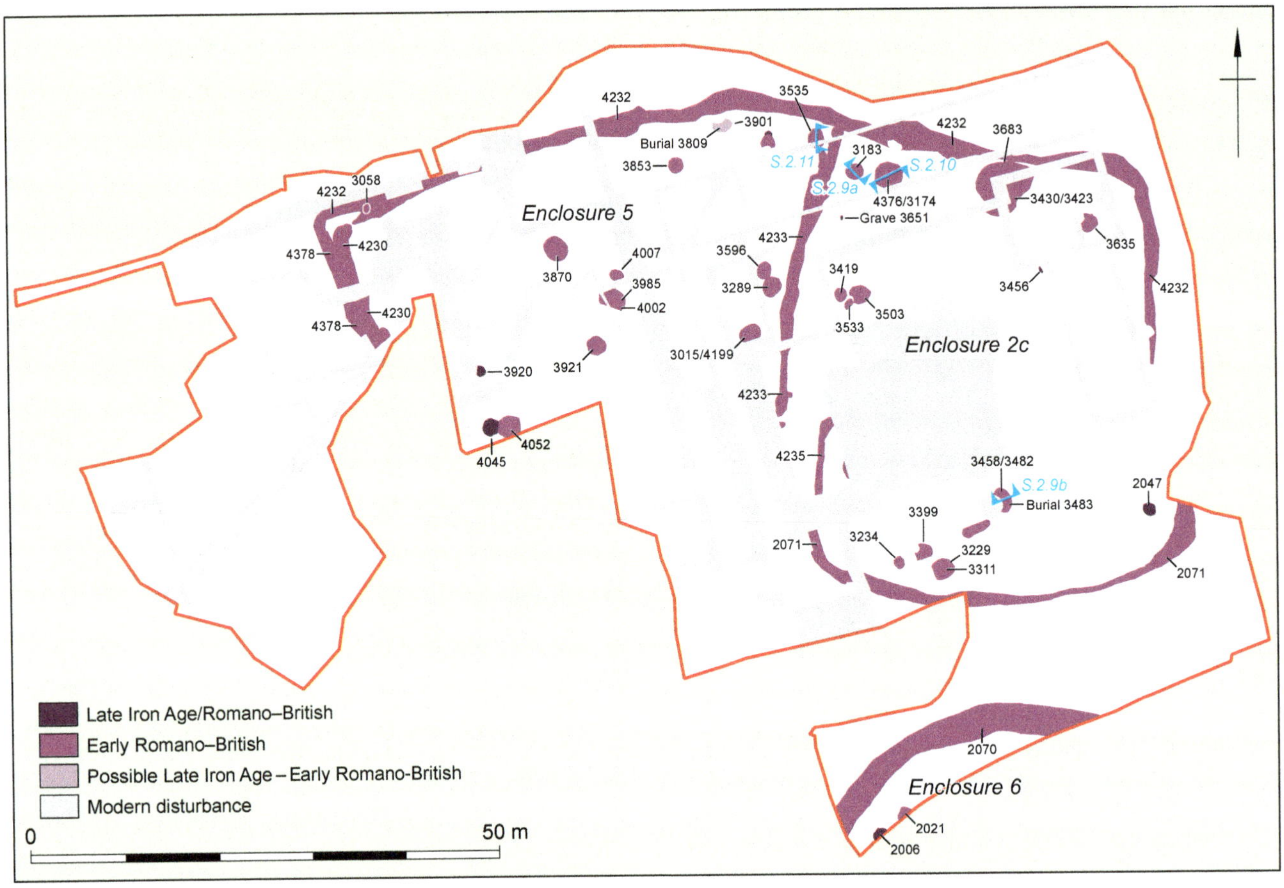

Figure 2.8 Features of the early Romano-British phase

Plate 2.6 Neonate burial (3483) in fill of early Romano-British pit 3458, viewed from the north

(ONs 97 and 104) possibly from a single boot, pieces of perforated, triangular fired clay objects (ON 155), worked flint, burnt flint and animal bone. A length of iron chain, comprising three figure-of-eight links (ON 94; Fig. 3.6, 10), recorded as coming from the underlying layer (3670), was found close to hobnail group ON 94, and may have been part of this deposit.

Layer 3669 was overlain by chalk rubble (3198), dumped from the pit's south-east side, then a more extensive charcoal-rich layer (3197), containing a complete copper alloy Colchester brooch (ON 89) (Fig. 3.6, 6), and further pottery (Late Iron Age/early Romano-British), fired clay, animal bone, worked flint and burnt flint, as well as briquetage and a piece of slag. A soil layer (3196) separated this from the upper charcoal-rich layer (3194), which contained the pit's only animal bone group, a partial neonate sheep skeleton (ABG 230), as well as further general waste material – similar quantities of which were also recovered from many of the overlying fills.

The association of the metal finds and the partial lamb skeleton with the charcoal-rich fills suggests that these three deposits were more than just dumps of waste from household and hearth. However, there was little formality of placement evident in the pit deposits, with the majority of fills, including the charcoal-rich ones, appearing to have been simply dumped, mostly from the south-east side, and with no apparent levelling.

Pit 3458/3482

This oval bell-shaped pit in the southern part of Enclosure 2c was 1.8 m deep, with a flat base and an eastern side with a distinctly sinuous profile (it was truncated by a modern feature at the west) (Figs 2.8 and 2.9). Apart from a thin lens of charcoal (3692) just above the base, it was filled to a depth of 1.3 m with a series of substantial but sterile soil deposits.

The uppermost fill (3465) which contained 41 sherds (937 g) of Late Iron Age/early Romano-British

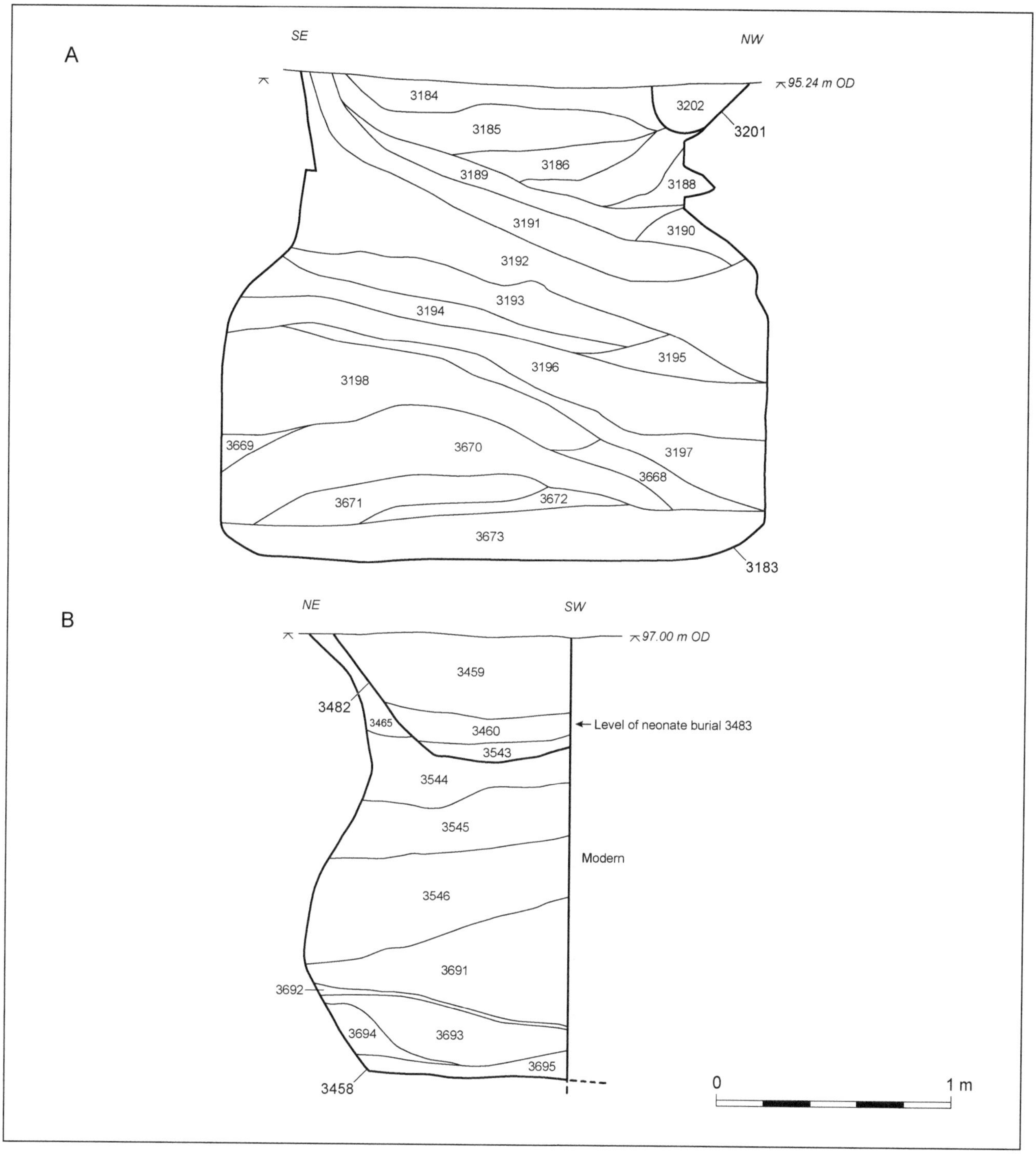

Figure 2.9 Sections of early Romano-British pits 3183 and 3458/3482

pottery, along with animal bone, stone and burnt flint, was cut by a shallower feature (3482), 0.5 m deep, with a charcoal-rich layer (3543) at its base containing small quantities of fired clay and animal bone. This was overlain by a layer containing large amounts of mid-reddish brown material, identified as natural iron deposits (3460), as well as early Romano-British pottery and an iron ferrule (ON 73).

Within this latter fill, or possibly on its surface, was a neonate burial (3483) laid with the head to the east (Pl. 2.6). The pit's two uppermost fills (3460, and 3459 overlying the burial) contained almost 100 sherds (1758 g) of pottery, of predominantly Late Iron Age/early Romano-British date, but including 24 early Romano-British sherds (429 g). Given the amount of pottery in the layer (3465) into which this feature was cut, it is likely that much of this pottery derives from that layer. However, it is possible that some of it was associated with the burial, although no relationship was noted during excavation.

Plate 2.7 Excavating the animal bone deposit (3711) in pit 3174, viewed from the west

Plate 2.8 Animal bone deposit (3537) in pit 3535

Pit 4376/3174

This originally bell-shaped pit, located in the north-western part of Enclosure 2c (Fig. 2.8), was one of the largest on the site. It was 2.8 m deep, narrowing from 2.6 m wide at the base to 1.9 m near the top, but probably originally narrower as the upper sides had eroded (Fig. 2.10). It contained a series of fills, the character and dating evidence from which suggest that this feature had a complex history - digging (4376), storage, removal of stored contents, refilling with waste, re-digging (3174) and refilling, including with animal and human burials.

A series of seven irregular dumps of material filled the bottom 0.2–0.6 m of the pit, three containing apparently domestic waste (Late Iron Age/early Romano-British pottery, animal bone, fired clay, worked flint, burnt flint and a bent, subsquare-sectioned iron bar (ON 136)), the others containing no finds. A partial lamb skeleton from one of these layer (4183) produced a radiocarbon date of *100 cal BC–cal AD 60 (SUERC-38161, 1990±35 BP at 95% probability)* which is consistent with the 1st century BC–1st century AD date range of the associated Late Iron Age/early Romano-British pottery, these lower fills, representing the re-filling of the emptied storage pit (4376).

The lower fills were overlain by a 0.4–0.6 m thick deposit (3711) which, along with all the later fills, has been assigned to the subsequent recutting (3174) of the pit (see below). Layer 3711 contained the butchered partial carcasses of 25–30 animals (Pl. 2.7), predominantly sheep/goat (of varying age), but including also cattle, a perinatal horse, two domestic fowl and a raven. There were also two dogs – one a large type (ABG 116), and the other of a smaller, lapdog type (ABG 131) (see Higbee, Chapter 3). Some pieces of egg shell were also recovered from this layer. It also contained 4510 g of ironworking slag, amounting to approximately half of all the slag recovered from the site, suggesting that ironworking may have taken place in its immediate vicinity; in fact, pit 3174 produced all the smithing slag from the site (see Andrews, Chapter 3). Other material, including pottery of predominantly early Romano-British date (as well as some residual Iron Age sherds) could represent domestic waste, but its incorporation within this bone-rich (and slag-rich) deposit may have given it with some additional symbolic significance.

A radiocarbon date of *cal AD 10–110 (SUERC-38158, 1900±35 BP at 95% probability)* was obtained for one of the small dog's bones, consistent with the 1st–2nd century AD date range of the early Romano-British pottery from layer 3711 (and the layers above). From modelling the radiocarbon dates pit 3174 was dug at some point during *50 cal BC–20 cal AD (at 68% probability modelled as First Dig pit 3174 or 95 cal BC–55 cal BC at 95% probability)*.

The difference in the pottery and radiocarbon dates between the basal layers and those above (and the absence of slag in the basal layers), is consistent with there being a significant interval between these two main phases of deposition. There is no indication that the pit had remained open for any length of time after the deposition of the basal layers; instead their clear interface with the bone-rich deposit above suggests that pit 4376 had been almost completely emptied before the subsequent deposit of animal carcasses was made. The near-level upper surface of these irregular dumps of material in the base gives the impression that they may have undergone some degree of levelling, presumably when the pit was re-emptied.

There may have been a concern, either practical or symbolic, to bury this large quantity of animal carcasses at depth, and in the absence, perhaps, of a readily available empty storage pit, this may have been most easily achieved by the near-complete re-emptying (to over 2 m depth) of a pit that had already

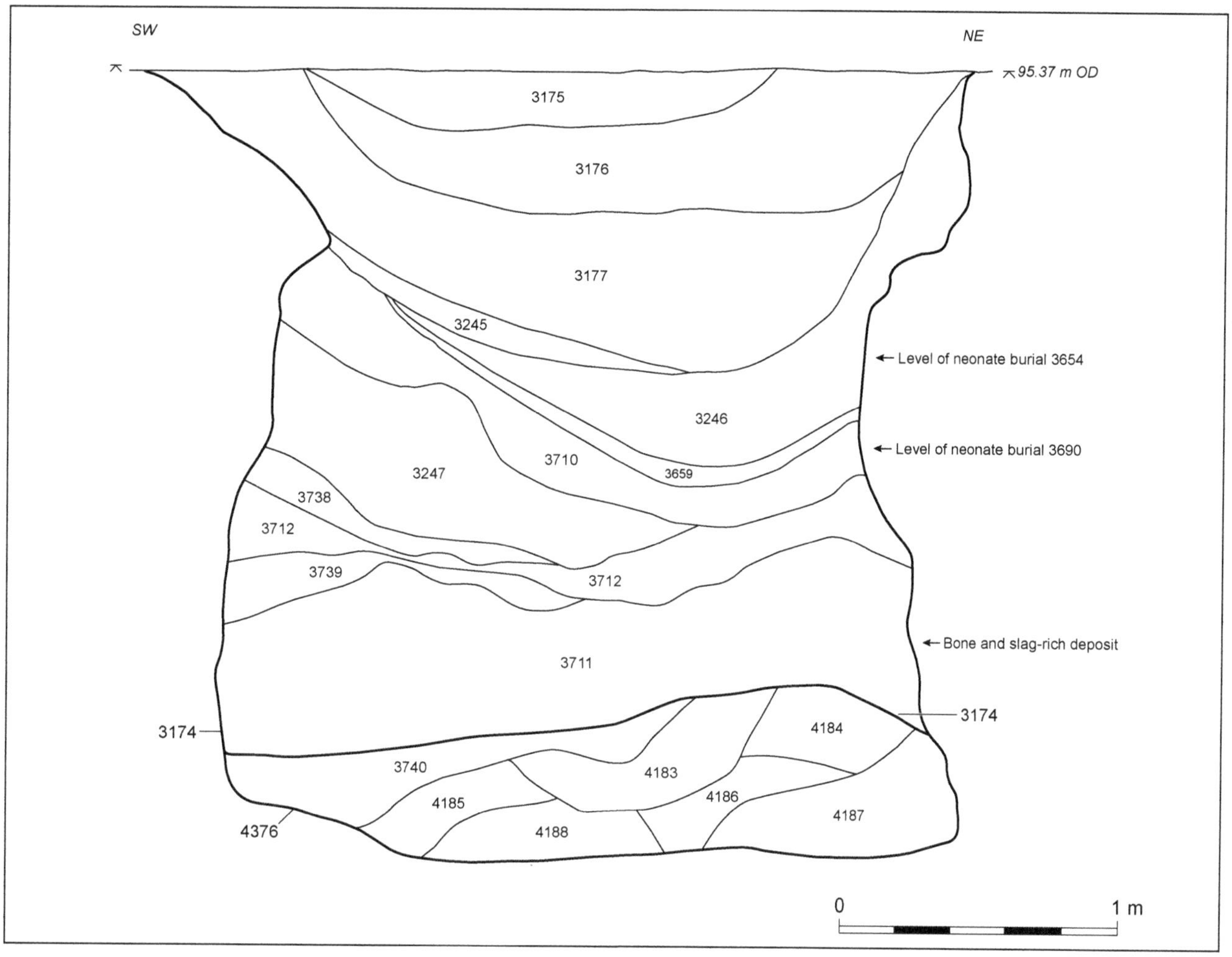

Figure 2.10 Section of Late Iron Age/early Romano-British pit 4376/3174

been (wholly or partly) refilled, rather than digging a new one. It should be noted, however, that many of the pits contained deposits which appear to have been deliberately levelled without any indication of emptying or recutting.

The bone deposit (3711) was sealed by a sequence of three sterile layers (3739, 3712 and 3738), above which at the side of the pit were recovered a number of neonate bones from a disturbed burial (3690, not visible in section). There were two further dumps of soil, the lower (3247), on the south-west side of the pit, containing a small quantity of domestic waste (pottery, slag, bone, worked flint and burnt flint), and the upper (3710) being sterile. Cattle bone (ABG 203) from layer 3247 was radiocarbon dated to *cal AD 20–130 (SUERC-38143, 1865±35 BP at 95% probability)*. These were covered by a thin charcoal-rich layer (3659) containing burnt pottery, fired clay, burnt bone, slag (2507 g), hammer-scale and pieces of iron, as well as a chalk spindlewhorl (ON 168). A similar quantity of slag was recovered from the overlying deposit (3246).

On top of layer 3246 was a second neonate skeleton (3654, also not visible in section), which appeared to have been laid on a loose stone setting of chalk and flint; an accompanying flint scraper and a pig's tooth may be deliberate or chance associations. The overlying layers all had marked concave profiles, probably reflecting their slumping as the deposit of animal carcases decomposed, and the layers compacted. They contained varying quantities of domestic waste, some of it (as indicated by the pottery) residual, but none of it apparently deliberately deposited; this included a sandstone whetstone (ON 167) in layer 3177. The latest pottery, from the uppermost fills, was of mid-1st–mid-2nd century AD date. Cattle bone (ABG 202) from layer 3177 was radiocarbon dated to *cal AD 50–170 (SUERC-38141, 1880±35 BP 95% probability)*.

Pit 3535

This large oval pit in the north-east corner of Enclosure 5 (Fig. 2.8), was 1.9 m deep and 2 m wide at its flat base, narrowing only slightly (to 1.8 m) towards the top (Fig. 2.11). On its base, against the eastern side, was the skeleton of a small dog (ABG 115), approximately 1 year old that had been laid with its head to the north facing into the pit. Behind its back and hind legs were sherds from an early Romano-British jar (ON 118) dated *c.* AD 70–90,

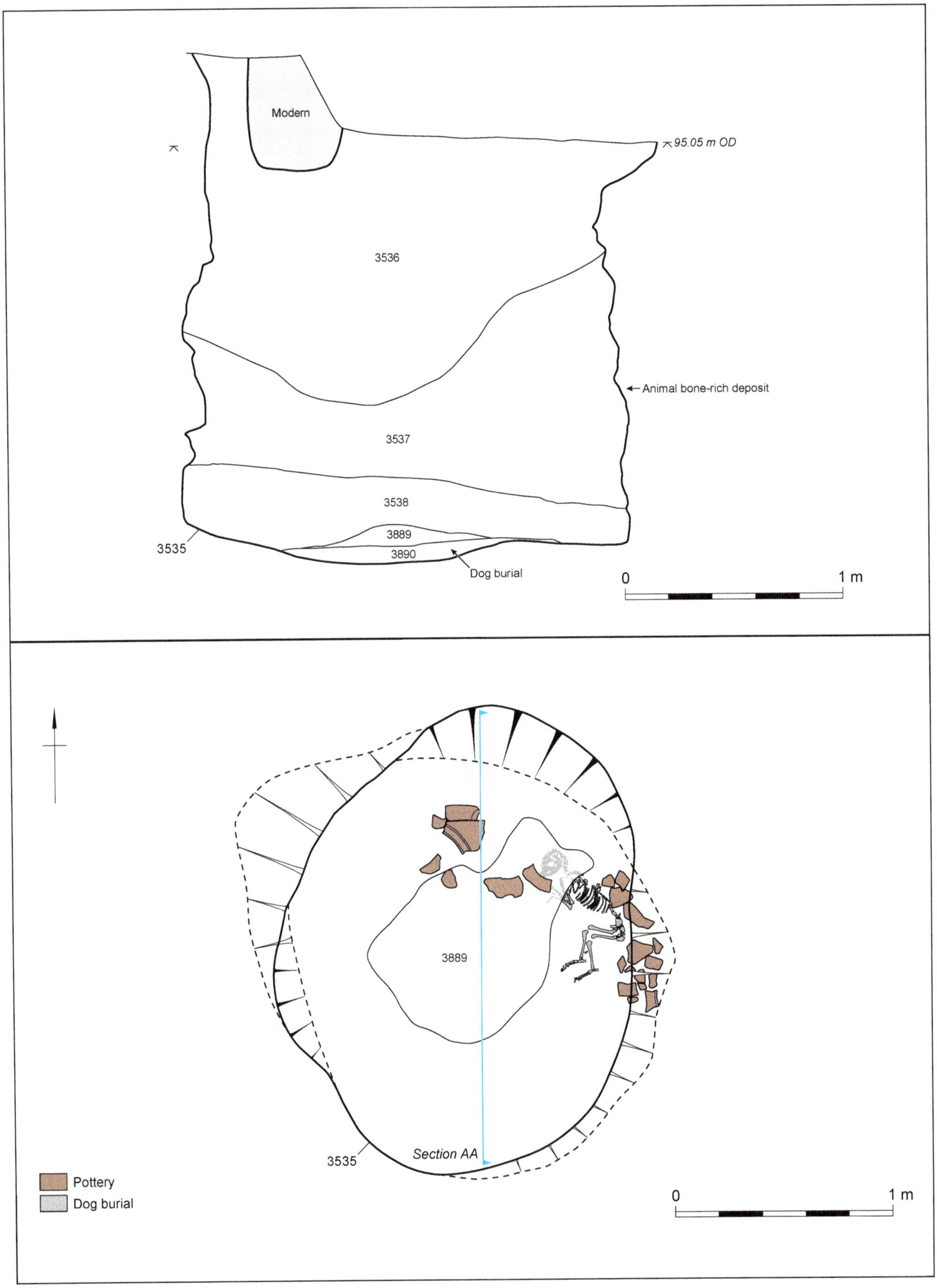

Figure 2.11 Section and plan of early Romano-British pit 3535

further large pieces of which, including most of its rim, lay in front of its head. The vessel appears to have held an ashy deposit (3889), containing the burnt remains of at least two lambs, as well as a fragment of an iron saw blade (ON 122; Fig. 3.6, 9). This material was spread across the centre of the pit, the edge of it apparently covering the dog's head. The sequence of deposition associated with this clearly placed deposit is not entirely clear. It is unlikely, for example, that the distribution of sherds (spread over 1.3 m), and the extent of the ashy deposit in the centre of the pit, could both have resulted simply from the natural breaking, or falling over of the vessel. Instead, it seems that the vessel was deliberately broken, with some of its sherds then being moved out of the way to the side of the pit, behind the dog.

The ashy deposit (3889) was recorded as overlying a thin spread of lighter soil (3890), which also surrounded the skeleton. It is possible that this material was already lying on the base of the pit, which may have lain open for some time between the emptying of its stored grain (if that had been its original function) and the act of deposition. These layers and deposited materials were covered by a 0.2–0.3 m thick layer of soil (3538) containing a small number of disarticulated cattle and pig bones. The upper surface of this layer was very even (although very slightly sloping), and this possible levelling may represent the final stage in this act of deposition/animal burial. The dog skeleton was radiocarbon dated to *50 cal BC–cal AD 70 (SUERC-38160, 1985±35 BP at 95% probability)*, earlier than the suggested date of the pot.

Above layer 3538 there was a thick deposit (3537) containing 15 separate animal bone groups, mostly complete skeletons, densely packed with no obvious positioning or arrangement (Pl. 2.8). They included four sheep (two lambs, ABGs 83 and 240; one subadult, ABG 83; and one adult, ABG 239), three dogs (two complete, ABGs 90 and 92; and one missing its skull, ABG 109; as well as a partial foetus, ABG 241), a fox (ABG 91), a horse skull (ABG 107), and cattle (one near-complete skeleton, ABG 100; skull, mandibles, vertebrae and ribs, ABG 101; an adult left foreleg, ABG 242; and a neonate right foreleg, ABG 243). One of the dog skeletons (ABG 90) was radiocarbon dated to *30 cal BC–cal AD 90 (SUERC-38153, 1955±35 BP at 94.9% probability)*.

Small quantities of other mostly residual finds (including sherds of Iron Age pottery) were recovered from layer 3537, probably in the soil backfilled over the animal remains, and similar material came from the overlying fill (3536) which filled the deep hollow left as the carcases decomposed and compacted.

Pit 3683

Early Romano-British pit 3683, which cut the top of the undated 'shaft' (3676, see above) (Fig. 2.2), was recorded as one of a cluster of adjacent, probably overlapping features (3423, 3430, 3434 and 3683) at the northern end of Enclosure 2c. It is unclear, however, whether this apparent cluster, which was cut into three parts by modern building foundations, actually comprised a number of discrete features, or instead was one large feature, possibly an area of quarrying. If the latter it would have measured approximately 5 m by 6 m, and been up to 1.7 m deep, with steep sides and an irregular base. Pit 3683 produced 18 sherds of Romano-British pottery (including two Middle Romano-British sherds from its uppermost fill), a Late Iron Age Nauheim-derivative brooch (ON 78) (Fig. 3.6, 8), a piece of ceramic building material, and small quantities of worked flint, burnt flint and animal bone.

Plate 2.9 Neonate burial (3652) in grave 3651, viewed from the south

Other Burials

As described above, two neonate inhumation burials (3654 and 3690) were found in pit 3174, and another in pit 3458. In addition, a redeposited neonate bone was found in the ditch (2070) of Enclosure 6, and a redeposited adult bone in Enclosure 5 ditch 4232. Two other features contained burials.

Grave 3651

A small subrectangular grave (3651) lay immediately next to ditch 4237 on the eastern side of Enclosure 2c (Fig. 2.8). It measured 0.4 m by 0.25 m, aligned

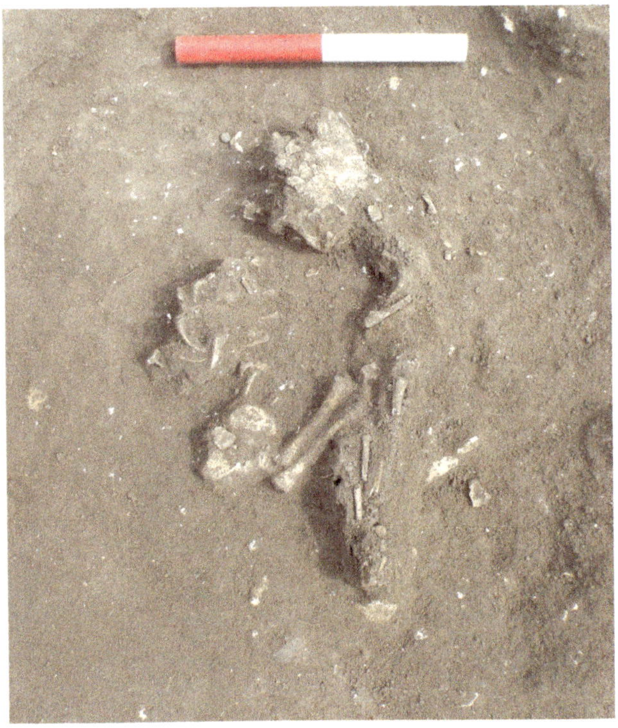

Plate 2.10 Neonate burial (3809) in upper fill of undated pit 3910, viewed from the west

north–south, and was 0.1 m deep. It contained a neonate burial (3652) placed flexed on its left side with the head to the north (Pl. 2.9). The grave contained a small quantity of residual worked flint and burnt flint, but no grave goods. A radiocarbon date of *50 cal BC–cal AD 80 (SUERC-39063, 1975±30 BP at 95% probability)* was obtained on the bone.

Burial 3809

A neonate burial (3809) was found in the upper fill of an undated, irregular pit (3901), laid crouched on the right side (Fig. 2.8; Pl. 2.10). The pit, which was 0.2 m deep, was recorded as pre-dating ditch 4232, and therefore probably of Late Iron Age or earlier date, but this relationship is by no means certain. The bone provided a radiocarbon date of *40 cal BC–cal AD 90 (SUERC-39062, 1955±30 BP at 93.2% probability)*. It is unclear at what stage during the pit's filling the burial was made, but no grave cut was visible in the pit's single fill.

Continuity and Change

The evidence for Early Iron Age activity, apparently unconnected with the Late Bronze Age ringwork enclosure but pre-dating the establishment of the enclosures revealed on this site, suggests a phase of possibly short-term open settlement. Enclosure 1 subsequently encompassed the area occupied by the roundhouse and square structure, as well as some of the early pits. However, the fact that other pits lay outside it suggests that it was not intended primarily as a boundary of the existing settlement area. Given the relatively insecure dating of the roundhouse, its continued occupation in this period cannot be ruled out. It would have been positioned (along with the square structure) towards the rear of Enclosure 1 and with its suggested west-facing entrance looking towards the entrance to the enclosure, which was similarly aligned.

There is no evidence for any significant break in the site's occupation from the Early/Middle Iron Age to the early Romano-British period. In fact, there appears to have been a high degree of continuity in both the layout of features, in particular in the arrangement of the enclosures, and in the range of activities undertaken within and around them. The eastern enclosure (Enclosure 2), which dates from the first phase of enclosure construction towards the end of the Middle Iron Age, largely kept its form, despite being gradually enlarged, into the early Romano-British period. The shape of the western enclosure (Enclosure 1) was substantially changed in the Late Iron Age, but then only saw minor modification in the early Romano-British period.

While no structures were identified relating to the Late Iron Age and early Romano-British occupation, and the extent of the associated settlement remains uncertain, the increase in the number and size of grain storage pits suggests an expansion in the settlement's productive capacity into the 2nd century AD. Associated with this is an increase in the frequency of formalised deposition, particularly involving a wide range of animal carcasses and other remains, but including also, in Late Iron Age pit 3998, the 'burial' of high status objects of likely symbolic significance, hinting at social as well as economic developments.

Chapter 3
Finds

Pottery

by Rachael Seager Smith

Overall, 3452 sherds of pottery, weighing 53,632 g, were recovered. These include one small group of Late Bronze Age date from a single feature (5010), as well as a handful of intrusive post-medieval/modern pieces (contexts 613, 3735 and 4198). The bulk of the assemblage, however, spans the period from the Early Iron Age (800–400 BC) to the early 2nd century AD.

The whole assemblage was recorded using an abbreviated version of Wessex Archaeology's standard recording system for pottery (Morris 1994), which follows the nationally recommended guidelines of the Prehistoric Ceramics Research Group (PCRG 2010) and the Study Group for Roman Pottery (Darling 1994). Within each context, sherds were divided by chronological period based on their fabric and form characteristics. Four generic fabric groups defined by their principal tempering agents (F: crushed burnt flint; S: fossil shell; G: grog; Q: quartz sand) were identified among the prehistoric material, and where appropriate were then subdivided into more specific fabric types based on their more minor inclusions. The later prehistoric fabrics were cross-referenced with the series constructed for north-west Surrey (Jones 2012, 117–24), and a site-specific vessel form series was then used to describe the rims present. The Romano-British fabrics and vessel forms were coded (Appendices 2 and 3) according to the system used by the Museum of London Archive (http://www.museumoflondonarchaeology.org.uk/Publications/Online-Resources/MOLA-ceramic-codes.htm), originally established to record the early Romano-British coarsewares from Southwark (Marsh and Tyers 1978), with subsequent additions and revisions (eg, Davies *et al.* 1994, 5–8). Within each fabric, the pieces were sorted into 'sherd families' – individual rims, bases, groups of joining sherds or, indeed, any group of sherds sharing certain characteristics, such as unidentifiable jar rim fragments or a mass of undiagnostic body sherds – dated and quantified by sherd count, weight (to the nearest whole gramme) and estimated vessel equivalence (EVE; calculated excluding pieces representing less than 5% of the diameter of the vessel). Other details, such as surface, treatment, decoration, manufacturing technique, cross-context joins, the presence of perforations and residues, and evidence for use, re-use and repair were also recorded, with all the data stored in a fully integrated Access database which forms part of the site archive.

In total, 12 later prehistoric and 12 Romano-British fabrics were identified, although in both cases the majority comprise broad groups identified on the basis of predominant inclusion types, rather than closely-defined fabric entities. Fabric descriptions are given in Appendix 2. The quantity of pottery present by chronological period is shown in Table 3.1 and by fabric type and phase in Table 3.2. In general, it survives in good condition, with relatively low levels of surface and edge abrasion. The mean sherd weight is 15.5 g, and was once considerably higher as many sherds exhibit fresh breaks indicating that they were broken during or shortly after excavation. Differences in mean sherd weight and EVE indicate some variation in condition between the different chronological periods, while material from ditches and gullies tended to be less well preserved than that from pits. Overall, 78% of the assemblage by sherd count (86% by weight) was recovered from pits.

It should also be reiterated here that the site phasing was undertaken at the feature level, rather than on an individual context basis (eg, a feature and all its fills were assigned to the same phase, even if the uppermost layers were not deposited until some considerable time later). With the possible exception of the enclosure ditches, most of the features on this

Table 3.1 Pottery totals by chronological period

Period	*No. sherds*	*Weight (g)*	*Av. weight (g)*	*EVE*
Late Bronze Age	15	109	7.2	0.06
Early Iron Age	233	3178	13.6	2
Early/Middle Iron Age	174	1314	7.5	0.67
Middle Iron Age	78	1269	16.3	1.54
Middle/Late Iron Age	572	13039	22.8	3.81
Late Iron Age	583	8865	15.2	7.42
Iron Age	145	441	3.0	0.25
Latest Iron Age/ Romano-British	1649	25354	15.4	20.98
Post-medieval/modern	3	63	21.0	–
Total	3452	53632	15.5	36/73

Table 3.2 Overall pottery quantities (number of sherds/weight in grammes) by fabric type and phase

	EIA and MIA open settlement		*MIA/LIA 1st phase enclosures*		*LIA 2nd phase enclosures*		*latest IA/R-B 3rd phase enclosures*		*Unphased*		*Total*	
Date/ware	No.	*Wt. (g)*	No.	*Wt. (g)*	No.	*Wt. (g)*	No.	*Wt. (g)*	No.	*Wt. (g)*	No.	*Wt. (g)*
Late Bronze Age												
F1	1	*8*	–	–	–	–	4	*21*	10	*80*	15	*109*
Iron Age												
BRIQ	–	–	14	*51*	2	*1*	1	*8*	–	–	17	*60*
G1	9	*96*	17	*170*	260	*3250*	21	*188*	–	–	307	*3704*
G2	–	–	5	*57*	–	–	4	*98*	–	–	9	*155*
SUG	–	–	7	*108*	–	–	1	*19*	–	–	8	*127*
Q1	166	*1706*	112	*817*	31	*198*	33	*271*	9	*34*	351	*3026*
Q2	173	*2302*	24	*273*	19	*176*	35	*225*	14	*93*	265	*3069*
Q3	18	*129*	3	*24*	–	–	1	*11*	1	*4*	23	*168*
Q4	2	*9*	8	*45*	–	–	3	*6*	–	–	13	*60*
Q5	7	*109*	1	*7*	1	*3*	–	–	–	–	9	*119*
S1	85	*789*	207	*10176*	328	*5670*	62	*263*	6	*30*	688	*16928*
S2	5	*119*	87	*539*	–	–	5	*66*	–	–	97	*724*
subtotal	*465*	*5259*	*485*	*12267*	*641*	*9298*	*166*	*1155*	*30*	*161*	*1787*	*28140*
Latest IA/R-B												
SAM LG	–	–	–	–	–	–	12	*75*	–	–	12	*75*
SAM CG	–	–	–	–	–	–	1	*6*	–		1	*6*
BAET	–	–	–	–	–	–	17	*2113*	3	*119*	20	*2232*
FN GRY	1	*1*	–	–	–	–	34	*293*	–	–	35	*294*
HWC	–	–	–	–	–	–	8	*28*	–	–	8	*28*
OXID	5	*39*	18	*38*	–	–	70	*514*	9	*28*	102	*619*
VRW	–	–	–	–	2	*107*	56	*1455*	6	*98*	64	*1660*
G100	1	*2*	7	*104*	3	*18*	241	*3485*	44	*474*	296	*4083*
G101	–	–	–	–	1	*9*	11	*134*	–	–	12	*143*
SAND	3	*12*	12	*34*	14	*124*	802	*11027*	30	*326*	861	*11523*
SHEL	–	–	–	–	5	*166*	227	*4441*	2	*22*	234	*4629*
TSK	–	–	–	–	–	–	2	*28*	–	–	2	*28*
subtotal	*10*	*54*	*37*	*176*	*25*	*424*	*1481*	*23599*	*94*	*1067*	*1647*	*25320*
Post-med./modern												
Refined w'ware	–	–	–	–	–	–	–	–	1	*37*	1	*37*
Flowerpot	–	–	–	–	–	–	–	–	1	*13*	1	*13*
Stoneware	1	*13*	–	–	–	–	–	–	–	–	1	*13*
subtotal	*1*	*13*	–	–	–	–	–	–	*2*	*50*	*3*	*63*
Total	477	*5334*	522	*12443*	666	*9722*	1430	*21583*	218	*2760*	3452	*53632*

site appear to have filled relatively rapidly, but the phasing methodology means that the ceramics from the various stratigraphic phases cannot be treated as discrete chronological groups. This limits the appropriateness of any discussion of the assemblage by phase, so the following discussion is based on the date of the sherds themselves, rather than stratigraphic phase.

Late Bronze Age

A single feature (pit 5010) to the east of the Late Bronze Age ringwork contained 10 flint-tempered sherds (Fabric F1) of Late Bronze Age date. These include part of a shouldered jar with a simple, upright rim (form R5) and seven unrelated plain body sherds in hard, fairly fine fabrics with very common, well-sorted flint, as well as two thin-walled, carinated body sherds probably from fineware bowls. The five other flint-tempered sherds (Table 3.1) are all undiagnostic plain bodies; four were found residually in later features, while the fifth came from Early Iron Age pit 3079. All these wares belong within the post-Deverel-Rimbury plainware tradition of the Late Bronze Age and are typologically comparable with material considered to be of 10th–8th century BC date from the ringwork (Adkins and Needham 1985, fabrics 2 and 7) and other sites in the vicinity (eg, Groves and Lovell 2002; Macpherson-Grant 2002; Jones 2012, 120–1).

Iron Age

Fabrics

Three principal fabric groups, tempered with shell (S), quartz sand (Q) and grog (G), were identified, together with a few pieces of oxidised sand and organic-tempered briquetage. Although the relative frequency of these groups varied considerably through time (Table 3.2), the fabric types and their proportions conform to the pattern seen in other local assemblages (eg, Cotton 2001; Jones 2012). The apparent absence of flint-tempered wares is, however, a matter of definition; although no Iron Age sherds tempered only with crushed, calcined flint were identified in this assemblage, significant quantities of sand and crushed flint-tempered ware (fabric Q2) do occur but are included here in the quartz sand-tempered group, as sand was considered to be the predominant inclusion type. All the tempering agents present within the assemblage are available within the locality, and there was no evidence from this assemblage to contradict the view (eg, Jones 2012, 117) that production of pottery in Iron Age Surrey was mostly undertaken on a small-scale, probably household, basis, with vessels predominantly made for highly localised consumption. Sherds in all three fabric groups were predominantly unoxidised (black, dark grey, brown in colour) although often with patchy oxidisation indicative of not very well-controlled bonfire or clamp kiln firing.

Overall, shell-tempered wares were the most numerous, representing 43% of the Iron Age assemblage by sherd count. The two fabrics (S1 and S2) can be paralleled amongst Jones' TUFA group (2012, 121), containing fluvial shell and tufa fragments derived from the calcareous grit-charged clays of the Thames/Colne hinterland and predominantly of Early to Middle Iron Age date. More locally, suitable clays containing fossil shell can be found in the Woolwich Beds which occur in the area around Ewell, approximately 5 km to the south-west of the site, although by the Late Iron Age, sources of supply may have been switching to the north Kent/south Essex coastal zone (*ibid.*, 121, SHEL group), where extensive production continued into at least the middle of the 2nd century AD. These wares predominantly contain fossil oyster or other marine shell, and should therefore be relatively easy to distinguish from the earlier group, but at this site, as elsewhere in the region (*ibid.*, 118), most of the sherds had at least partially lost their calcareous content, leaving only voids and thus preventing any reliable identification of source.

The five sandy fabrics together represented 37% of the Iron Age assemblage by sherd count. This group was dominated by a wide range of handmade, mostly dark-fired, naturally sandy wares (fabric Q1), spanning the whole of the period. The sand and flint-tempered wares (Q2) can be compared with many of the CALC and SAND fabrics at Lea Thorpe Nurseries, particularly CALC2 and SAND 2A and B (Jones 2012, 120 and 124), and represent a continuation of the use of flint-gritted pottery, a tradition apparent from the Neolithic onwards in the west London area. Although present in far smaller quantities, the fabrics containing reddish-brown iron minerals, probably limonite (Q3), organic material (Q4) and glauconite (Q5) also form part of the standard range of wares seen in the area. As at Lea Thorpe Nurseries, Fabric Q3 represented approximately 1% of the Iron Age assemblage (*ibid.*, 122), while its relative frequency in features of the open settlement (Table 3.2) suggest that it is predominantly of Early to Middle Iron Age date. No featured sherds were present amongst the sand and organic-tempered sherds (Q4), but further comparisons with the Lea Thorpe Nurseries assemblage suggest that these wares and the glauconitic (Q5) sherds are slightly later, perhaps belonging within the 3rd to 1st centuries BC (Middle/Late Iron Age; *ibid.*, 122–3, ORG and GLAUC groups).

Although occasionally used in earlier phases of the Iron Age, grog-tempered fabrics were not common in this area until the mid–late 1st century BC (Thompson 1982; Cotton 2001, 12). Overall, these wares (fabrics G1, G2 and SUG) represent 18% (by count) of the Iron Age sherds. Some handmade vessels were noted but most were at least wheel-finished and all were predominantly dark-fired. The most common fabric (G1) contained occasional calcined flints, quartz sand and/or ferrous particles in addition to the grog, while a few pieces of Middle to Late Iron Age date contained fossil shell inclusions as well as grog, itself sometimes shell-tempered (fabric G2). The small group of East Sussex grog-tempered (SUG; Green 1980) sherds were identified here on the basis of their vessel forms and distinctive decoration (shallow-tooled standing arcs or eyebrows); other less, diagnostic pieces may be present within the assemblage but their fabrics were not readily distinguishable from the bulk of the G1 material. These vessels have been assigned a 1st century BC to *c.* AD 70 date in Sussex (*ibid.*, 69–72); locally, Late Iron Age examples occurred at Reigate Road, Ewell (Cotton 2001, 14), while others are known in 1st century AD contexts in London (Davies *et al.* 1994, 117, fig. 101, 671–2).

The briquetage sherds (salt containers) occur in handmade sandy fabrics with variable quantities of organic material, probably dung. All were fully oxidised and bright orange or pink in colour, sometimes with white or cream surfaces typical of this material type. Similar fabrics are known from other sites in Carshalton (eg, Macpherson-Grant 2002, 81) and these vessels are likely to be traded items, carrying pre-dried salt from production zones in the lower Thames estuary or on the south coast, for example. Although not closely dated, most probably belong within the 2nd–1st centuries BC.

Forms

The Iron Age vessel forms were dominated by jars, although neutral-profiled vessels, bowls and cups were also represented. The assemblage clearly included both coarse- and fine-ware forms, albeit with a strong bias towards the coarse. Such divisions were not always clear-cut, however, necessitating a consideration of a combination of attributes, including the presence of finer, better sorted inclusions, vessel form, wall thickness, the presence of surface treatments (eg, smoothing, burnishing, surface coating with a slip or slurry to disguise inclusions) and decoration.

Jars

R1 shouldered jar with short, upright neck and irregular rim, Fig. 3.1, 3

R2 weakly shouldered jar with simple, unelaborated, upright rim, Fig. 3.1, 2

R3 weakly shouldered jar with upright, flat-topped, internally bevelled rim, Fig. 3.1, 4

R4 externally-expanded rim from a large vessel; plain or finger-pinched along outer edge of rim (*cf.* Jones 2012, 132, fig. 5.32, 103 (tufa 2 fabric), Fig. 3.1, 5

R5 shouldered jars with simple upright rims – plain, finger-impressed or slightly expanded, Figs 3.1, 1; 3.1, 7; 3.2, 11

R6 proto-bead rimmed jar; often flat-topped and internally thickened but without external beading (*cf.* Thompson 1982, type C3), Figs 3.2, 13 and 14; 3.3, 26; 3.4, 35

R8 simple, slightly inturned, rounded or flat-topped rim – probably from an ovoid jar. Plain or decorated, Fig. 3.1, 6

R9 weakly shouldered jar with a concave neck and a finger-pinched (alternate sides), flat-topped rim

R11 narrow-necked, shouldered jar with an externally-expanded rim; neck sometimes decorated with finger-tip impressions

R12 bead rim jars; profiles vary but generally high rounded shoulders and simple rounded, pointed or slightly triangular bead rims, Figs 3.2, 17; 3.3, 18; 3.3, 22; 3.3, 29; 3.3, 31

R13 high shouldered jars with simple, upright 'pulled' bead rims; often internally thickened at neck/shoulder junction

R19 shouldered S-profiled jars with slightly everted rims, Figs 3.2, 8–10; 3.3, 27

R20 large storage jar with high, rounded shoulder, upright neck and everted rim. Top of shoulder has multiple cordons; incised grooves around point of greatest girth, Fig. 3.3, 24

R21 shouldered jar with almost horizontal, out-turned rim; little or no discernible neck, Fig. 3.4, 33

R26 jar with an everted rim and a corrugated profile; no cordon at base of neck but angled neck/shoulder junction, bulging rounded shoulder, cordon, bulge, another cordon, Fig. 3.3, 25

R27 inverted pear-shaped jar with high, rounded shoulder, corrugated neck and slightly externally expanded (B1) base (*cf.* Thompson 1982, 117, type B2-1, but this code is used for rims only), Fig. 3.4, 37

R28 round-bodied cordoned jars with a narrow neck and an everted rim (*cf.* Thompson 1982, 155, type B3-5), Fig. 3.4, 32

Jars/bowls

R7 jar/bowl with a high, rounded shoulder and a simple, upright rim, Fig. 3.3, 20 and 21

R15 round-shouldered jar/bowl with sloping neck and everted rim; decorated with finely tooled 'eye-brow' motifs on shoulder. East Sussex Grog-tempered ware (Green 1980; Cotton 2001, 13, fig. 5, 7–13), Fig. 3.2, 15

R17 plain (not externally beaded), upright rim from a necked jar/bowl form

R18 globular-bodied jars/bowls with upright or slightly everted rims, cordons at base of neck; flat base; similar to Thompson 1982, type B1-3 jars, Fig. 3.4, 36

R23 sharply-shouldered bowl with a simple, upright or slightly flaring rim; tripartite form. C5th–3rd BC

R24 inverted pear-shaped bowl/jar, Fig. 3.3, 28

Bowls

R10 upright or slightly everted rim from a fineware bowl; often red-finished

R14 round shouldered bowl with an upright or slightly everted 'pulled' bead rim and a short, vertical neck, Fig. 3.2, 12

R25 round-bodied, wide-mouthed bowl with an, upright, cordoned neck; terminal of rim slightly beaded, Fig. 3.4, 34

Miscellaneous

R16 briquetage cup with plain, rounded rim; straight or flared walls; flat base, Figs 3.2, 16 and 3.3, 23

R22 lids; details of profiles vary

These forms find parallels other published groups from the region (eg, Cotton 2001; Proctor 2002; Leivers with Every and Mepham 2010; Jones 2012) and their frequency by fabric type is summarised in Table 3.3.

Function and use

In the main, the uses of Iron Age vessels can only be presumed; the finer vessels can be assumed to have been tablewares, and while it is likely that the coarsewares divide into storage and cooking pots, this cannot be detected in most instances. Sooting and burnt residues (both internal and external) survived on just 24 Iron Age sherds or groups of joining sherds, six on Early and Middle Iron Age forms R1, R5, R9 and R19 and 12 on bead (R12), proto-bead (R6), and upright-rimmed (R7) jars of Middle and Late Iron Age date, suggesting cooking or the preparation of foodstuffs and other materials in these vessels.

Post-firing perforations were noted in the walls or bases of the five of Iron Age vessels. These are generally interpreted as indicative of a change in the use of a vessel and the practice is widely known in Late Iron Age and Romano-British contexts across

*Table 3.3 Iron Age vessel forms by fabric type (number of rims and total EVE shown. * = <5% only)*

Form	*BRIQ*	*G1*	*G2*	*SUG*	*Q1*	*Q2*	*Q3*	*Q5*	*S1*	*S2*	*Total no.*	*Total EVE*
R1	–	–	–	–	1	6	–	–	4	–	11	0.53
R2	–	1	–	–	–	–	–	–	–	–	1	0.1
R3	–	–	–	–	–	1	–	–	1	–	2	*
R4	–	–	–	–	–	–	–	–	2	–	2	0.07
R5	–	–	–	–	1	6	–	–	1	–	8	0.94
R6	–	–	–	–	1	1	–	–	12	–	14	2.64
R7	–	1	–	–	5	–	1	–	–	1	8	1.07
R8	–	–	–	–	2	2	–	–	–	–	4	0.37
R9	–	–	–	–	–	1	–	–	–	–	1	0.05
R10	–	–	–	–	4	1	–	–	–	–	5	0.07
R11	–	–	–	–	–	1	–	–	–	–	1	0.1
R12	–	2	1	–	1	1	–	–	15	1	21	3.61
R13	–	–	–	–	–	–	–	–	1	–	1	0.07
R14	–	–	1	–	–	–	–	–	–	–	1	0.1
R15	–	–	–	1	–	–	–	–	–	–	1	0.2
R16	4	–	–	–	–	–	–	–	–	–	4	0.46
R17	–	–	–	–	2	–	–	–	–	–	2	0.05
R18	–	8	–	–	1	–	–	–	–	–	9	0.6
R19	–	2	–	–	2	–	1	1	–	–	6	1.17
R20	–	–	–	–	–	–	–	–	1	–	1	0.38
R21	–	1	–	–	–	–	–	–	–	–	1	0.25
R22	–	–	–	–	1	–	–	–	–	–	1	*
R23	–	–	–	–	–	1	–	–	–	–	1	0.05
R24	–	1	–	–	–	–	–	–	–	–	1	0.65
R25	–	1	–	–	–	–	–	–	–	–	1	0.32
R26	–	1	–	–	–	–	–	–	–	–	1	0.3
R27	–	1	–	–	–	–	–	–	–	–	1	0.56
R28	–	1	–	–	–	–	–	–	–	–	1	0.9
Total	4	20	2	1	21	21	2	1	37	2	111	15.72

southern England. It is traditionally associated with the production of cheese (Harding 1974, 88), although such vessels could have been used to drain/strain solids from liquids in a wide variety of industrial and domestic contexts, or put to more exotic uses as time-pieces or as flower pots, for example, while others may have been rendered useless in more ritualistic ways (Fulford and Timby 2001, 294–6). Four of these vessels were perforated through the base (Figs 3.3, 21, 27 and 28, and 3.6, 36), while the fifth (Fig. 3.3, 24) had at least six perforations arranged in two slightly off-set rows drilled through its wall, just below the point of its greatest girth. It may be significant that all these vessels formed part of deliberate, structured deposits (pits 3220, 3513, 3053 and 4313, see Chapter 2), although other vessels from the site apparently used in similar ways showed no such mutilations or, indeed, any distinctive physical characteristics.

At least three vessels of 2nd–1st century BC date (pits 3341, 3513 and 4313) had also been repaired in antiquity with a thick, dark greyish brown or black adhesive substance. These repairs survived as thick, resinous deposits, with dull or glossy lustres, sometimes with a bubbly appearance, on the broken edges of sherds and/or along the margins of the break, where the liquid glue had spread onto the adjacent surfaces as the sherds were pushed together during the repair process. Increasing numbers of glue-repaired pots are now known from south-eastern Britain, particularly Kent, although the practice is more commonly associated with Romano-British vessels (Marter Brown and Seager Smith 2012, 5). Similar repairs of Iron Age date are, however, known from a variety of sites on the Isle of Thanet (Jones 2009, 25; Seager Smith 2015) and around Ashford (Wessex Archaeology 2014) in Kent, while further afield, glued repairs to Iron Age horse harness fittings are known from Wetwang, East Yorkshire (Stacey 2004) and pottery vessels used in the production and storage of adhesive materials have been identified at Grand Aunay, France (Regert *et al.* 2003). Although not undertaken here, chemical and/or elemental analysis has consistently identified birch bar tar, produced by heating birch bark to temperatures in excess of 300/400°, as the principal ingredient of these adhesives (eg, Charters *et al.* 1995; Stacey 2004; Wicks and Shillito 2009), which sometimes contain other materials, such as beeswax (Regert *et al.* 2003), animal fat (Dudd and Evershed 1999) or clay (English 2005), as plasticisers and/or binding agents. Although the reasons why certain vessels were considered worthy of repair remain obscure, the glue-repaired vessels provide clear evidence for the care and curation of 'everyday' ceramics and it may be of particular significance that lumps of birch bark tar were included in the *pars pro toto* deposit of iron objects in Middle/Late Iron Age pit 3998 (see Chapter 2), this material perhaps being symbolic of the restoration of the deliberately broken objects.

Table 3.4 Overall pottery quantities (number of sherds/weight in grammes) by chronological period and phase

	EIA and MIA open settlement		*MIA/LIA 1st phase enclosures*		*LIA 2nd phase enclosures*		*latest IA/R-B 3rd phase enclosures*		*Unphased*		*Total*	
	No.	*Wt.*	No.	*Wt.*	No.	*Wt.*	No.	*Wt.*	No.	*Wt.*	No.	*Wt.*
Late Bronze Age	1	*8*	–	–	–	–	*4*	*21*	10	*80*	15	*109*
Iron Age												
Early Iron Age	213	*2942*	14	*204*	2	*20*	*3*	*9*	1	*3*	233	*3178*
Early/Middle Iron Age	103	*825*	23	*159*	7	*65*	*25*	*172*	16	*93*	174	*1314*
Middle Iron Age	24	*497*	42	*671*	7	*60*	*1*	*15*	4	*26*	78	*1269*
Middle/Late Iron Age	28	*253*	361	*11009*	145	*1477*	*38*	*300*	–	–	572	*13039*
Late Iron Age	65	*642*	16	*148*	462	*7623*	*41*	*477*	1	*9*	585	*8899*
Iron Age	32	*100*	29	*76*	18	*53*	*58*	*182*	8	*30*	145	*441*
Iron Age subtotal:											*1787*	*28140*
Latest Iron Age/Romano/British	10	*54*	37	*176*	25	*424*	*1481*	*23599*	94	*1067*	1647	*25320*
Post-medieval/modern	1	*13*	-	-	-	-	-	-	2	*50*	3	*63*
Total	477	*5334*	522	*12443*	666	*9722*	*1651*	*24775*	136	*1358*	3452	*53632*

Distribution

Early Iron Age

Sherds belonging within this period, broadly considered to be the 8th–5th centuries BC, accounted for approximately 7% of the assemblage by sherd count (233 sherds, 3178 g or 6% by weight). The majority were from contemporary features, mostly pits, within the Early and Middle Iron Age open settlement (Table 3.4).

The fabrics were dominated by the sand and flint-tempered wares (Table 3.5; 48% of the sherds of this date), continuing in the post-Deverel-Rimbury traditions of the area with smaller, but approximately equal quantities, of other sandy and shell-tempered fabrics. These wares were virtually absent from the flint dominated Late Bronze Age assemblages recovered from the nearby sites at Queen Mary's Hospital (Adkins and Needham 1985; Mepham 2002), and Westcroft Road (Macpherson-Grant, 2002, 79), although some parallels are known in the assemblage from Heathrow (Leivers with Every and Mepham 2010), for example. Elsewhere in north-west Surrey, the introduction of these sandy and shell-tempered wares marks a point late on in the post-Deverel-Rimbury sequence, probably during the Early Iron Age (Jones, 2012, 121 and 124, table 5.3).

Vessel forms consisted largely of coarseware jars, mostly of bipartite form with flat or slightly externally expanded bases, rough or vertical finger-smeared surfaces and, occasionally, finger-impressed shoulders and/or rims. These, too, clearly belong within the post-Deverel-Rimbury repertoire, but have a fairly lengthy currency throughout the Late Bronze Age and Early Iron Age periods, although the handful of fine, carinated body sherds and rims from at least two fineware bowls, both with traces of 'red-finishing' (pits 3079 and 3178), indicate the Early Iron Age nature of this group. The affinities of this material place it within Cunliffe's 'Park Brow – Ceasar's Camp' and 'Darmsden–Linton' ceramic groupings of the 8th–5th centuries BC (1991, 69–72, 561, 565).

Of the 24 Early and Middle Iron Age features containing pottery of this date, only seven (grave 3052 and pits 3011, 3178, 3940, 4131, 4333 and 4341) contained more than 10 sherds or 100 g, and of these, only grave 3052 and pits 3178, 3940 and 4333 had sufficient diagnostic sherds to merit description.

Grave 3052

All the pieces (19 sherds, 203 g) were from a single, predominantly unoxidised, shell-tempered shouldered jar (Fig. 3.1, 1), but it remains unclear whether this vessel

Table 3.5 Pottery quantities of the Iron Age fabric types (number of sherds/weight in grammes) by chronological period

	Early Iron Age		*Early/Middle Iron Age*		*Middle Iron Age*		*Middle/Late Iron Age*		*Late Iron Age*		*Iron Age*		*Total*	
Fabric	No.	*Wt.*	No.	*Wt.*	No.	*Wt.*	No.	*Wt.*	No.	*Wt.*	No.	*Wt.*	No.	*Wt.*
BRIQ	–	–	–	–	–	–	4	*24*	1	*8*	12	*28*	17	*60*
G1	1	*19*	–	–	–	–	14	*96*	288	*3556*	4	*33*	307	*3704*
G2	–	–	–	–	4	*53*	2	*33*	3	*69*	–	–	9	*155*
SUG	–	–	–	–	–	–	8	*127*	–	–	–	–	8	*127*
Q1	54	*573*	47	*345*	13	*328*	124	*875*	86	*807*	27	*98*	351	*3026*
Q2	113	*1997*	105	*779*	4	*29*	18	*176*	2	*7*	23	*81*	265	*3069*
Q3	4	*34*	10	*40*	4	*58*	2	*19*	–	–	3	*17*	23	*168*
Q4	2	*9*	–	–	–	–	8	*45*	–	–	3	*6*	13	*60*
Q5	–	–	–	–	9	*119*	–	–	–	–	–	–	9	*119*
S1	59	*546*	11	*107*	40	*606*	304	*11091*	204	*4422*	70	*156*	688	*16928*
S2	–	–	1	*43*	4	*76*	88	*553*	1	*30*	3	*22*	97	*724*
Total	233	*3178*	174	*1314*	78	*1269*	572	*13039*	585	*8899*	145	*441*	1787	*28140*

represented a deliberate grave offering or was merely coincidentally included.

Pit 3178

Although fairly small, the pieces (35 sherds, 380 g) from this feature comprised a comparatively wide range of fabrics and forms indicative of domestic debris. Shell-tempered and sandy wares each represented approximately one third of this assemblage by sherd count (13 and 10 pieces respectively) with smaller quantities of sand and flint- (six sherds), sand and limonite- (four sherds) and sand and organic- (one sherd) tempered fabrics. A single grog-tempered sherd, from a weakly shouldered jar with simple, unelaborated, upright rim (Fig. 3.1, 2), came from backfill deposit 3180 which also included two fine, red-finished fineware bowl sherds, confirming the Early Iron Age date of this group, as well as rims from four jars (eg, Fig. 3.1, 3 and 4) in coarser sandy and shell-tempered wares. Just one rim (Fig. 3.1, 5) occurred amongst the 14 sherds from the basal fill (3181).

Pit 4333

Three joining sand and flint-tempered sherds formed the more or less complete profile of small ovoid jar (Fig. 3.1, 6), also likely to be of 8th–5th century BC date. Other sherds from this feature consisted of 11 unrelated body sherds (119 g) in sandy, shell-, and sand and flint-tempered fabrics.

Pit 3940

Sherds (26 pieces, 703 g) from a single Early Iron Age sand and flint-tempered vessel (Fig. 3.1, 7) with a roughened, slightly sooted exterior surface, were found in the secondary fills (layers 4064 and 4065) of pit 3940 as well as in layer 3941/4120 which sealed this feature and the adjacent pit 4066. These three layers also incorporated other Early Iron Age sherds (19 pieces, 390 g), mostly jar bodies in sand and flint- (Q2; 14 sherds, 318 g) and shell- (S1; 4 sherds 58 g) tempered fabrics, along with a single shoulder sherd (5 g) from a carinated fineware bowl (Q1). Pit 4066, on the other hand, contained just one sherd (8 g), from the shoulder of a grog-tempered, necked, cordoned jar likely to be of Late Iron Age date. This jar sherd was assigned to the same layer (4074) as the La Tène I brooch (Fig. 3.5, 1), but is considered to be intrusive or mistakenly attributed to this context in view of the otherwise consistent dating evidence from these features (see Chapter 2), which, based on the date of the brooch, may fall towards the end of the Early Iron Age period, perhaps within the 6th/5th–4th centuries BC.

Early/Middle Iron Age

The majority of sherds assigned to this period were undiagnostic body and base fragments that could not be dated with any precision. These sherds represent 5% of the assemblage by sherd count (2% by weight) and occurred in 49 features, mostly within the Early and Middle Iron Age open settlement (Table 3.4). Sand and flint-tempered fabrics (Q2) continued to be dominant (60% by sherd count; Table 3.5) but only four rims, totalling 0.67 EVE, were present amongst this group.

Middle Iron Age

Middle Iron Age sherds, broadly dating to the 4th/3rd–2nd centuries BC, were comparatively poorly represented (just 2% of the assemblage by sherd count; Table 3.1), and it is therefore difficult to gauge relative fabric proportions within this period. Although shell-tempered wares were overtly dominant (Table 3.5), 34 of the 40 sherds derived from a single, semi-complete vessel (pit 3231, Fig. 3.2, 13), thus over-emphasising their importance. However, by this time, the sand and flint-tempered fabrics occurred only residually, with a corresponding rise in the importance of the sandy and shell-tempered wares and the use of a wider range of tempering agents overall. Both jars and bowls were characterised by more rounded profiles (eg, R7, R12, R14, R19, and R23), marking a distinct change from the earlier, angular profiles. Rims tended to be upright, everted or beaded while bases continued to be flat. No decorated sherds were present, but the vessels were more carefully finished than in proceeding periods, with smoothed or silkily burnished surfaces.

Most were found in features associated with the first phase enclosures (Enclosure 1 and 2a) (Table 3.4) but only two pits contained significant groups of this date.

Pit 4315

A broad date in the 4th/3rd–2nd centuries BC was indicated by 23 sherds (468 g), although earlier, residual, sherds and 11 pieces assigned broad Middle/Late Iron Age dates also occurred. Most of the Middle Iron Age sherds were well-burnished sandy wares (eight sherds, 255 g of Q1, four, 58 g, of Q3 and seven, 109 g of Q5), and included rims from at least four S-profiled jars (Fig. 3.2, 8–10), a jar/bowl with a high, rounded shoulder and a simple, upright rim (type R7) and a coarser, sand and flint-tempered shouldered jar (Fig. 3.2, 11). Plain body sherds in shell- (S1, 2 sherds, 14 g) and shell and grog- (S2; two sherds, 32 g) tempered fabrics were also included in this group, which is likely to represent domestic refuse.

Pit 3231

In all, 43 sherds (664 g) were recovered, including five undiagnostic sherds assigned Early/Middle and Middle/Late Iron Age dates. Part a round shouldered bowl with a short neck and an upright rim (Fig. 3.2, 12) in a grog and shell-tempered fabric came from the basal fill of this feature (layer 3598), while a more or less complete, shell-tempered, proto-bead rim jar (Fig. 3.2, 13) came from layer 3232. Both vessels are likely to belong within the 2nd century BC, broadly consistent with the 2nd–1st century BC radiocarbon determinations obtained on two of the articulated ABGs found in these deposits (Barclay, Chapter 4, and Table 4.4). Although it is possible, even likely, that the more or less complete jar formed part of the structured deposits within layer 3232, there is nothing exceptional about the jar itself, and unfortunately, no information concerning its relationship to the articulated animal bone was recorded.

Middle/Late Iron Age

Most sherds assigned to this period, considered to be the 2nd–1st century BC, occurred in features associated with the first and second phase enclosures (Table 3.4). However, as befitting a widely dated group, approximately one third of all the pieces were chronologically undiagnostic plain body or base sherds. Although the first phase enclosures (Enclosures 1 and 2a) were probably constructed at about this time, their ditches contained very little pottery, just 23 un- or poorly-diagnostic sherds (191 g), spanning the whole of the Iron Age. Significant groups of this date, however, did occur in three contemporary pits.

Pit 3341

Overall, 45 sherds, 675 g, were recovered from this feature. Rims from a shell-tempered proto-bead rim jar (Fig. 3.2,14) and a decorated East Sussex Grog-tempered ware jar/bowl (Fig. 3.2, 15) were found in the primary fill (3749), while a decorated jar/bowl shoulder sherd in this fabric also occurred in layer 3249. Eight other, joining, grog-tempered (G1) body sherds from layers 3749 and 3728 came from a vessel repaired in antiquity with birch bark tar adhesive and made in a fabric not readily distinguishable from that of the East Sussex Grog-tempered wares. Although lacking the distinctive decoration, it is therefore possible that these sherds also belonged to the East Sussex Grog-tempered ware vessel(s). Other pieces from the lower fills of this feature included sherds from a small sandy proto-bead rimmed jar (3285) as well as undiagnostic body sherds in sand and flint- and shell-tempered fabrics. The material from these deposits can be compared with that from pit 1 at Reigate Road, Ewell (Cotton 2001, 13, fig. 5, 7–13, 15, 16 and 18), and its date is consistent with the two 2nd–1st century BC radiocarbon dates obtained on ABGs in layers 3728 and 3263 (Barclay, Chapter 4, and Table 4.4).

In addition to the East Sussex Grog-tempered ware sherd noted above, two rims, each less than 5% of the diameter, from sandy bead rim jars, the more or less complete profile of a small briquetage cup (Fig. 3.2, 16) and the flat base of a medium/large shell-tempered jar were recovered from layer 3249, where they were associated with a slightly later, 1st century BC, radiocarbon date (Barclay, Chapter 4). However, once again, the pottery from this feature did not appear to have been used as part of the structured deposits but rather represented domestic waste.

Pit 3998

A large, shell-tempered storage jar (Fig. 3.2, 17) of 2nd–1st century BC date may have formed part of the *pars pro toto* deposit of iron objects (Fitzpatrick, see below) recovered from this feature. Sherds from every part of this vessel were present, but it is too friable to be fully reconstructed and it remains unclear whether it was deposited in pieces or as a complete vessel. Six sherds (322 g) were assigned to the basal fill (4115), where the head of an iron set hammer (Fig. 3.5, 2) was found, while the rest (106 sherds, 8632 g) came from the upper fill (3999), where at least some of them apparently formed a single layer separating 3999 from the underlying charcoal-rich deposit 4114. The iron nave hoop, the socketed spearhead (Fig. 3.5, 3 and 4) and the bundle of birch bark tar and twisted fibres were recorded as resting on this layer of sherds, although the possibility that they were originally contained within the vessel cannot be ruled out. Other sherds from layer 3999 (20 pieces, 129 g) included rims from a smaller, shell-tempered bead rim jar (Fig. 3.3, 18) and a jar/bowl with a high, rounded shoulder and a simple, upright rim (R7) in a sandy fabric, the base of a finely-made, grog-tempered, neutral-profiled vessel (Fig. 3.3, 19), as well as undiagnostic body sherds in sandy and sand and flint-tempered fabrics.

Pit 3513

No pottery came from the basal fill (3696) of this feature, but two Middle/Late Iron Age vessels had been deposited, probably deliberately, at higher levels. Both were jars/bowls with high, rounded shoulders and simple, upright rims. The first (ON 86; Fig. 3.3, 20), made in shell and grog-tempered fabric had apparently been placed in the centre of the pit, on the surface of charcoal-rich layer 3647. Although now fragmentary (86 sherds, 523 g), most of the breaks are fresh, so it is probable that the vessel was deposited in an at least semi-complete condition, but no sherds from the base or lower walls were present. The second vessel (ON 85; Fig. 3.3, 21; 60 sherds, 491 g), in a sandy fabric, was recovered from layer 3552. This vessel had been repaired with birch bark tar adhesive and five post-firing perforations, each 5 mm in diameter and set in a quincunx arrangement, had been drilled through its base. Other pottery, including two rims from shell-tempered bead rim jars (Fig. 3.3, 22), pieces from at least two briquetage vessels (including Fig. 3.3, 23) and undiagnostic body sherds in sand and flint- (1 sherd, 3 g) and shell- (16 sherds, 23 g) tempered fabrics, from these lower fills confirm their 2nd–1st century BC date. However, the uppermost fill (3514), contained 30 early Romano-British sherds (103 g), in addition to four residual Iron Age pieces (3 g); this later material probably accumulated in the hollow resulting from the compaction of the lower fills over time.

Late Iron Age

The Late Iron Age (1st century BC, perhaps extending into the early decades of the 1st century AD) witnessed the not only the introduction but the rapid rise to dominance of the grog-tempered wares (Table 3.5; 49% by sherd count; 41% by weight), with the shell-tempered fabrics continuing to hold 35% (by sherd count) of the market. The importance of sandy fabrics, however, declined during this century; these wares accounted for just 15% of the Late Iron Age sherds. Vessel forms comprised a variety of high-shouldered, bead- and proto-bead rimmed jars as well as necked, cordoned jar and jar/bowl forms with upright or slightly everted rims. Profiles varied in detail but most belonged within widely-distributed types (eg, Thompson 1982, types B1-3, B2-1, B3-5, B5, C3, and C6-1). By this time, most vessels were at least partially burnished or smoothed, but decoration continued to be rare and largely confined to horizontal cordons or bulges, incised grooves or simple, burnished line motifs (grouped parallel lines, vertical lines between cordons or intersecting arcs).

Sherds belonging within this period were predominantly associated with the second phase of enclosure construction (Enclosures 2b, 3 and 4; Table 3.4). The ditches again contained remarkably little pottery (26 sherds, 337 g), mostly undiagnostic or poorly diagnostic sherds spanning a wide date range (Early Iron Age to early Romano-British), although a further 36 pieces (382 g) were recovered from one short length (cut 3498) of ditch 4237 on the western side of Enclosure 2b, at the point where this feature cut the earlier, Enclosure 1 ditch (4242). Some cross-context joins were noted between sherds assigned to ditch 4242 (cut 3498 and the upper fill (3490) of cut 3493), but the material is broadly consistent with the radiocarbon dates for these features, of *100 cal BC–cal AD 80 (SUERC-38151, 2005±35 BP at 95% probability)* for ditch 4242 (cut 3493), and *130–1 cal BC (SUERC-38152, 2095±35 BP at 95% probability)* for the primary fill (3496) of ditch 4237 (cut 3498); it is also comparable with the assemblage from pit 2 at Ewell (Cotton 2001, fig. 6). Grog-tempered wares were more frequent than the shell-tempered fabrics (53% and 42% by sherd count), while the vessel forms also provide a contrast between the two wares, with necked, cordoned jars/bowls (R18; 0.15 EVE) present in the grog-tempered fabrics and proto-bead rim (R6: 0.14 EVE) and bead rim (R12; 0.18 EVE) jars in the shelly wares. The only other sherd consisted of a bead rim jar fragment (0.09 EVE) in a sand and flint-tempered fabric.

Overall, Late Iron Age sherds were recovered from 19 contemporary pits but only seven contained significant groups (20 or more sherds, weighing at least 200 g). One of these, pit 3737, appeared to contain a purely domestic assemblage (28 sherds, 221 g), consisting only of shell-tempered body sherds, along with two grog-tempered pieces (21 g). Five of the other pits contained pottery used as part of formal, structured deposits, in three instances (pits 3053, 3220 and 4313) associated with articulated animal bone groups and two without (pits 3088 and 4135). The status of the assemblage from pit 3579 was more uncertain, however.

Pit 3053

The majority of sherds from this feature derived from the perforated shell-tempered storage jar noted above (Fig. 3.3, 24; 56 sherds, 1328 g), which was associated with three articulated animal bone groups. Other sherds from this feature (28 pieces, 445 g) were mostly from the upper fill (3054) and were derived from general domestic waste. Shell-tempered fabrics were the most common (16 sherds; 57%), dominated by plain bodies with a single rim from a pulled bead rim jar (R13). The 11 grog-tempered sherds included rims from a bead rim jar and a globular-bodied jar/bowl with an upright rim (Thompson 1982, type B1-3); the only other sherd present was a single sandy body sherd, also of Late Iron Age date.

Pit 3088

A large, natural flint nodule placed centrally on the base of this feature separated groups of sherds from two vessels, both now fragmentary but probably deposited in at least a semi-complete condition. These comprised a grog-tempered, everted rim jar with a corrugated profile (Fig. 3.3, 25; 104 sherds, 382 g), broadly comparable with Thompson's type B3-1 vessels (1982, 139) and a shell-tempered, proto-bead rimmed jar (Fig. 3.3, 26; 29 sherds, 747 g). Two small (5 g), sandy ware body sherds of Middle/Late Iron Age date and two crumbs (1 g) of briquetage were the only other ceramics from this feature.

Pit 3220

Just three plain body sherds (22 g) in grog- (2 pieces) and shell- (1 piece) tempered fabrics were found in the basal fill of this feature. However, sherds from two grog-tempered vessels (Fig. 3.3, 27 and 28), both with post-firing perforations through the base, were found in association with an articulated animal bone deposit (ABG 231) in layer 322. One of these vessels (Fig. 3.3, 28) was unusually hard and highly fired, its multi-coloured surfaces perhaps indicating that it had also been burnt prior to its deliberate deposition. Both vessels were incomplete (approximately 50% of each), but the pit was not fully excavated.

Pit 3579

Overall, 63 sherds (1731 g) were recovered. The rim of a shell-tempered bead-rimmed storage jar (Fig. 3.3, 29) and a dish base (Fig. 3.5, 30), along with sherds from two more or less complete vessels, a shell-tempered bead rimmed jar (Fig. 3.3, 31) and a grog-tempered, narrow-necked, cordoned jar (Fig. 3.4, 32), were found in the basal fill (3609). This latter vessel is broadly comparable with Thompson's type B3-5 (1982, 155) and indicates a date in the final decades of the 1st century BC or early 1st century AD for the group, prior to the arrival of imports or the more 'Romanised' fabrics and forms. All the sherds from 3609 were recorded by the excavator as being from a single vessel (ON 81), perhaps implying that the sherds occurred in a close-knit group. Two other rims, from another shell-tempered bead rim jar and a small, grog-tempered shouldered jar with an out-turned rim (Fig. 3.4, 33) came from layer 3617, but, unusually, no stray body or base sherds were found in this feature. This, coupled with the inclusion of two more or less complete vessels, may indicate the deliberate selection of material for disposal in this feature, although the possibility that it simply results from the partial excavation of this pit cannot be ruled out.

Pit 4135

Eleven pieces (312 g) from a grog-tempered, round-bodied bowl with an upright, cordoned neck (Fig. 3.4, 34) were found associated with charred wood fragments on the base of this feature, while two further sherds (11 g) from this vessel were assigned to overlying layer, 4140. The freshly broken nature of the sherds and the absence of companion pieces suggest that the bowl was originally deposited in a far more complete condition; this, coupled with its positioning on the base of the feature suggest that it represents part of a formalised, perhaps ritual action. Stray body and base sherds from the overlying layers (4138 and 4140) mostly consisted of grog-tempered wares (13 sherds), along with single pieces in sandy and shell-tempered fabrics.

Pit 4313

Although not fully excavated, 101 Late Iron Age sherds, 1575 g, were recovered. Just six plain bodies (65 g; five grog- and one shell-tempered), came from the basal fill (layer 4366), where three ABGs (ABGs 250–2), all from foetal or neonatal animals, were found. The remaining sherds were from overlying layer 4314. However, another 80 sherds (779 g) assigned to layer 4319 in Middle Iron Age pit 4315 probably belonged to this deposit; the nature of the material from 4314 and 4319 is exactly comparable and numerous cross-context joins were noted between sherds from the two layers. Furthermore, there were no similarities or cross-context joins between the sherds assigned to 4319 and others from pit 4315. It seems most likely, then, that the 4319 sherds were incorrectly numbered, and the two groups are therefore considered together here (175 sherds, 2289 g).

The majority of these sherds derived from three semi-complete vessels, one in each of the three main Late Iron Age fabrics. These comprised a shell-tempered proto-bead rim jar (70 pieces, 496 g; both contexts; Fig. 3.4, 35), a necked, cordoned jar/bowl in a sandy fabric (58 pieces; 568 g; Fig. 3.4, 36) and a grog-tempered, inverted pear-shaped jar (20 sherds, 366 g; both contexts; Fig. 3.4, 37). Post-firing perforations in the base of the sandy jar/bowl and its badly spalled and worn surface, indicated that this vessel had been extensively used prior to its deposition. Unfortunately, no details concerning the arrangement of these vessels or their relationship(s) with the ABGs in the underlying layer were recorded, but it remains feasible that they too represented structured deposition.

The remaining sherds consisted of shell-tempered wares (19 pieces, 782 g) along with eight (77 g) pieces in sandy fabrics. These included a single rim from a bead rim jar (0.15 EVE), while the shelly sherds included rims from two other proto-bead rim jars (0.18 EVE), one with evidence of a glued repair, and flat base sherds from a medium/large jar.

Iron Age

Sherds assigned to this broad period (Table 3.1) mostly comprised small undiagnostic body sherds. Approximately 60% (by count) occurred in Iron Age features, either alone or alongside more closely dated pieces, the remainder being residual in later, Romano-British features. All were made in fabrics present among the wider Iron Age assemblage so do not merit further discussion here.

Latest Iron Age and Romano-British

It is now well recognised that there are no clear boundaries between Iron Age and Romano-British material culture in southern Britain (Fulford 2010). Although ceramics and other distinctive items, such as decorative metalwork, were imported from Gaul and other parts of the Mediterranean world, these reached only a minority of sites, and in material culture terms there is generally little to distinguish a late 1st century BC 'pre-Romano-British' settlement from one of later 1st century AD, early 'Romano-British' date. Ceramically, local fabrics and vessel forms established by the end of the 1st century BC continued to be manufactured with little change until well after the Roman Conquest, and in the absence of imports, more diagnostic materials and/or an independently dated ceramic sequence, the dating of context groups within this transitional period can be problematic. Although somewhat arbitrary, the beginning of the 1st century AD has been taken as marking the end of the Late Iron Age, with the term 'latest Iron Age/early Romano-British' used to describe material broadly of 1st century AD date, and 'early Romano-British' being used only when there was more conclusive evidence for a post-Conquest date. However, as the composition of the ceramic assemblage changed comparatively little during this period, it is described here as a single entity.

Composition of the assemblage

Overall, 1649 sherds, 25,354 g (Table 3.1), extending from the early decades of the 1st century AD to the mid-/late 2nd century AD, were recovered, providing evidence for a considerable increase in the intensity of activity at this time compared with that of proceeding periods. Imports, however, were scarce, accounting for just 2% of the assemblage (Table 3.2). The samian, all from Southern and Central Gaulish sources, is of mid-/late 1st to 2nd century AD date. Diagnostic Southern Gaulish pieces included a pre-Flavian form 24/25 cup (primary fill of cut 3105 of ditch 4232), bases from a form 18 platter and a cup or small bowl (pits 3503 and 3683, respectively) and a decorated sherd from a form 30 bowl (pit 3419). The single Central Gaulish sherd comes from a form 33 cup found in pit 3683. Dressel 20 amphora sherds were found in pits 3174 and 3503, feature 2059 and ditch 3313 as well as in three contexts in evaluation trench 6. These vessels were used to transport olive oil from southern Spain from the 1st to at least the mid-3rd century AD, but were often subsequently re-used, and probably widely traded in their own right, as empty containers (Callender 1965, 23; Van der Werff 2003; Evans 2007, 179). To facilitate this re-use, the upper part of the vessel (rim/neck/handles) was often removed, to provide a wider, more easily accessible opening, and it may be of some relevance that both pits contained pieces from these upper zones, although neither bore any unequivocal evidence for deliberate removal.

British-made, fine, tableware vessels were similarly restricted, limited to the few Fine Greyware and Highgate C ware sherds. The fine greywares included six pieces (55 g) from London-type ware vessels which enjoyed a floruit during the Trajanic period (Davies *et al.* 1994, 151). Two pieces, comprising part of a carinated bowl with a flared wall and an out-turned rim (Lon IVD; *cf.* Marsh 1978, fig. 6.20, 44.19) from ditch 4150 and a body sherd (ON 126) from pit 3985, displayed the incised decoration typical of this ware; the others were plain, derived from bowl (pit 3289) and beaker (pit 4052) forms. The remaining Fine Greyware sherds were mostly derived from beakers; one body sherd with rouletted decoration (pit 3921) may be from an imitation butt beaker of pre- to early Flavian date, while rims from two vessels with short sharply everted rims (LON IIIC) and three carinated beakers (LON IIIG) of later 1st century AD date came from pits 3503, 4002, 4052 and 4199. The only other form in these wares was a round-bodied jar with a thickened rim (LON IIB), represented by a small group of joining sherds from pit 3503. The Highgate C wares carried the fine grey beaker tradition into the 2nd century AD, a poppy-head beaker rim (LON IIIF) being found in pit 3921, while two barbotine-dot decorated body sherds probably from similar forms came from ditch 4378.

The oxidised wares, however, represented a range of intermediate quality vessels falling between the fine tablewares and the more utilitarian, generally unoxidised, kitchen wares, and were probably used in a variety of food/liquid serving and storage roles. Together, the two fabrics making up this category, the miscellaneous oxidised wares (OXID) and the regionally-traded Verulamium region whitewares (VRW), accounted for 10% of the assemblage by sherd count. The miscellaneous oxidised wares (OXID) encompassed a range of different fabrics, some white-slipped, representing the products of several different centres. While most of these were probably British, five flagon body sherds in a hard, fine white fabric with a burnished exterior (pit 3419) could represent continental imports, perhaps from the Lezoux region. A small number of butt beaker body sherds (enclosure ditch 4233, pit 4199 and layer 4213) probably belonged within the middle decades of the 1st century AD (*c.* AD 40–70/80), while a possible girth beaker sherd, decorated with a red-painted band with wavy and horizontal lines incised through it (Fig. 3.4, 39), was recovered from pit 3174. Most of the other unsourced oxidised ware sherds probably derived from flagons, although diagnostic pieces were scarce. Rims were limited to a ring-necked flagon with a prominent upper ring, probably belonging within the first half of the 2nd century AD (LON IB4) and a narrow-necked jar (R101), both from feature 2059, and a carinated bowl (Fig. 3.4, 40; Marsh 1978, 178, fig. 6.19 and 20, type 44) from pit 3174.

The Verulamium region whitewares were also predominantly from flagons, although again diagnostic sherds were scarce. A rim from a large, wide-mouthed flagon/jug/pitcher form (LON IH) broken at neck/shoulder junction came from segment 3796 of ditch 4378, while a ring-necked flagon rim came from pit 4199 and jar rims (LON IIG and IIH), both characteristic products of this industry, were found in the secondary fill of Late Iron Age ditch 3764 and evaluation trench 7 respectively. The only mortaria identified within the entire assemblage were also made in this region; a rim (LON HOF) came from unphased feature 3101 and a body sherd from Late Iron Age pit 3225, both surviving in a very worn, abraded condition. These wares are present in pre-Boudiccan contexts in London, but production peaked in the Flavian-Trajanic period, declining sharply after *c.* AD 140 (Davies *et al.* 1994, 41).

The remainder of the assemblage consisted of unoxidised coarsewares which included vessels suited for a wide variety of roles, from food preparation and storage to 'everyday' serving vessels of intermediate quality. The coarsewares continued to consisted of three broad fabric groups; grey/brown sandy wares (52%), grog-tempered wares (19%) and shell-tempered wares (14%) in order of prevalence by sherd count (Table 3.2). The two latter groups, tempered with grog and shell, represented the continuation of 1st century BC ceramic traditions;

both out-lasted the Conquest (Cotton 2001, 12; Jones 2012, 121 and 123) but their frequency appeared to decline relatively rapidly thereafter, Pollard dating their demise in west Kent, at least, to the period *c.* AD 75–120 (1988, 64). Conversely, the wheel-made grey/brown wares increased dramatically from the middle of the 1st century AD and thereafter continued as the principal coarseware type throughout the Romano-British period. Most of these wares derived from the Alice Holt/Farnham industry (Lyne and Jefferies 1979), located on the Surrey/Hampshire borders, although some may be from more local sources or those supplying London (Davies *et al.* 1994, 91).

Perhaps unsurprisingly, these wares showed the most diverse range of forms. Bead rims jars (LON IIA) formed a significant element of the assemblage (19% by EVE) but necked jars, often with cordons and/or burnished decoration (LON IIC and D; eg, Fig. 3.4, 38 and 41), were by far the most common (61% by EVE). The paucity of beaker and bowl forms throughout the coarseware assemblage was also reflected in this group, with just two rims from imitation butt beakers (pits 8183 and 3870; Fig. 3.4, 45) and a two further rims from bowls; one with a with a reed-rim (LON IVF; secondary fill of segment 3814 of Late Iron Age/early Romano-British ditch group 4232), the other of Atrebatic style (LON IVK) from unphased pit 3504. Part of a strainer bowl (Fig. 3.4, 48) with pre-firing perforations was found in pit 3870. A flat base from another open form, found in the uppermost fill of pit 3503, attested to the continued use of birch bark tar glue to repair pottery vessels. Other Romano-British examples of this practice have been noted elsewhere within the county, at the King William IV site, Ewell, at Manor Farm, Guildford (English 2005) and in Staines (McKinley 2004a, 31), for example. The presence of at least small quantities of sandy ware post-dating AD 120/130 was highlighted by rims from an everted rim jar (LON IIF; pit 3413) and a shallow, plain rimmed dish (LON IVJ; pit 3472), while the two definite pieces of Thameside greyware (TSK), both from straight-sided bowls/dishes with triangular rims (LON IVH; feature 2059 and pit 3683) may indicate the presence of other, less diagnostic, products of this industry amongst the sandy wares.

Most the grog-tempered wares (fabrics G100 and G101) were similar in appearance to Highgate B wares (Davies *et al.* 1994, 74), although there was no certain evidence to suggest that they were made there. At least 15 (341 g) of the G100 sherds, some from thick-walled storage jar forms, were made in fabrics with distinctive oxidised surfaces, a grey core and a speckling of black inclusions, probably charcoal, in addition to grog and a little sand; these may be classed as 'Patchgrove ware' (Ward-Perkins 1939, 176–8), but they were not separately quantified due to the difficulties of reliably distinguishing fabrics by firing colour. Locally, small quantities of Patchgrove ware were also identified in the assemblage from Reigate Road, Ewell (Cotton 2001, 12). Another small but distinct group contained greater quantities of sand alongside the grog (fabric G101), but no diagnostic sherds were present amongst this material. Overall, necked, cordoned jar forms (LON IIC and D) were prevalent, representing 49% by EVE, while bead rimmed jars (LON IIA and B; Fig. 3.4, 46) formed just 19%. Other forms included rims from at least three necked storage jars (6% by EVE; LON IIL) and single rims from an upright necked jar (LON IIG; 3%), a shouldered jar with an almost horizontal, out-turned rim (R21; 6%), and beakers with sharply everted (LON IIIC; Fig. 3.4, 44; 10%) or beaded (R106; 7%) rims.

As in proceeding periods, the shell-tempered wares remain largely unsourced, although some probably derived from the north Kent or south Essex coastal zones. All 16 rims belonged to bead rim jar forms (LON IIA; eg, Fig. 3.4, 42), although detail of vessel shape did vary; most were high-shouldered but examples with internally thickened, large and rounded or small, pointed rims were all noted. Rim diameters also showed a wider range than the other coarseware forms, varying from 80 mm (two vessels from early Romano-British pit 3458) to 200 mm (pit 3174) in diameter, with the main cluster between 120–160 mm. The use of shell as a tempering material declined rapidly in this assemblage, from 35% by sherd count of the Late Iron Age (1st century BC) sherds, to just 9% of those assigned an early Romano-British date, which, coupled with the limited range of forms, suggests an early demise for these wares, perhaps in the third quarter of the 1st century AD.

Distribution

The majority of the latest Iron Age and Romano-British sherds came from pits, with 20% by sherd count (333 sherds, 3856 g), recovered from the ditches forming enclosures 2C, 5 and 6. Of these, just 13 sherds, 113 g, were recovered from primary fills. These comprised the mid-1st century AD samian form 24/25 cup (0.2 EVE), from the northernmost ditch (4232, cut 3105), as well as less diagnostic but broadly contemporary grey/brown sandy sherds, including bead rimmed and necked cordoned jar fragments (0.13 EVE), from the same feature (cut 3674) and a shelly ware jar base and a grey/brown sandy ware body sherd from ditch 2071 (cut 3006) on the southern side of Enclosure 2C. Residual, Iron Age, sherds (76 pieces, 318 g) as well as one of Late Bronze Age date (4 g, Enclosure 6) occurred amongst the material from the upper fills, although the remaining sherds were predominantly of later 1st–early 2nd century AD date, indicating that the ditches were out of use and filling up by this time. This process, however, continued into the period after *c.* AD 120/130, with some of the ditches (eg, ditch 2071, cut 2030, and ditch 4378, cut 3092 and 3796) also containing material of mid-/late 2nd century AD date. These assemblages were characterised by the overwhelming dominance of sandy fabrics, some fired to the blue/grey hue typical of the later Alice Holt products, together with unsourced oxidised ware, Verulamium region whitewares and a few Highgate C poppy-head beaker; grog- and shell-tempered fabrics were completely absent from these groups.

Latest Iron Age or Romano-British pottery was found in 38 of the pits considered to be contemporary with Enclosures 2C, 5 and 6, with three others (pits 3058, 3295 and 3819) containing residual Iron Age sherds only. Most only contained small quantities, with just 14 pits containing more than 20 sherds or 200 g of this date (pits 3015/4199, 3174/4376, 3183, 3289, 3412, 3458, 3503, 3533, 3535, 3870, 3921, 3985 and 4052). Most sherds appeared to represent normal domestic debris, although the practice of making formal, structured deposits in pits continued into this period, with deliberately placed ABGs, metalwork and other artefacts occurring in 12 of the pits assigned to this phase. These included six of the ceramically-rich features (pits 4376/3174, 3183, 3535, 3870, 3921 and 4052), but more or less complete pottery vessels seem only to have used as part of these deposits in pits 4376/3174 and 3535.

1st century AD

Pit 3535

A decorated, grey/brown sandy ware necked cordoned jar (Fig. 3.4, 38; 48 sherds, 1240 g) deposited in this feature contained part of an iron saw blade (Fig. 3.6, 9) and the burnt remains of at least two lambs. This vessel, probably of late 1st century AD date (*c.* AD 70–90) and an Alice Holt product (*cf.* Lyne and Jefferies 1979, fig. 6, 1.13), appeared to have been deliberately broken over the remains of the dog (ABG 115), radiocarbon dated to *50 cal BC–cal AD 70 (SUERC-38160, 1985±35 BP at 95% probability)*, placed on the base of the pit. The base of the vessel was severely scuffed, suggesting it had seen considerable use prior to deposition. It may also have been deliberately holed; the central part of the base was substantially missing, but there was evidence for at least four small, post-firing perforations set in a square. Although not deliberately altered in this way, a similar necked, cordoned jar had been used to contain burnt sheep/goat bones at Reigate Road, Ewell (Cotton 2001, 10, fig. 11.2). The six remaining Romano-British sherds from this feature comprised miscellaneous body and base sherds in a range of sand and grog-tempered fabrics, with three residual Late Bronze Age (layer 3537) and Iron Age pieces from layers 3536 and 3890.

Pit 4376/3174

In total, these pits contained 237 sherds, weighing 5841 g. None of the pieces from the deposits filling the original pit (4376; 8 sherds, 80 g) were closely datable, although, with the exception of a single, small (5 g), residual, Early/Middle Iron Age body sherd in a sand and flint-tempered fabric from layer 4188, all probably belonged within the 1st century AD. The other pieces from layer 4188 comprised two body sherds (13 g each) in shell- and grog-tempered fabrics, while a single shell-tempered jar shoulder sherd (18 g) came from layer 3740. Fragments representing than 5% of the diameter of a lid and a plain upright necked jar/bowl, both in sandy fabrics (16 g), and two grog-tempered body sherds (15 g) came from layer 4183, where a radiocarbon date of *100 cal BC–cal AD 60 (SUERC-38161, 1990±35 BP at 95% probability)* was obtained for a partial lamb skeleton.

The pottery from the later recut (3174; 229 sherds, 5761 g) was predominantly of Flavian to Trajanic date (*c.* AD 70–120). This material was dominated by the grey/brown sandy wares (153 sherds; 2519 g; 67% by count; 45% by weight), with rims from at least six necked, cordoned forms (2.43 EVE) and three bead rimmed jars (0.65 EVE), all likely to be products of the early Alice Holt industry. The other shell- and grog-tempered coarsewares were present in much more minor quantities (17% and 2% by sherd count respectively; 40 sherds, 1279 g and 4 sherds, 41 g), vessel forms consisting of just two shelly bead rimmed jars (0.41 EVE). Similar fabric and form proportions occurred in City of London assemblages only after *c.* AD 100 (Davies *et al.* 1994, 199–204). Continental imports included two sherds from a South Gaulish samian cup, as well as two Dressel 20 amphora sherds (942 g), one representing approximately half of the rim/neck and one upper handle stump of the vessel. Other Romanised fabrics comprised Verulamium region whitewares (9 sherds, 703 g), and unsourced oxidised wares (9 sherds, 58 g), one with red-pained decoration (Fig. 3.4, 39) probably from a girth beaker and five from a carinated bowl (Fig. 3.4, 40) imitating samian form 29 (eg, Marsh 1978, 178, fig. 6.19 and 20, type 44).

Although now fragmentary, a grey/brown sandy ware necked, cordoned jar and large, shell-tempered jar (Fig. 3.4, 41 and 42) may have been deposited in an at least semi-complete condition in layer 3246. The bead rim jar base was smoothed and abraded as if the vessel had been much used. Two plain body sherds of Verulamium region whiteware from this context probably derived from a globular-bodied flagon (Fig. 3.4, 43) assigned only to the cut number (3174) of this pit, and may indicate that it, too, came from this layer. The base of this vessel had been deliberately perforated, while the base plate of the necked, cordoned jar was the only part of this vessel to be completely missing. For the most part, however, the pottery from this feature represented only small parts of whole vessels. Numerous cross context joins were noted, including the two pieces of samian (layers 3711 and 3247), a large, grey/brown sandy ware necked, cordoned jar (layers 3175, 3177, 3245, 3247 and 3711) and a smaller necked, cordoned jar/bowl (layers 3177 and 3711), while the two amphora sherds found in layer 3711 may also have been from the same vessel. These factors suggest that most of the pottery from this feature represented redeposited material, initially disposed of in another location before being incorporated into these deposits, an interpretation supported by the considerable quantities of other material types (eg, metalworking debris, burnt flint, fired clay, shell) found in these layers. However, the remains of between 25 and 30 animals found in layer 3711 at the bottom of this feature, and the range of species included (mostly sheep/goat with two dogs, a foal, two domestic fowl and a raven; Higbee, see below), as well as other ABGs and two human neonate skeletons found at higher levels (layers 3177, 3246, 3247 and 3710), highlight the symbolic or ceremonial significance of this pit, in a way not readily apparent from the ceramics, although it is possible that the two holed vessels could have been deliberately broken in a symbolic gesture forming part of 'a wider Romano-British chthonic ritual' (Fulford and Timby 2001, 296). The presence of apparently undifferentiated domestic debris in otherwise 'ritual' features has already been noted elsewhere – in the slightly later, mid-Roman, ritual shaft at Springhead, Kent (Seager Smith *et al.* 2011, 65), for example, while similar dichotomies in the treatment of animal and ceramic assemblages have also been observed at Snow's Farm, Haddenham, Cambridgeshire (Evans and Hodder 2006), Coleshill, Warwickshire (Booth 2006) and Uley, Gloucestershire (Leach 1993), where unusual aspects associated with animal bone deposits were not routinely reflected by the other material categories.

Pit 3870

The ceramics (72 sherds, 1586 g), were again predominantly of Flavian-Trajanic date. The grey/brown sandy wares accounted for 40% of the assemblage by both sherd count and weight, with grog- and shell-tempered fabrics representing 32% and 19% by count. The rest of the assemblage comprised five Verulamium region whiteware sherds and two residual Iron Age pieces. This feature was predominantly filled with successive dumps of burnt domestic and/or industrial waste material, including fired clay and burnt flint, although at least some ritualised use of this feature is indicated by the complete skeleton of a terrier-type dog (ABG 137) and the head/back of an adult horse (ABG 114) in layer 3771. The pottery, however, showed no obvious signs of burning, and appeared to represent domestic debris although several unusual forms were present.

Just seven sherds (133 g, layer 4112) were recovered from the basal fills, comprising one residual East Sussex grog-tempered sherd and six miscellaneous early Romano-British body sherds in grey/brown sandy and grog-tempered fabrics. Grog- and shell-tempered body sherds were also found in layers 3956 and 3958, along with two small rim fragments from bead rimmed and necked round-bodied jars (Marsh and Tyers 1978, 556–7, types IIA and IIB). Sherds from a grog-tempered beaker (Fig. 3.4, 44), were found in layer 3871 while part of a globular-bodied imitation butt beaker in a grey/brown sandy fabric (Fig. 3.4, 45), and a second necked round-bodied jar (Fig. 3.4, 46) came from layer 3950 above. A flagon rim (Fig. 3.4, 47), similar to examples from Elmsleigh Centre, Staines (Jones with Poulton 2010, fig. 2.3, 640 and fig. 2.40, 864) was also found in this deposit. Comparable forms were made by the early Alice Holt industry but usually in fabrics containing grog; this example is in a light brown sandy fabric although the exterior is so well burnished that it feels as if it is grog-tempered. Three joining sherds from the complete profile of a strainer bowl (Fig. 3.4, 48; *cf.* Lyne and Jefferies 1979, 46–7, fig. 33) came from layer 3949 above; abraded wear on the lower part of this vessel suggest that it was much used. Although part of the standard range of Romanised forms, strainer bowls were never common, but evidence from eastern England suggests that they were used to make infused native or 'Celtic' beer (Sealey 1999, 123), in the serving of mead or other herbal infusions. Although each of these vessels was represented by only a small part of the whole and not all were found in the same deposit, it remains curious that a complete set of drinking vessels – a strainer for preparation, a flagon for serving and beakers for consumption – occurred together, with only minor parts of other, more everyday vessels.

2nd century AD activity

Pottery from four isolated features (feature 2059 and pits 3015, 3412 and 3683) indicated continued activity into the mid-/late 2nd century AD. Together, these features contained 170 sherds (1565 g), again dominated by the sandy wares (62% by count), many in the more Romanised blue/grey fabrics. The shell- and grog-tempered wares occurred in smaller but almost equal quantities (21 and 19 sherds respectively), along with a handful of pieces in the oxidised fabrics and 13 sherds of Dressel 20 amphora from feature 2059. Overall, however, diagnostic sherds were limited to just 11 rims (0.93 EVE). In addition to small, residual pieces from necked, cordoned and bead rimmed jars, mid-/late 2nd century AD forms included the Central Gaulish samian form 33 cup fragment (pit 3683), an oxidised ring-necked flagon (LON IB4; feature 2059), an everted rim jar (LON IIF; pit 3412) and a shallow, plain rimmed dish (LON IVJ; pit 3015), both in greyware fabrics, as well as the only definite Thameside greyware sherds present within the assemblage, both from straight-sided bowls/dishes with triangular rims (LON IVH; feature 2059 and pit 3683). No evidence for formal, structured deposits was encountered in these features, the pottery and other finds recovered from them appearing to represent normal domestic debris.

List of illustrated sherds

Fig. 3.1

1. Shouldered jar with simple, upright rim; shell-tempered ware; Early Iron Age grave 3052, context 3051, ON 54, PRN 482
2. Weakly shouldered jar with simple, unelaborated rim; grog-tempered ware; Early Iron Age pit 3178, context 3180, PRN 21
3. Shouldered jar with short, upright neck and irregular rim; shell-tempered ware; Early Iron Age pit 3178, context 3180, PRN 22
4. Weakly shouldered jar with upright, flat-topped, internally bevelled rim; sand and flint-tempered ware; Early Iron Age pit 3178, context 3180, PRN 20
5. Externally-expanded rim from a large vessel; shell-tempered ware; Early Iron Age pit 3178, context 3181, PRN 23
6. Ovoid jar with a simple, slightly inturned rim; sand and flint-tempered ware; Early Iron Age pit 4333, context 4334, PRN 1092
7. Shouldered jar with simple, upright rim; sand and flint-tempered ware; Early Iron Age pit 3940, contexts 3941 (PRN 179) and 4064 (PRN 177)

Fig. 3.2

8. S-profiled jar with a slightly everted rim; sandy ware; Middle Iron Age pit 4315, context 4321, PRN 426

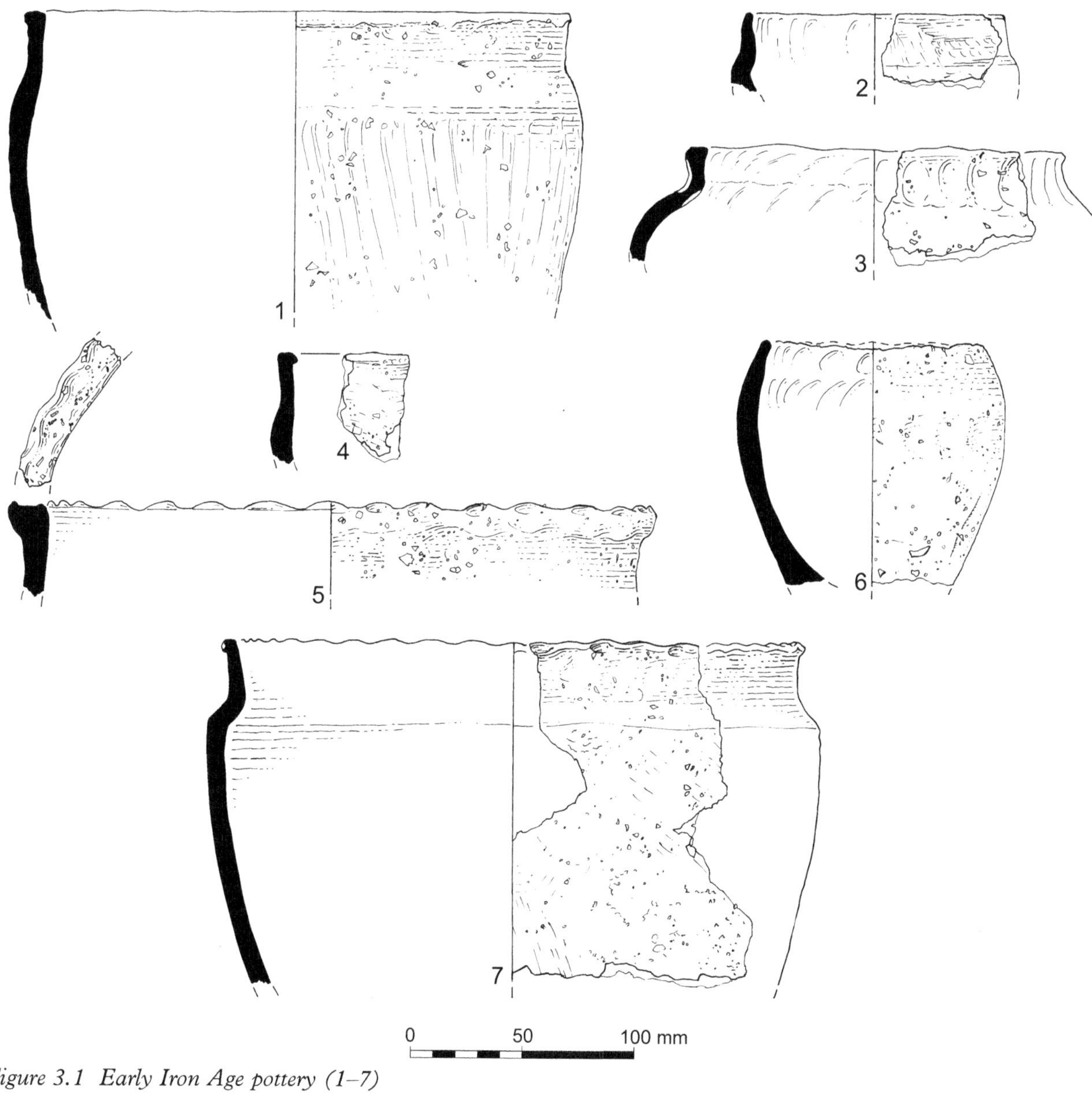

Figure 3.1 Early Iron Age pottery (1–7)

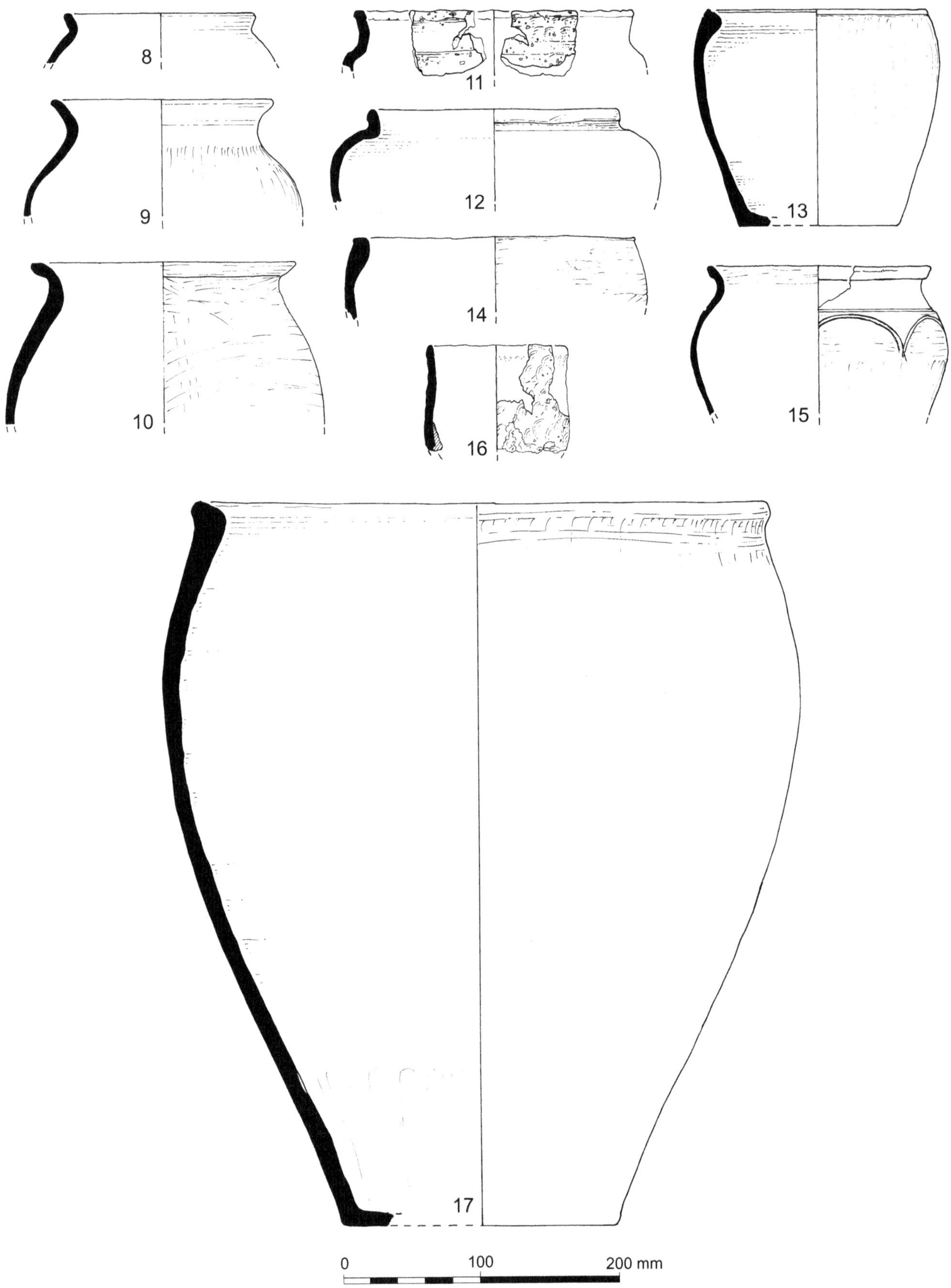

Figure 3.2 Middle and Middle/Late Iron Age pottery (8–17)

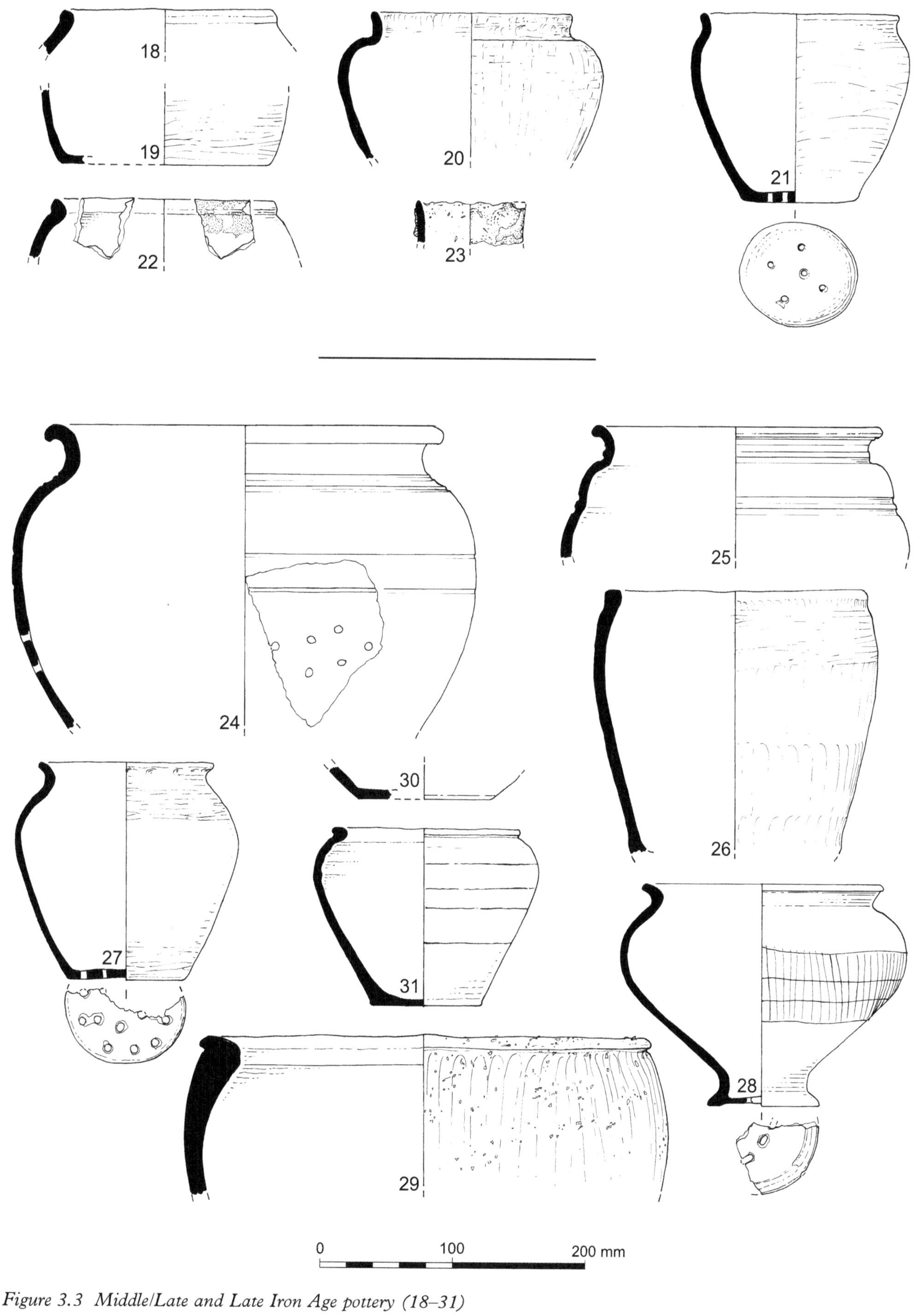

Figure 3.3 Middle/Late and Late Iron Age pottery (18–31)

9. S-profiled jar with a slightly everted rim; glauconitic sandy ware; Middle Iron Age pit 4315, context 4332, PRN 431
10. S-profiled jar with a slightly everted rim; sandy ware; Middle Iron Age pit 4315, context 4332, PRN 434
11. Weakly shouldered jar with simple, unelaborated rim; sand and flint-tempered ware; Middle Iron Age pit 4315, context 4320, PRN 417
12. Round shouldered bowl with a pulled bead rim and a short, vertical neck; grog and shell-tempered ware; Middle Iron Age pit 3231, context 3598, PRN 151
13. Proto-bead rimmed jar; shell-tempered ware; Middle Iron Age pit 3231, context 3232, PRN 148
14. Proto-bead rimmed jar; shell-tempered ware; Middle/Late Iron Age pit 3341, context 3749, PRN 164
15. Round-shouldered jar/bowl with finely tooled 'eye-brow' motif on shoulder; East Sussex grog-tempered ware; Middle/Late Iron Age pit 3341, context 3749, PRN 165
16. Briquetage cup; Middle/Late Iron Age pit 3341, context 3249, PRN 155
17. Bead rimmed storage jar; shell-tempered ware; Middle/Late Iron Age pit 3998, contexts 3999 (PRN 395) and 4115 (PRN 394)

Fig. 3.3

18. Bead rimmed jar; shell-tempered ware; Middle/Late Iron Age pit 3998, context 3999, PRN 397
19. Finely made, well-finished base from a neutral-profiled vessel, possibly a saucepan pot; grog-tempered ware; Middle/Late Iron Age pit 3998, context 3999, PRN 401
20. Jar/bowl with a high, rounded shoulder and a simple, upright rim; shell and grog-tempered ware; Middle/Late Iron Age pit 3513, context 3647, ON 86, PRN 392
21. Jar/bowl with a high, rounded shoulder and a simple, upright rim; sandy ware. Post-firing perforations in base; glued repair to vessel wall; Middle/Late Iron Age pit 3513, context 3552, ON 85, PRN 382
22. Bead rimmed jar; shell-tempered ware; Middle/Late Iron Age pit 3513, context 3647, PRN 391
23. Briquetage cup; Middle/Late Iron Age pit 3513, context 3647, PRN 388
24. Large, necked storage jar; shell-tempered ware. Post-firing perforations in vessel wall; Late Iron Age pit 3053, context 3055, PRN 446
25. Jar with an everted rim and a corrugated profile; grog-tempered ware; Late Iron Age pit 3088, context 3089, PRN 372
26. Proto-bead rimmed jar; shell-tempered ware; Late Iron Age pit 3088, context 3089, PRN 373
27. S-profiled jar; grog-tempered ware; post-firing perforations in base; Late Iron Age pit 3220, context 3222, PRN 855
28. Inverted pear-shaped jar/bowl; grog-tempered ware; post-firing perforations in base; Late Iron Age pit 3220, context 3222, PRN 856
29. Bead rimmed jar; shell-tempered ware; Late Iron Age pit 3579, context 3609, ON 81A, PRN 449
30. Base from an imitation Gallo-Belgic platter; grog-tempered ware; Late Iron Age pit 3579, context 3609, PRN 453
31. Bead rimmed jar; shell-tempered ware; Late Iron Age pit 3579, context 3609, ON 81B, PRN 450

Fig. 3.4

32. Round-bodied, necked, cordoned jar; grog-tempered ware; Late Iron Age pit 3579, context 3609, ON 81C, PRN 451
33. Shouldered jar with almost horizontal, out turned rim; grog-tempered ware; Late Iron Age pit 3579, context 3617, PRN 455
34. Wide-mouthed, round-bodied, necked, cordoned bowl; grog-tempered ware; Late Iron Age pit 4135, context 4136, PRN 1050
35. Proto-bead rimmed jar; shell-tempered ware; Late Iron Age pit 4313, contexts 4314 (PRN 407) and 4319 (PRN 413)
36. Globular-bodied jar/bowl; sandy ware; post-firing perforations in base; Late Iron Age pit 4313, context 4319, PRN 416
37. Inverted pear-shaped jar with high, rounded shoulder and a corrugated neck; grog-tempered ware; Late Iron Age pit 4313, contexts 4314 (PRN 412) and 4319 (PRN 414)
38. Round shouldered, necked, cordoned jar; grey/brown sandy ware, probably Alice Holt; post-firing perforations in base; early Romano-British pit 3535, context 3889, ON 118, PRN 663
39. Probable girth beaker body sherd; oxidised ware; early Romano-British pit 3174, context 3175, PRN 516
40. Carinated bowl probably based on samian form 29; oxidised ware; early Romano-British pit 3174, context 3246, PRN 542
41. Necked, cordoned jar with a sharply carinated shoulder; grey/brown sandy ware, probably Alice Holt; base possibly deliberately holed; early Romano-British pit 3174, context 3246, ON 106, PRN 547
42. Bead rimmed jar; shell-tempered ware; early Romano-British pit 3174, context 3246, PRN 546
43. Globular-bodied flagon; Verulamium-region white ware; post-firing perforation in base; early Romano-British pit 3174, ON 63, PRN 508
44. Globular-bodied beaker; grog-tempered ware; early Romano-British pit 3870, context 3871, PRN 676
45. Imitation butt beaker with a globular body; grey/brown sandy ware; early Romano-British pit 3870, context 3950, PRN 691
46. Necked jar with a thickened out-turned rim; grog-tempered ware; early Romano-British pit 3870, context 3950, PRN 697

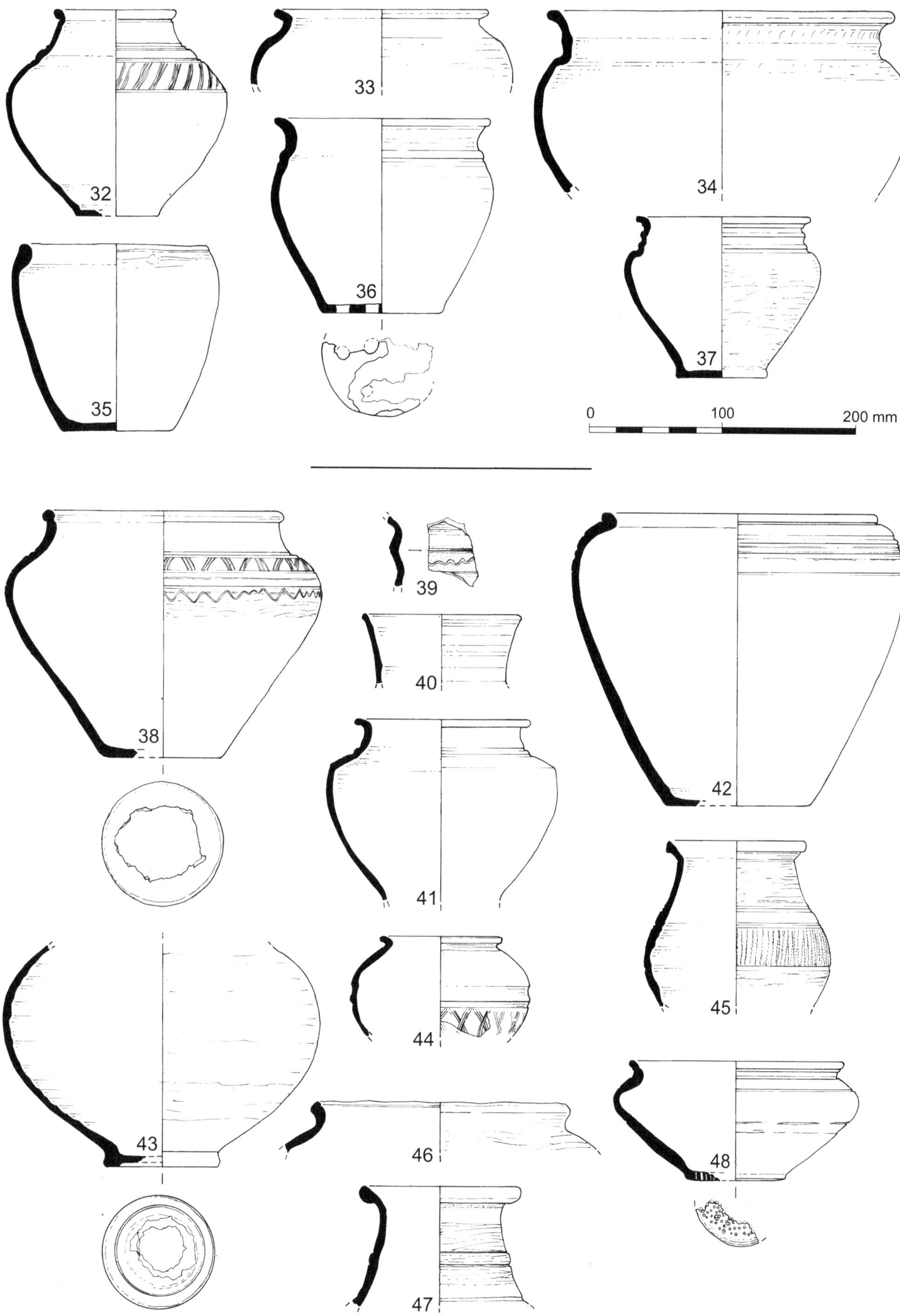

Figure 3.4 Late Iron Age/early Romano-British pottery (32–48)

47. Flagon with a lid-seated, off-set rim and a slightly flaring, cordoned neck; grey/brown sandy ware, possibly Alice Holt; early Romano-British pit 3870, context 3950, PRN 692
48. Sharply shouldered strainer bowl with a short, flared, internally lid-seated rim; grey/brown sandy ware, possibly Alice Holt; pre-firing perforations in base; early Romano-British pit 3870, context 3948, PRN 690

Fired Clay

by Rachael Seager Smith

This material includes pieces from objects as well as amorphous fragments likely to be of structural origin. Most are probably derived from ovens/hearths and, together with the metal-working debris and burnt flint, provide clear evidence for moderate- to high-temperature pyrotechnical activities, including iron smithing, occurring in the immediate vicinity, even although no clear *in situ* remains of such heating structures were encountered during the excavations.

Six broad fabric groups were identified, based on the principal inclusion types, all of which are locally available:

Fabric 1: fine sandy fabrics with rare red/black ferrous inclusions; one or two large (up to 40 mm across) calcined flints, chalk particles and organic inclusions noted in some fragments;
Fabric 2: generally fairly soft, pale orange or buff, sand and chalk-tempered; chalk generally less than 7 mm across but larger fragments up to 15 mm across also noted;
Fabric 3: fine sand and organic-tempered, with rare red/black ferrous inclusions and very occasionally, flint, chalk and/or grog inclusions;
Fabric 4: very fine, soapy, almost inclusion-free fabrics;
Fabric 5: fine sandy fabrics, generally oxidised, with a powdery texture;
Fabric 6: fine sand and grog/clay pellet-tempered fabrics.

Fabrics 3 and 5 were comparatively uniform, but the range, size and relative proportions of inclusions in the other fabrics varied considerably, suggesting that many of the incidental inclusions were incorporated accidentally. Most pieces were only softly fired at relatively low temperatures but were made in well-mixed, relatively dense fabrics, while a minority were poorly wedged. Surface colour indicates that the firing conditions were predominantly oxidising, but many pieces had unoxidised cores, suggesting that they were fired for relatively short periods of time, insufficient for full oxidisation.

Overall quantities of the fired clay fabrics are summarised by phase in Table 3.6. The fine sandy fabrics with rare red/black ferrous inclusions (Fabric 1) were by far the most numerous, occurring in all phases, while Fabrics 3, 4 and 6 were comparatively uncommon. Within these four fabrics, at least 83 pieces (11475 g) were identified as coming from triangular objects with perforations piercing the corners, 72 (10847 g) in Fabric 1, nine (433 g) in Fabric 3, and one each (173 g and 22 g, respectively) in Fabrics 4 and 6. Although lacking diagnostic features, such as perforations and/or corners, it is feasible that most of the other fragments in these fabrics derive from similar objects, although it is difficult to gauge exact numbers even within a single feature, as few refits could be made. Perforated triangular objects are a well-known form, common in Iron Age contexts across the whole of southern Britain and remaining current well into the 2nd century AD (Wild 2002, 10). Traditionally, they have

Table 3.6 Quantification of the fired clay fabrics by phase (count/weight in grammes)

	Fabrics						
	1	2	3	4	5	6	
Phase	*No. Wt.*	*No. Wt.*	*No. Wt.*	*No. Wt.*	*No. Wt.*	*No. Wt.*	Total
Uncertain	62/3244	7/90	–	1/173	–	–	70/3507
Early Iron Age	67/4588	–	6/162	–	–	1/22	74/4772
Early/Middle Iron Age	4/111	–	–	–	–	–	4/111
Middle Iron Age	15/546	2/14	7/105	–	1/50	–	25/715
Middle/Late Iron Age	23/474	29/362	4/25	–	–	1/26	57/887
Late Iron Age	123/2167	11/52	–	–	–	2/154	136/2373
Late Iron Age/early Roman	27/1792	12/234	–		–	–	39/2026
Early Roman	208/10262	201/1547	–	1/15	11/768	1/7	422/12619
Total	*539/24069*	*262/2299*	*17/292*	*2/188*	*12/818*	*5/229*	*837/27895*

been interpreted as loomweights but it is now considered more likely that they were associated with ovens and/or kilns, perhaps as linings or pedestals (Lowther 1935; Poole 1995). Most of the examples from this site were crudely formed with irregular surfaces. None are complete or even preserve complete side lengths, but nine objects are between 55 mm and 66 mm thick, one is 75 mm thick (ON 145; Early Iron Age pit 3219), while a large fragment from early Romano-British pit 3183 (ON 163) is 90 mm thick and a minimum of 160 mm high, with a horizontal perforation just below the apex.

Perforated triangular object fragments were found in features belonging to all phases, but although present in some of the features which contained structured deposits, they do not appear to have been directly associated with such deposits, mostly occurring in other layers within these features. Only five features contained significant quantities (over 1 kg). These include Early Iron Age pits 3219 and 3820, which both contained diagnostic parts of at least two perforated triangular objects (ONs 145 and 103, 105/110, respectively), all of Fabric 1. Nine diagnostic fragments (corners and/or perforations; including ONs 155, 163–6) in similar fine, sandy fabrics with rare red/black ferrous inclusions (Fabric 1) were also recognised among the 74 pieces (5759 g) from early Romano-British pit 3183, while parts of at least three perforated objects (totalling 1450 g and including ONs 150 and 156) were found in early Romano-British pit 3870. Unfortunately, the material from pit 3183 was too fragmented to permit even an estimate of the original number of objects represented.

In addition, 52 rough, abraded fragments (2466 g) probably from one or more perforated object, in fine, sandy fabrics with rare red/black ferrous inclusions, were recovered from dump layer 3318 in unphased feature 3317, where they were associated with over 3 kg of burnt flint. It may also be of relevance to the interpretation of these objects as oven furniture that the 15 pieces (959 g) derived from at least two perforated objects, one of Fabric 1 (ONs 121, 123, 128, 129 and possibly 149) and one grog-tempered (ON 124; Fabric 6), from the upper fill (layer 3941), of Early Iron Age pit 3940, were associated with large quantities of burnt flint and other heat-affected materials, including charcoal. Indeed, significant quantities (over 1 kg) of burnt flint were also recovered from pits 3183, 3820 and 3870, while 45% (by weight) of the perforated object fragments from pit 3183 were derived from three charcoal-rich deposits (layers 3192, 3197 and 3669), probably representing dumped material raked-out of ovens or hearths.

The only other recognisable object made in Fabric 1 was a short piece (surviving length 45 mm) from a roughly triangular bar, each face approximately 30 mm across, which was found in Late Iron Age pit 3874. This item, too, is likely to represent kiln or oven furniture, bars being the most frequent objects of this type encountered in Late Iron Age and Romano-British contexts (Swan 1984, 62).

Small featureless fragments made in the pale orange or buff, sand and chalk-tempered fabrics (Fabric 2) made up just under one-third of the assemblage by fragment count (8% by weight). These were found in 19 features, dating from the Middle Iron Age onwards, but only seven (Middle/Late Iron Age pit 3998, Late Iron Age/early Romano-British pit 4376 and early Romano-British pits 3174, 3183, 3458, 3870 and 3921) contained more than 100 g of this material. Although lacking the straw inclusions typically added to the sand and clay mixture used for cob-walling, much of this material may have had a structural origin, particularly as wattle impressions occurred in a handful of the larger pieces from Middle/Late Iron Age pit 3998 and early Romano-British pit 3870. Other pieces, such as those from dump layer 3659 in pit 3174, may derive from oven/hearth linings. Most of the 102 fragments (309 g) from this deposit were burnt or over-fired to some degree, with one or two having almost vitrified surfaces. Significant quantities of metalworking debris from this deposit (Andrews, see below), suggest that these fired clay fragments derive from one or more iron smithing hearths.

Twelve other pieces in the powdery sandy fabrics (Fabric 5) may also derive from oven/hearth linings. One featureless fragment (50 g) with a single flattish surface came from posthole 3982, part of the Middle Iron Age square structure 4247; the others (768 g) were all from early Romano-British pit 3183. One of the pieces from this feature appeared to be from a roughly circular object, approximately 60 mm thick with a chamfered outer edge, perhaps a perforated oven plate (*cf.* Poole 1984, 118), while a second piece had two opposing flattish surfaces and was 35 mm thick.

Coin

by Nicholas Cooke

A single copper alloy coin (ON 138), a small corroded late Roman 'Urbs Roma' issue of the House of Constantine, struck between AD 330 and AD 345, was recovered from section 3816 of enclosure ditch 4232. Its size suggests that it is likely to be a contemporary copy of an 'official' issue. Episodes of copying were a feature of the late 3rd and 4th centuries AD, and copies were probably struck to compensate for gaps in the supply of coinage to Britain, to provide sufficient small change for the province's needs. It is unclear whether these copies were officially sanctioned, but they are not uncommon and seem to have circulated in the same fashion as officially struck coins.

Objects of Metal

by A. P. Fitzpatrick

Iron Age

Twelve objects were found in Iron Age contexts. The only object from the Early–Middle Iron Age is a La Tène I brooch (ON 134). From the Middle–Late Iron Age there is the terminal of an unidentified object (ON 50), and a small hoard of three items (ON 132–3 and 135). A small length of rectangular bar (ON 117) from a Late Iron Age pit (3852) could be from an ingot and be associated with iron working. The remaining objects were a fragment of bar, fragments of four nails, and a post-medieval iron buckle (ON 139) intrusive in ditch 3969. The terminal of the small object (ON 50) from pit 3025 is of unknown purpose and although it has some similarity to medical instruments, this could be fortuitous. Full details are held in the project archive.

Pit 3998

The small hoard or deposit in pit 3998 can be dated to 2nd–1st centuries BC. The hoard was found alongside large sherds from a single pot that were also placed deliberately. The relationship between the deposit and the charred materials, which included birch tar and twisted fibres but also crop-processing waste, is not clear. The iron objects appear to represent a *pars pro toto* deposit in which objects were deliberately broken and only parts of them deposited (to represent the whole). Set hammers were struck with iron sledge hammers, but only the set hammer was put in the pit. Nave hoops bound together the ends of the wheel naves into which the ends of the axle fitted, so each nave had two hoops, but only one is present. If the hoop was attached to the wheel when it was deposited, only part of the wheel was present (though the complete wheel, which is likely to have been in the range of 0.7–0.9 m in diameter could have fitted into the pit). If the whole spear was deposited, the location of the metal head near the middle of the pit indicates that the shaft, which would have been at least 2 m long (Brunaux and Rapin 1988, 88–94), must have been broken. As metal ferrules are rare in Iron Age Britain, the absence of one from the pit does not indicate that the spear was incomplete. The spearhead itself is unusual in that it is decorated with bronze appliqués, and is one of only a very few decorated spearheads from Iron Age Britain. It may be better seen as a standard or ensign.

Pars pro toto deposits of metal objects are widely recognised in continental Europe, often in Late Iron Age burials but are not usually recognised in Iron Age Britain, although the placing of broken objects of other materials in special deposits within settlements is well known (Hill 1995). The spear or ensign and the smithing hammer may both be regarded as objects used by males; who would have used the wheeled vehicle that the nave hoop is from is less clear. In Yorkshire, at least, chariots or carts were placed in the graves of high status women and men.

Illustrated Iron Age objects

Fig. 3.5

Costume

1. Brooch ON 134, Early Iron Age pit 4066, context 4074; length 50 mm.

   An iron La Tène I brooch, with the hinge or spring and part of the pin missing, although as the tip of the pin is *in situ* in the catchplate it is likely that the brooch was complete on deposition in the pit. Many brooches of this type have a ball-like decoration near the end of the foot and it is likely that this example originally had one, possibly a separate element which is now lost or if it was integral to the foot, it is now corroded beyond recognition. The corrosion means that it is not clear if the end of the foot touched the bow or not. However, the foot and the top of the bow have well-defined transverse grooves and those on the bow are filled with a red coloured inlay. This inlay is not coral and although it does not appear to be vitreous, it is similar to other examples of degraded enamel or red glass (Virginie Defente pers. comm.).

   The high arch of the bow suggests that this brooch belongs to Hull and Hawkes Type 1A, which dates to between *c.* 450–375 BC but because the foot is so badly preserved an exact identification to type is not possible. Most Type 1A brooches currently known are of bronze and their bow is often decorated, sometimes with a simple cord-like pattern. However, one of the relatively few iron examples of Type 1A is from Crickley Hill, Gloucestershire, and it also has transverse grooves on the bow that could have held an inlay (Hull and Hawkes 1987, 83–4, no. 6759, pl. 24, 6759).

Tools

2. Hammerhead ON 135, Middle–Late Iron Age pit 3998, context 4115; length 86 mm; width 31 mm; thickness 29 mm; weight 291 g.

   The rectangular eye, which is typical of Iron Age hammers, is offset towards the striking face, and the sides of the hammer swell slightly by the eye. The face is round and as it is well burred through use it may originally have been rectangular, like the cross pane at the other end whose face has also become worn and its outline softened by use.

   The offset eye would affect the balance of the tool as a double faced hand hammer. Therefore, it is likely

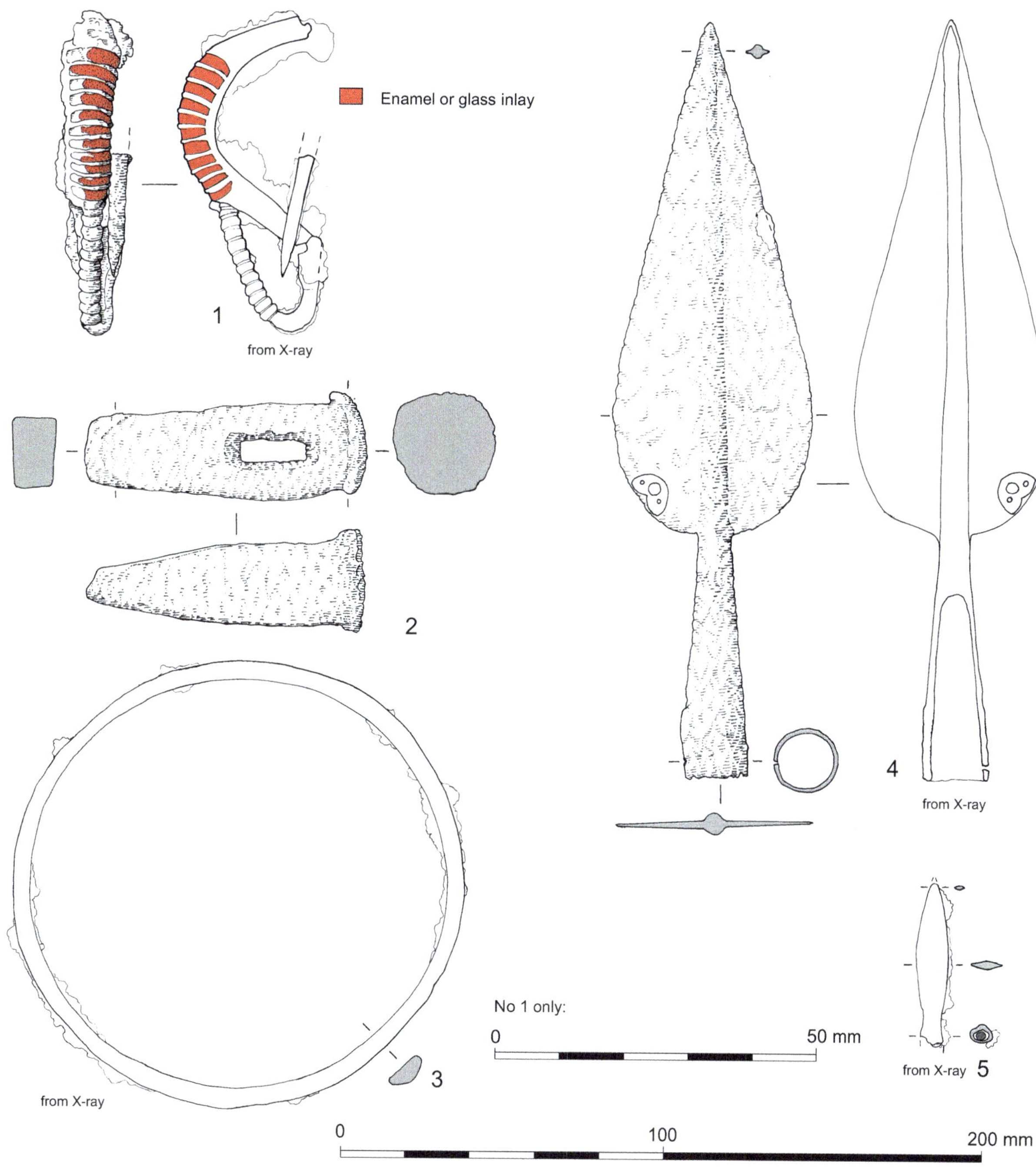

Figure 3.5 Iron Age metal objects (1–5)

that it is either a small set hammer or a single-faced striking hammer. Set hammers are forging tools that were not swung on their own but were struck with a sledge hammer. This allows the set hammer to be positioned more accurately. Most hammerheads from Iron Age Britain are made of medium-carbon steel and were often quenched.

Several of the hammers known from Iron Age Britain come from hoards and the closest parallel to this example is the slightly larger example from Bigberry, Kent, from the 1st century BC deposits. It is annealed suggesting that it had been used to work hot metals (Fell 1998, 218, app. no. 8, fig. 2, 8). The Bigberry iron work is badly corroded and the hammer now weighs 326 g.

Transport

3. Wheel nave hoop ON 133, Middle–Late Iron Age pit 3998, context 3999; external diameter 141 mm, deep 13 mm, thickness 8 mm.

The wheel nave holds the axle and both ends of the nave were usually secured with iron hoops that were sometimes covered by bronze sheet. This complete example is D-shaped in section and the overlapped welded join of the strip is visible in the X-ray.

Similar D-shaped nave hoops are known from sites of Middle and Late Iron Age date in England and Wales (Stead 1979, 40–4, fig. 11; 1991, 41, fig. 33, 3–4; Cunliffe and Poole 1991, 352, fig. 7.20; Jay *et al.* 2012). Examples from settlements include both pairs and singletons.

Weaponry

4. Spearhead or ensign ON 132, Middle/Late Iron Age pit 3998, context 3999; length 230 mm, width 63 mm.

A leaf-shaped spearhead with a pronounced midrib and long socket in which there is a hole for the rivet that fixed the shaft. The rivet is missing although there are small quantities of mineral-replaced wood in the socket. Near the bottom of each side are small crescent-shaped bronze appliqués that stand proud of the iron. There is a circle in the centre of each appliqué, which may originally have been a hole but which is now filled with corrosion products. On either side of this are single bronze rivets made from a different, lighter coloured alloy.

British Iron Age spearheads are not yet well dated but related forms, although often with slightly wider blades, are common in Middle La Tène contexts (La Tène B2–C1) in France and Switzerland (eg, Brunaux and Rapin 1988, 122–4, fig. 61) dating to *c.* 225–175 BC.

Iron Age decorated spearheads are not common and although decoration is more commonly typically incised (Duval 1982), a number of examples with perforated decoration are known (Brunaux and Rapin 1988, 126, fig. 62). The number of holes on some of these blades means that they cannot have been used effectively as projectiles and so are more likely to have been ensigns or standards, as were the 'spearheads' with wavy outlines and openwork decoration.

The only decorated spearheads previously known from Britain are from the River Thames and Danebury, Hampshire. This spearhead is similar in shape to the one from the Thames but it is slightly smaller (230 mm against 302 mm) and its ornament is much less elaborate. The appliqués are placed in the same place on both sides of the blade, as are those on the example from the Thames, and its form may be seen as two overlapping symmetrical lobes, a motif that is common in the British Iron Age. The different alloys of the appliqués and the rivets would have contrasted with the colour of the blade but this would only have been visible at close quarters. If the appliqués originally surrounded a hole in the blade it is possible that a chord passed through it allowing something to be suspended from it.

The example from the Thames is unique in having four bronze sheets each with slightly different incised decoration ornament riveted to the blade (Jope 2000, 282, pl. 217, a–c, correcting Fox's (1958, 49) attribution of the find to the Thames 'near Datchet'). The Danebury weapon has single bronze rivets either side of the midrib, halfway up the blade and was found in a Late Iron Age (ceramic phase 7) context (Sellwood 1984, 361, fig. 7.19, 2.100).

Appliqués also occur occasionally on Iron Age sword scabbards, usually of Middle La Tène date. A small number of these are on the side of the scabbard in a manner reminiscent of the present spearhead (*cf.* Lejars 2003, 18–20, fig. 5, 9–10; Landry and Blaizot 2011). It may also be noted that the shape of the appliqués resembles some sword stamps or armourer's mark which represent stylised human faces. Only one such example is known amongst the small number of stamps recorded from Britain, recovered from an old course of a tributary of the Thames at Shepperton Ranges, Spelthorpe, some 20 km to the north-west from this site. This stamp is crescentic and has three dots within it, although it also has a line across the cartouche (Stead 2006, 48–9, fig. 11, 127; 84, 127). The sword probably dates to late in La Tène II or early in La Tène III, towards the end of the 2nd century or early 1st century BC.

Unknown

5. Handle terminal ON 50, Middle/Late Iron Age pit 3025, context 3026.

The linguate-shaped end of a small and finely made object whose function is uncertain. It is too small and narrow to be a very small, or even miniature, spearhead, and it also lacks the central midrib that almost all spears possess. Arrowheads are not known from Iron Age Britain and the contemporary Mid–Late Iron Age ones from central Europe are much larger and typically have a single barb. While it is possible that this object is a tang for the wooden or horn handle of a small tool, these are typically rectangular in section and are not finely made (Guillaumet 1983).

What the object does resemble is the end of a medical instrument from the grave at Kisköszeg, Baranya vm, Hungary which may be either a double-ended spatula or a periosteal elevator, an instrument used to lift tissue from the bone (de Navarro 1955, 244, fig. 3, a) and the end of the instrument, possibly a scalpel or rasp from grave 520 at St Pölten, Austria (Neugebauer 1992, 53, Abb. 17, 6; Künzl 1991, 372). The Kisköszeg grave probably dates to the Late Iron Age. As so few medical instruments are known from Iron Age Britain and Europe (Jackson 2007), the resemblance of the current object may be fortuitous.

Romano-British

Some 24 objects or groups of objects were found in contexts of Late Iron Age/early Romano-British or early Romano-British date. The majority are fittings from timber, either nails (12) or staples (1) that were used to fix objects or parts of buildings and these were evenly distributed across the excavation area.

There are three brooches, all of well-known types that are typical of 1st century AD settlements in the region (Bayley and Butcher 2004; Mackreth 2011); a complete Dolphin type (ON 89), a slightly damaged strip brooch (ON 125), and the bow and catchplate only of a Nauheim derivate (ON 78). None need be later than Flavian in date (AD 69–96) and all were found in pits.

Other finds include part of a hand saw for woodworking (ON 122) from deposit 3889 in pit 3535, although its inclusion in it may be accidental, and some originally articulated lengths of chain (ON 94) from pit 3183, which also contained the Dolphin brooch. Two separate groups of hobnails (ONs 97 and 155) from pit 3183 may well be from part of a single boot. The remaining objects were a possible small ferrule from the tip of an object (ON 73), from pit 3458. The other two objects were small fragments of a bar (ON 136) from pit 4376, and of a loop (ON 10) from pit 2021.

Illustrated Romano-British objects

Fig. 3.6

Costume

6. Bronze two-piece Dolphin (Colchester-derivative) brooch, ON 89, early Romano-British pit 3183, context 3197; length 56 mm; spring has 12 coils with the outer coil passing through a hole in the lug at the top of the curved bow.
7. Bronze strip-bow brooch, ON 125, early Romano-British pit 4002, context 3986; length 50 mm; has a hinge not a spring, and the central groove is filled with oblique punch marks.
8. Bronze Nauheim-derivative brooch, ON 78, early Romano-British pit 3683, context 3677; length 50 mm; only the bow and perforated catchplate, and a single coil of the spring, are present.

Tools

9. Fragment of a hand saw, ON 122, early Romano-British pit 3535, context 3889; length 29 mm; width 49 mm; teeth clearly visible in X-ray (*cf.* Manning 1985, 19–21, pl. 9, B21-3; Jones 2011, 39–41, fig. 22, 7).

Utensils

10. Chain, ON 94, early Romano-British pit 3183, context 3670; three fragments of chain with figure-of-eight shaped link; lengths 44 mm, 57 mm and 63 mm.

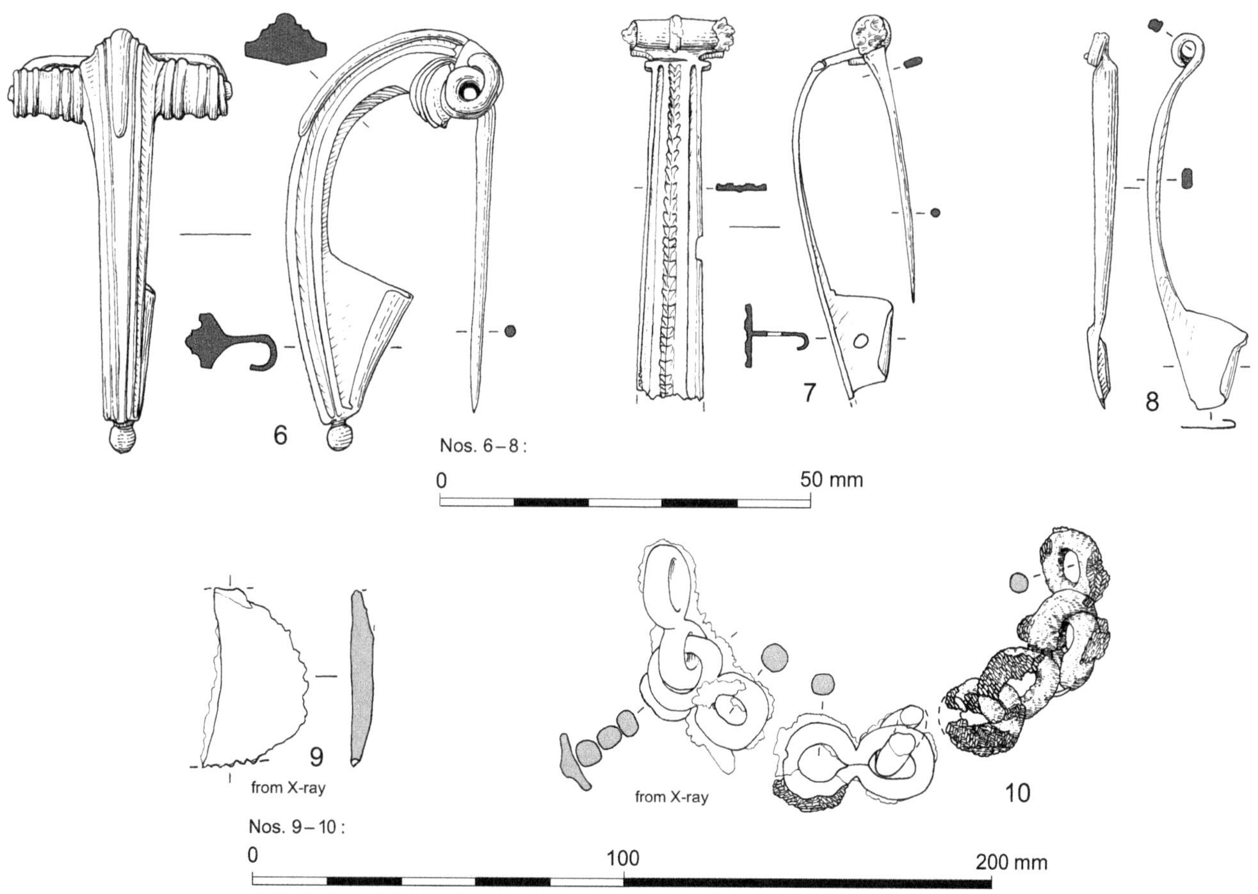

Figure 3.6 Romano-British metal objects (6–10)

Slag

by Phil Andrews

Approximately 9.3 kg of metalworking slag or related debris has been identified and recorded. The condition of the material is fresh to moderate, with the majority of the slag fragments unabraded or only slightly abraded around the edges. All of the material was examined visually or by the use of a hand lens to identify type and form. Hammerscale was collected by running a magnet over environmental samples sieved to 4–2 mm and 2–0.5 mm. A summary of the identifications is presented in Table 3.7.

Results

Approximately 9.1 kg of the slag, all from early Romano-British pit 3174, derives from ironworking. Although much of this material is undiagnostic, it is most likely to be debris from iron smithing. The slag is typically highly vesicular and rather amorphous, although there are a number of relatively thin, somewhat 'brittle' pieces, many of which have become broken, probably during deposition and burial. There are occasional denser fragments, but these too are likely to derive from iron smithing. A further 108 g of undiagnostic material, occurring in small quantities in three other contexts, is possibly also a product of smithing.

Table 3.7 Ironworking debris by feature and/or context (weight in grammes)

Feature	*Context*	*Smithing*	*Smithing?*	*FAS*	*Other*	*Totals*
–	605	–	23	–	–	23
–	608	–	84	–	–	84
Ditch 3050	3049	–	1	–	–	1
Grave 3052	3051	–	–	–	4	4
Pit 3088	3089	–	–	4	–	4
Pit 3174	3246	2087	–	–	–	2087
	3659	2507	–	–	–	2507
	3711	4510	–	–	–	4510
Pit 3250	3251	–	–	1	–	1
Pit 3344	3356	–	–	13	–	13
Pit 3436	3441	–	–	5	–	5
	3455	–	–	28	–	28
Total weights		9104	108	51	4	9267

Table 3.8 Details of smithing hearth bottoms (SHBs) from pit 3174

Context	*Weight (g)*	*Dimensions (mm)*	*Notes*
3246	412	100 x 90 x 45	–
	209	75 x 75 x 30	–
	150	–	fragment
	113	–	fragment
	106	–	fragment
	72	–	fragment
3659	236	85 x 85 x 30	–
	230	90 x 70 x 30	–
	228	120 x 100 x 35	–
	169	125 x 70 x 30	–
	138	80 x 80 x 20	fragment
	105	65 x 60 x 30	–

The slag assemblage from pit 3174 includes as many as 12 smithing hearth bottoms (SHBs), as well as numerous other pieces which are probably fragments of SHBs (Table 3.8). These SHBs are the hemispherical bowl-shaped accumulations of slag which formed at the base of smithing hearths. All of them are relatively small and moderately vesicular, varying in size from 65 x 60 x 30 mm to 100 x 90 x 45 mm, and their weights ranging between 105 g and 412 g.

Plate- or flake-hammerscale was present in some quantity (along with oak charcoal) in the sample from deposit 3659 (pit 3174), which produced the second largest quantity of slag from the site. However, none was identified in two other layers in the same pit which also contained notable amounts of slag (see below).

Also from deposit 3659 was a small quantity of very fragmentary material which has been subjected to intense heat and is almost certainly the remains of the lining from one or more smithing hearths (see Seager Smith, above); there were also a few fragments of probable mould, but these are too small to allow identification of what copper alloy object(s) might have been cast.

Five contexts (none from pit 3174) produced a total of 51 g of pale grey, vesicular, fuel ash slag (FAS) which is likely to have formed as a result of a high temperature process, perhaps an intense fire, but is not necessarily a product of metalworking. Other finds include an offcut from a square-section iron rod (ON 117) (see Fitzpatrick, above), perhaps the raw material for smithing, although it came from pit 3852 (context 3849), and not pit 3174. A small (4 g) pyrites nodule from grave 3052 is unlikely to have had a metallurgical connection.

Discussion

Overall, the quantity of ironworking slag is relatively small, but there was a clear concentration in early Romano-British pit 3174, which produced nearly all of the smithing slag (9104 g) and all 12 SHBs. The largest quantity (4510 g) of slag came from the deposit of animal carcases (3711) at the base of the suggested pit recut (see Chapter 2), although this material was very broken up and included no identifiable SHBs. Deposit 3659, a relatively thin charcoal-rich layer at a higher level within the pit, produced 2507 g of slag, including six SHBs, as well as a concentration of hammerscale indicative of iron forging, suggesting material disposed of directly from smithing activity nearby. Context 3246, immediately above 3659, contained 2087 g of debris including a further six SHBs. The quantities of possible ironworking debris from other features are negligible.

The available evidence from Surrey more generally indicates that Romano-British metalworking, and specifically iron smithing, is always likely to have been small-scale, supplying little more than local needs. This is the case in Staines (McKinley 2004a), the only semi-urban centre in the county, as well as in the smaller settlements, villas and rural sites, all of relatively modest status. The likely source of the iron is the mining and smelting sites of the Sussex Weald. The smithing debris (slag and hearth lining) at this site may represent the waste left by an itinerant smith, although the quantity suggests that it represents a number of smithing episodes.

What is particularly interesting is that virtually all the debris came from three layers in a single early Romano-British pit (3174) which also contained a variety of unusual and probably significant deposits, including animal bone, human bone, pottery and possible mould fragments from casting copper alloy, which together suggest more than just the casual deposition of domestic rubbish (see below).

Worked Flint

by Phil Harding

An assemblage of 518 pieces was recovered from 182 contexts, and has been quantified by type (Table 3.9). The worked flint is dominated by flakes, which account for 73% of the assemblage, with only 7% blades and bladelets. The flint is a cherty mottled grey/black material, probably sourced from surface nodules from the local Chalk, and flaking quality ranges from relatively good to pieces riven with thermal fractures. There was also some Bullhead flint, a result of the contact between the Chalk and overlying Thanet Sand, which is also of variable quality.

There was a relatively low density of pieces from the excavated features (a mean of 2.8 pieces from all excavated contexts), the largest single group, from Iron Age pit 3223 (Fig. 2.6), comprising 26 pieces. Much of the material is considered likely to be residual, although a small collection of flakes and debitage from Early Iron Age pit 3759 includes two pairs of refitting flakes, suggesting that that these were contemporary with the filling of the pit.

The earliest pieces are two Mesolithic tranchet axe sharpening flakes. There is also the distal end of a notched blade, which may represent failed microburin technique. Mesolithic blades, flakes and cores are believed to have been recovered from the immediate area during previous excavations (Lowther 1944–5) and further material, including occasional microliths, is known from the wider area (Wymer 1977).

Table 3.9 Flint totals by type

Type	*Number*
Flake/broken flake	379
Flake core/core frag	36
Blade/broken blade	34
Bladelets	3
Rejuvenation tablet	2
Scrapers	4
Other tools	1
Miscellaneous retouch	9
Axe thinning flake	3
Microdenticulate	1
Debitage	32
Chips/microdebitage	14
Total	518

A small number of patinated pieces are probably of Neolithic or Early Bronze Age date. They include some of the blades, and artefacts with traces of platform abrasion as a means of core preparation. Among them is a partially patinated discoidal implement, possibly a scraper or knife, which is made on a thermal fragment. Most of the flakes are unpatinated; of these a number are characterised by a glossy surface and frequently with slight traces of post-depositional edge damage. This material includes a microdenticulate, probably also Neolithic.

Part of the assemblage is likely to include Late Bronze Age residual material, as well as some of Early Iron Age date. These pieces grade into flakes and cores that are in mint condition with no hint of surface gloss. The characteristics of the group include hard hammer percussion, poorly prepared flake cores often with incipient cones of percussion on the striking platform, relatively frequent primary flakes that hint at cores with relatively limited productivity, and flakes with cortical butts which also reflects poorly prepared cores. Retouched pieces are absent. Small quantities of mostly poorly stratified Late Bronze Age material were recovered from earlier excavations (Bruce and Giorgi 1994).

Burnt Flint

by Andrew B. Powell

Over 153 kg of burnt unworked flint was recovered from the site. This material type is intrinsically undatable, but is frequently associated with prehistoric activity, and may derive from either domestic or craft/industrial activities. It is noticeable that five of the eight pits containing over 4 kg of burnt flint were of Early Iron Age date, and located in the western part of the site – pits 4333 (4.6 g), 3940 (5 kg), 3825 (6.6 kg), 3011 (8 kg) and 3820 (11.2 kg). It is possible that this reflects some specific or general activity undertaken in this period that declined in later periods.

Stone

by Lorraine Mepham

The two complete chalk spindlewhorls (ONs 93 and 95) came from the same context in Late Iron Age pit 3341. One is of flattened globular shape, and the other is bun-shaped or sub-conical; both have central drilled perforations and each weighs 19 g. In addition, a possible roughout (from early Romano-British pit 3174) consists of half of a roughly disc-shaped piece of chalk with a central perforation (ON 168).

A whetstone (ON 167) in Kentish Ragstone, a hard calcareous sandstone from the Lower Cretaceous Hythe Beds of the Maidstone area, was also found in pit 3174. It is of flattish, subrectangular form, slightly waisted, and with one end broken off; there are no obvious wear marks.

Two fragments of sandstone, from Early Iron Age pit 3820 and trackway gully 4241), could derive from quernstones. Both are of Lower Greensand, one from the Bargate Beds, accessible either locally or from Farnham, while the other is probably Lodsworth Greensand from West Sussex. In addition, two fragments of lava, from ditches 2071 (Enclosure 2c) and 4378 (Enclosure 4), derive from lava quernstones, which were imported from the Rhineland during the Romano-British period (then also from the middle Saxon into the medieval period).

Worked Bone

by Lorraine Mepham

One small piece of worked bone decorated with incised ring-and-dot motifs was found among the domestic debris from Middle/Late Iron Age pit 3599. It is slightly curved but appears to have been lightly burnt.

Human Bone

by Kirsten Egging Dinwiddy

Human bone from 15 contexts was analysed (summarised in Table 3.10). The deposits include the remains of seven *in situ* burials of neonates made in five pits, two graves and three ditches. Redeposited bone was also recovered from some of the features containing the *in situ* remains, as well as from other ditches and pits. The remains are fairly dispersed across the site and range ranging in date from Early Iron Age to early Romano-British. Three burials were radiocarbon dated – as Late Iron Age (3466) and Late Iron Age/early Romano-British (3652 and 3809) (see Barclay, Chapter 4); the rest were dated, where possible, on the basis of artefactual and stratigraphic evidence.

The degree of erosion to the bone was recorded using McKinley's system of grading (2004b, figs 6.1–7). Age was assessed from the stage of tooth and skeletal development, and measurements of long bone shafts (Beek 1983; Scheuer and Black 2000). Sex was ascertained from the sexually dimorphic traits of the skeleton (Bass 1987; Buikstra and Ubelaker 1994); where the quantity and quality of the sexing criteria were compromised, the sex indicated is qualified (possible: ??).

Results

Some of the deposits had been disturbed both in antiquity and during excavation. A number of possible grave cuts could not be identified, probably as they were backfilled with the same material into which they were cut. The fact that *in situ* burial remains were recovered from ditches and pits implies that the corpses had been covered without delay, perhaps initially being placed within a shallow grave, otherwise unobservable during excavation. Therefore, many of the depths at which the *in situ* burial remains were encountered (0.03–1.3 m) are unlikely to be representative of the original grave depths. Overall, the bone from both the *in situ* and redeposited assemblages is in good condition (most grades 0–1, some up to grade 3), although the remains found within the fills of pit 3901 fared less well (grades 2–4), indicating a difference in the burial environment. Skeletal recovery from the *in situ* burial remains is generally good, with at least 50% of the skeleton recovered from five examples (71.4%). The major factors in the lower rates of recovery include disturbance and/or truncation, with decay and deterioration being of little consequence. Fragmentation is most often localised and slight; a good proportion of skeletal elements are complete or near complete.

Demography

A minimum of 11 individuals (MNI) were identified within the assemblage, comprising 11 neonates (0–6 months) and one adult (Table 3.10). Based on the osteological and contextual evidence, some of the redeposited skeletal material could not be attributed to the seven *in situ* burials or the other redeposited remains, and are therefore considered to represent a further four individuals (three neonates and the

Table 3.10 Summary of the human bone by phase

Cut	Context	Deposit	Quantification (approx.)	Age (approx.)/sex	Pathology
Early/Middle Iron Age					
Grave 3052	3051	redeposited = 3057	3 bones a.l.	neonate 37–38 weeks/ ??female	
	3057	inhumation burial = 3051	90%	neonate 37–38 weeks/ ??female	
Late Iron Age					
Ditch 4242 (cut 3580)	3466*	inhumation burial	10% a.l.	neonate 40 weeks	
Pit 3220	3222	redeposited	1 bone & frags a.	neonate birth–6 months	
	3813	redeposited = 3809	17 frags. s.a.u.	neonate 38 weeks	
Early Romano-British					
Ditch 2070 (cut 2009)	2010	redeposited	1 bone l.	neonate 38 weeks	?periosteal new bone – right femur
Pit 3174	3246	redeposited = 3690	15% s.u.l.	neonate 38 weeks	
	3654	inhumation burial = 4215	80%	neonate 38–39 weeks	
	3690	inhumation burial (disturbed)	15%	neonate 39–40 weeks	
	4215	redeposited = 3654	1% s.a.u	neonate birth	
Pit 3458	3483	inhumation burial	65%	neonate 39–40 weeks/ ??female	endocranial new bone
Grave 3651	3652*	inhumation burial	65%	neonate 40–41 weeks	enamel hypoplasia; generalised hyperporosity
Pit 3901	3809*	inhumation burial = 3813	50%	neonate 38 weeks	generalised hyperporosity
Ditch 4232 (cut 3485)	3487	redeposited	1 shaft frag. l.	adult > 18 years	
Undated					
Pit 3553	3554	redeposited	10%	neonate birth–3 months	

Key: * – radiocarbon dated; s. – skull, a. – axial skeleton, u. – upper limb, l. – lower limb (skeletal area represented where all are not present)

adult). The redeposited adult bone is probably Late Iron Age or earlier, and is probably derived from an inhumation burial either outside the confines of the excavation, or one obliterated by subsequent activity.

Where a defined age could be calculated, most of the remains indicate that the neonates died between approximately 37–41 weeks – around the natural full-term period of around 40 weeks' gestation. For other material, the lack of osteological evidence meant it was only possible to determine a broader age range. Although there is an apparent tendency for a slight increase in gestational age over time, this may also reflect a small increase in birth size, and/or variation between the sexes. It is difficult to determine the sex of neonatal skeletal remains unless certain traits are observed in their extreme. On this basis, the possible sex is only indicated for three of the neonates (each having noticeably female traits), although it is likely that the remains of both sexes are present in the assemblage.

Pathology

Pathological lesions were seen in the remains of three neonates, with more ambiguous changes seen in one further neonate (Table 3.10). These comprise enamel hypoplasia, and probable periosteal and endocranial new bone deposits. Diffuse feathering, pale discolouration and general hyperporosity of the most recent bone surface deposits observed in two of the neonates (3652 and 3809) may be periosteal new bone growth or perhaps indicative of poor mineralisation. However, current advice suggests that only histological examination has the potential to distinguish between pathological and normal growth in such young individuals (Egging Dinwiddy 2011, 130). Potential causes of such changes include various deficiencies, infection and trauma (Lewis and Roberts 1997). In such young infants, the health and/or nutritional status of the mother would be a primary factor.

Discussion

The Late Iron Age practice of disposing of infants and neonates in ditches and other features, widespread in rural settlement sites in southern England, continued into the early Romano-British period (Philpott 1991, 98; McKinley pers. comm.). It is well recognised that in the latter period neonates and young infants were commonly excluded from more formal cemeteries used by other members of the community, preferred locations tending to be agricultural or domestic settlement sites, often associated with structures. Possible reasons for such a disparate burial rite range from their lack of social recognition as a 'person' until they could, for example, walk and talk, with the result that they did not require the same rituals, to keeping them close to the living world (Philpott 1991, 101; Scott 1999, 115; McKinley 2009, 16).

The site lies within a landscape rich in Romano-British archaeology, including the temples at Farley Heath, 'ritual' shafts and pits at Ewell, and the Looe storage pits. Some of the pits and shafts from the latter two sites contained a series of seasonally differentiated deposits, occasionally incorporating cremated human bone (Bird 2004, 133–50), and neonatal burial remains (Cotton 2001). There may be some parallels between these features and some of those this site, particularly pit 3174 from which the remains of two *in situ* neonate burials were recovered.

Animal Bone

by L. Higbee

Introduction

The assemblage comprises 28,461 fragments (or 107,205 g) of animal bone and includes material of Early/Middle Iron Age (5%), Late Iron Age (35%) and early Romano-British date (40%). Once conjoins are taken into account the raw count is reduced to 11,126 fragments (Table 3.11). The site is characterised by large numbers of pits many of which contain rich deposits of animal bone including significant numbers of associated bone groups (hereafter ABGs; for definition see Grant 1984, 533; Morris 2008, 34–35; 2010, 12; 2011, 12–13).

All anatomical elements were identified to species where possible, with the exception of ribs, which were assigned to general size categories. Where appropriate the following information was recorded for each fragment; element, anatomical zone, anatomical position, fusion data, tooth ageing data, butchery marks, metrical data, gnawing, burning, surface condition, pathology and non-metric traits. This information was directly recorded into a relational database (in MS Access) and cross-referenced with relevant contextual information. The site archive includes the database, a detailed methods statement, and additional tables and figures of summary data.

Quantification methods applied to the assemblage include the number of identified specimens (NISP), minimum number of elements (MNE), and minimum number of individuals (MNI). An adjusted NISP count, which considers each ABG as one specimen, was also calculated to reduce the over-representation of ABGs in the standard NISP count (Table 3.12).

As an additional means of assessing the relative importance of livestock species, meat weight estimates (MWE) were also calculated (after Boessneck *et al.* 1971 and following Bourdillon and Coy 1980; Bond and O'Connor 1999; and Dobney *et al.* 2007). The following live weight values were used; 275 kg for cattle, 37.5 kg for sheep and 85 kg for pig.

Results

Preservation condition

Bone preservation is very good and the majority (98%) of fragments have intact cortical surfaces that show little or no signs of physical or chemical weathering. Pits include a higher proportion of well-preserved bones than ditches, but this is because most of the ABGs are from pits rather than ditches. The presence of reworked and re-deposited bones is apparent from differences in the preservation condition of fragments from a few ditch fills, but this is not considered to be a major problem since most of the suspected residual material is unidentifiable due to fragmentation, erosion and attrition.

Gnaw marks were recorded on 2% of bone fragments. This is a relatively low incidence but is unsurprising given the number of ABGs deposited directly into pits. The proportion of gnawed bones is higher for ditches (6%) than for pits (2%), and this coupled with the differences in preservation condition between feature types noted above, suggests that bones recovered from ditches largely represent random bits of surface detritus deposited into ditches via a range of processes. Pits on the other hand were deliberately targeted as receptacles for refuse disposal and as a focus for structured ritual deposition.

A small proportion of the gnaw mark evidence is characteristic of rodent, rather than carnivore gnawing. Various rodent species have been identified

Table 3.11 Number of identified specimens (or NISP) present by period

Species	*E/MIA*	*LIA*	*ERB*	*Unphased*	*Total*
Cattle	54	211	489	28	782
Sheep/goat	110	384	2494	22	3010
Sheep	2	7	52	–	61
Goat	–	1	1	–	2
Pig	12	240	42	4	298
Horse	14	172	53	4	243
?Donkey	–	1	–	–	1
Dog	1	405	1140	3	1549
Cat	–	4	–	–	4
Red deer	–	3	–	–	3
Roe deer	2	–	–	–	2
Deer	–	1	–	–	1
Fox	–	1	143	1	145
Hare	–	–	1	–	1
Mole	–	12	–	–	12
Weasel	–	–	6	–	6
Wood mouse	1	6	6	–	13
Pigmy shrew	–	1	–	–	1
Common shrew	–	–	1	–	1
Field vole	–	24	16	1	41
Vole	2	–	3	–	5
Domestic fowl	–	–	35	–	35
Crow/rook	–	–	4	–	4
Raven	–	65	50	–	115
Frog/toad	14	268	119	13	414
Total identified	*212*	*1806*	*4655*	*76*	*6749*
Large mammal	128	496	517	63	1204
Medium mammal	123	245	893	18	1279
Small mammal	1	158	131	–	290
Mammal	77	736	758	31	1602
Bird	–	–	2	–	2
Total unidentifiable	*329*	*1635*	*2301*	*112*	*4377*
Overall total	541	3441	6956	188	11126

Table 3.12 Number and percentage of bones from Associated Bone Groups (or ABGs). Adjusted NISP calculated as follows: total NISP minus total NISP for ABGs plus number of ABGs per species

Species	*Total NISP*	*No. of ABGs*	*Total NISP for ABGs*	*% NISP for ABGs*
Cattle	782	23	259	33
Sheep/goat	3073	74	1887	61
Pig	298	6	201	67
Horse	243	8	136	54
Dog	1549	18	1522	98
Cat	4	1	4	100
Fox	145	1	142	98
Domestic fowl	35	2	34	97
Raven	115	2	115	100
Other	505	0	0	0
Total identified	6749	135	4300	64

from the assemblage, the majority of which are from pits and probably represent pitfall victims (Piper and O'Connor 2001).

Spatial distribution

As already indicated a large proportion (92%) of the assemblage came from pits, and the majority of the rest is from the various phases of the enclosure ditch. The amount of bone recovered from each pit varies considerably, as does the nature of the bone deposit. There are pits that contain small amounts of general waste and those that contain complex structured deposits comprising complete animal skeletons, burnt animal bone, and large-scale feasting deposits, sometimes in association with human remains, pottery and other objects. Spatial patterning is difficult to discern because the interior of the enclosure(s) was heavily truncated, but most of the surviving pits with complex structured deposits lie close to the enclosure ditches where they are tucked into corners and bends (eg, pits 2061, 2047, 3053, 3174 and 3535). Most apparent is the concentration of pits containing ABGs and/or human remains in the northern central part of the site area where the three main phases of enclosure ditch converge. This patterning could indicate a concern with boundaries and transitional spaces (Evans 2006, 247).

Due to the unequal distribution of bones between feature types and the specific nature of the pit deposits, it has only been possible to look at gross differences between pits and ditches. The most obvious difference is in the relative proportions of the three livestock species; pits include significantly more sheep bones (78% NISP) than ditches (37%) which are characterised by a higher proportion of cattle bones (53%). One possible explanation for this spatial patterning is that large carcasses were butchered at the periphery of the settlement where more space was available, while smaller carcasses were butchered closer to domestic areas (Wilson 1996, 17–35). While this explanation has some merit when considered together with the taphonomic evidence, it is perhaps overly simplistic for sites such as this where the patterns of deposition are complex and probably related to activities or beliefs that are outside normal everyday processes such as carcass processing, and food preparation and consumption.

Species range

Approximately 61% of fragments are identifiable to species, and the number of identified fragments from each period varies from 212 to over 4000 (Tables 3.11 and 3.12). Twenty separate species have been identified from the assemblage. Bones from livestock species predominate and account for 62% NISP. Sheep are by far the most common livestock species, followed by cattle and then pig. Other domestic mammals (goat, horse, dog and cat) and fowl account for 27%, and wild mammals (red deer, roe deer, fox and hare) and birds (crow/rook and raven) a further 4% NISP. The remaining 7% NISP is made up of small mammals (mole, weasel and various rodents) and amphibians (frog/toad), all of which are considered to be pit-fall victims and part of the general environmental background to the site. If the latter are removed from the equation and the NISP counts are adjusted to take account of ABGs, the predominance of livestock species (92%) and in particular sheep (61%) is confirmed (see Table 3.12). The adjusted NISP figures therefore appear to negate some of the bias presented by the ABGs and are considered to represent a closer approximation to a 'normal' economic assemblage than the raw NISP count.

Livestock species

Relative importance by phase

The minimum criteria required for detailed analysis of the relative importance of livestock species is an NISP count (ie, cattle+sheep+pig) of over 300 and a MNI count of over 30 (see Hambleton 1999, 39–40). The Late Iron Age and early Romano-British assemblages fit the criteria for NISP and MNI, but the Early/Middle Iron Age assemblage falls short of this mark, and this should be kept in mind during the following discussion.

The pattern of relative importance is fairly consistent over the sequence of occupation and indicates that the pastoral economy of the site was primarily based upon sheep farming (Fig. 3.7). The raw and adjusted NISP counts both indicate that sheep accounted for between 59%–63% of livestock in the Early/Middle Iron Age, 47%–58% in the Late Iron Age and 72%–83% in the early Romano-British period. Cattle are the second most important livestock species in the Early/Middle Iron Age and early Romano-British period, at between 16%–34%

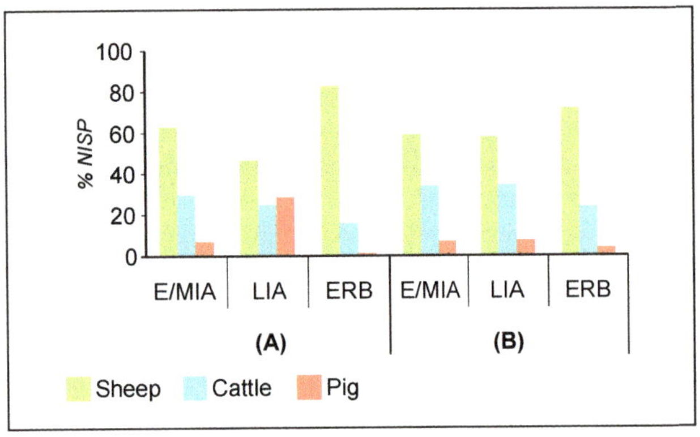

Figure 3.7 Relative importance of livestock species per phase by NISP (A = total count and B = adjusted count)

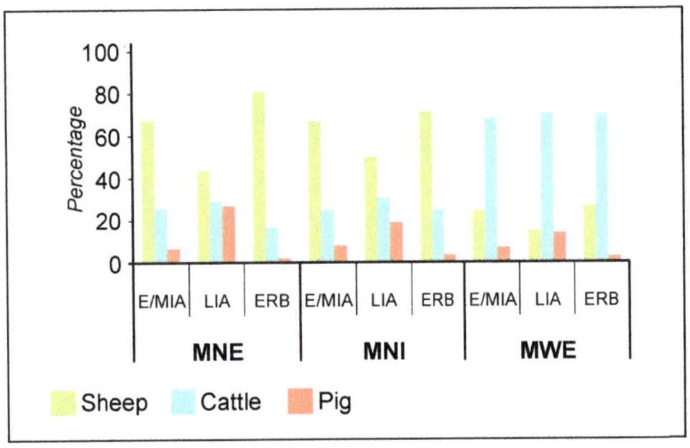

Figure 3.8 Relative importance of livestock species per phase by MNE, MNI and MWE

NISP, followed by pigs, at between 1%–7% NISP. For the Late Iron Age, the raw NISP count indicates that pigs were slightly more important than cattle, at 29% NISP, however this is due to a number of pig ABGs; when the figures are adjusted it is clear that cattle (35%) were far more important than pigs (8%).

The MNE and MNI methods of quantification (Fig. 3.8) show a similar pattern with sheep dominating the assemblages for each period. Despite this it is clear from the meat weight estimates that cattle provided the majority (68%–70%) of meat.

Comparison with other sites in the region

The adjusted NISP counts obtained for each period were compared to a range of contemporary sites in south-east England. This analysis was undertaken in order to establish if the pattern outlined above fits with general regional farming patterns for the periods under consideration and to assess the factors that might have affected or influenced any deviation from expected trends. The sites were compared on the basis of broad chronological period (Fig. 3.9) and site type (Fig. 3.10) using mean NISP values. Individual sites were also compared for each period, with the selection of sites for comparison focused on open and enclosed settlements similar to this site, as well as sites with a religious or ritual component (Fig. 3.11).

The results of this analysis indicate that species proportions for the two Iron Age phases at this site are similar to those from contemporary sites in the region, particularly in terms of sheep bone frequencies, which are around the 50% mark. Species proportions for the early Romano-British assemblage are significantly different from the mean period values (Fig. 3.9), with sheep accounting for 72% of livestock compared with a mean value of just 37% at other sites. As the NISP figures used in this analysis have already been adjusted to take account of the large number of sheep ABGs the high sheep bone count appears to be a genuine aberration from general trends. Most early Romano-British assemblages from sites in the south-east region are characterised by high cattle bone frequencies – indeed the mean value for other sites is 50% compared to just 24% at this site. The only site with a similar high sheep bone count is Harlow Temple in Essex (Legge and Dorrington 1985).

In terms of site type (Fig. 3.10), species proportions for the Iron Age assemblages are most similar to other open and enclosed settlements in the region, while for the early Romano-British assemblage the closest parallels are with hillforts and ritual/religious sites. The similarity between the early Romano-British assemblage and temple sites has already been mentioned above and no doubt reflects the unusual nature of the majority of the animal bone deposits.

Figure 3.11 shows the NISP results for individual sites by period. The sites have been graded according to sheep bone frequency, since this is the most common species in all three periods at this site. Most of the Early/Middle Iron Age (85%) and Late Iron Age (58%) sites included in the study have high sheep bone frequencies similar to this site. The closest regional parallels are with the Middle Iron Age open settlement at Recreation Way, Mildenhall in Suffolk (Higbee forthcoming), the Middle Iron Age banjo enclosure at Bramdean in Hampshire (Clutton-Brock 1982), and the Late Iron Age enclosed settlements at Wardy Hill and Haddenham IV in Cambridgeshire (Davis 2003; Serjeantson 2006a). The early Romano-British assemblage on the other hand has the highest sheep bone frequency of the settlement sites included in the study. Most (45%) have high cattle bone frequencies (>50% NISP), while only 28% have high sheep bone frequencies. The closest regional parallels are with the settlements at Orton Hall Farm (King 1996) and Grandford (Stallibrass 1982) in Cambridgeshire, and Baldock in Hertfordshire (Chaplin and McCormick 1986). However, these settlement sites have sheep bone frequencies of 60% NISP, a figure well below the 76% recorded for this site. Due to the unusual nature of some of the deposits, the early Romano-British assemblage was also compared to a number of ritual/religious sites in the region (Fig. 3.12), most of which have high sheep bone frequencies similar to this site, including the temple site at Harlow in Essex (Legge and Dorrington 1985; King 2005, 335–6), where sheep account for 84% NISP.

The overall result of this analysis confirms that although there is considerable variation in species proportions between sites at the intra-regional level (Hambleton 1999, 46–7), most Iron Age sites have sheep-dominated assemblages. Early Romano-British sites in the region also show a diversity of species proportions but the general trend is significantly different from the pattern recorded at this site, with its high sheep bone frequency similar to that recorded at some temple sites in the region, a general reflection of the unusual nature of some of the pit deposits.

Body parts

The skeletal element data for sheep (Fig. 3.13) clearly show that all parts of the carcass are represented in the assemblage, which is a general reflection of the large number of complete sheep ABGs and a pattern that indicates local slaughter and consumption. There are a few absences of small skeletal elements (eg, axis vertebra, incisors and phalanges) from the Early/Middle Iron Age assemblage but this is probably due to the small size of the assemblage and recovery methods.

The most common sheep bone in all phases is the tibia, the lower half of which is usually discarded as butchery waste together with the foot (Maltby 1985, 26). Other common elements in these Iron Age sheep bone assemblages include the radius and metatarsal. These elements are all fairly robust and resistant to fragmentation as such they generally show a good survival and recovery rate in most assemblages of animal bone (Hambleton 1999, 31). Sheep skulls are the second most common skeletal element in the early Romano-British assemblage, and this is probably because of the large numbers of processed sheep carcasses from pit 3174.

Analysis of the cattle body part information (Fig. 3.13) is limited due to small sample size, particularly for the Iron Age period. However, all parts of the carcass are represented in the assemblage so it is at least possible to suggest that cattle were slaughtered and consumed locally during all three main occupation phases. The most common cattle bones are the humerus and mandible.

The most common elements in the small pig bone assemblage are the humerus, tibia, pelvis and mandible. These elements are robust and generally survive well in most assemblages (Hambleton 1999, 31). Overall the pig body part data indicates that like the other two livestock species, whole carcasses are represented indicating local slaughter and consumption.

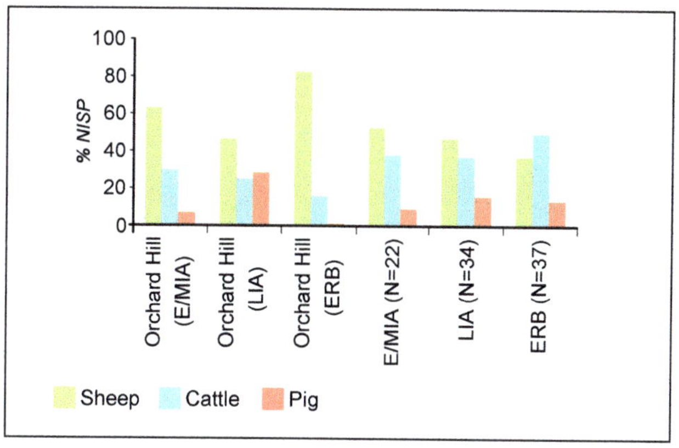

Figure 3.9 Relative frequency of livestock species from the site based on the adjusted NISP count compared to Early/Middle Iron Age, Late Iron Age and early Romano-British sites in south-east England. Data for other sites is based upon average values per period. Only sites with NISP of over 300 (ie, cattle+sheep+pig) have been included (see Appendix A). Sample size in parenthesis. Site data after Albarella and Pirnie (2008), and Hambleton (1999 and 2009)

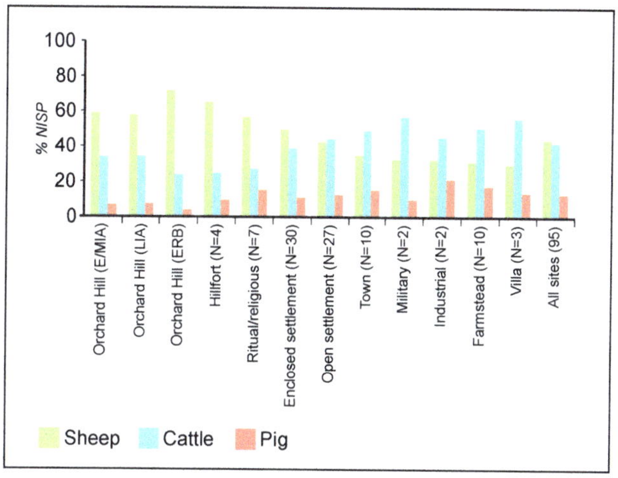

Figure 3.10 Relative frequency of livestock species from the site based on the adjusted NISP count compared to Early/Middle Iron Age, Late Iron Age and early Romano-British sites in south-east England by site type. Data used for other sites is based upon the average value per period. Only sites with NISP of over 300 (ie, cattle+sheep+pig) have been included (see Appendix A). Sample size in parenthesis. Site data after Albarella and Pirnie (2008), and Hambleton (1999 and 2009)

Mortality profiles

Mandibles

The mortality profile (Fig. 3.14) for Iron Age sheep shows a peak of slaughter at mandibular wear stage (MWS) E, which is equivalent to 2–3 years of age (Payne 1973). Over half of Iron Age sheep were therefore killed at the optimum age for prime meat. The mortality profile for early Romano-British sheep,

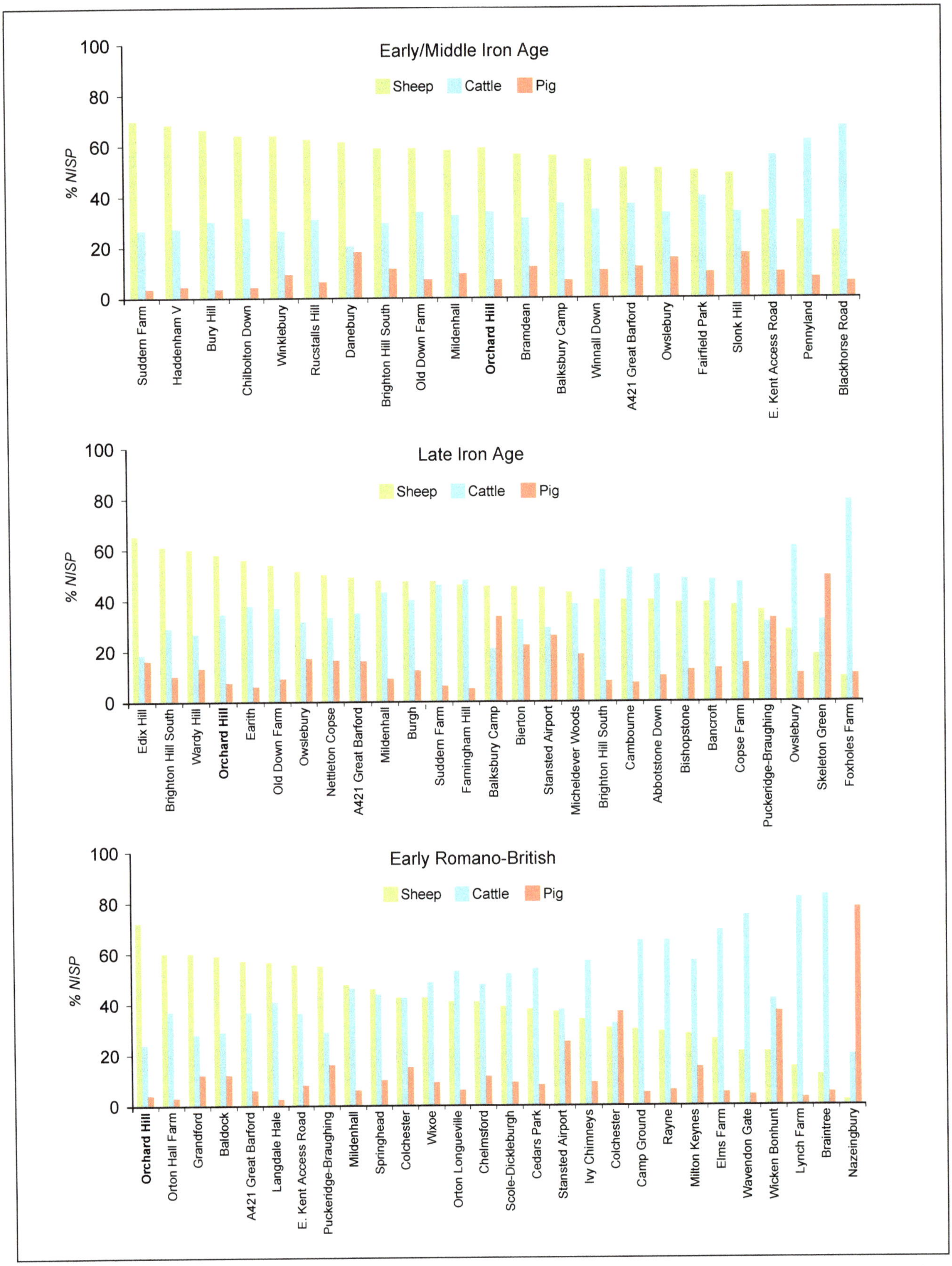

Figure 3.11 Relative frequency of livestock species from the site based on adjusted NISP count compared to a selection of Early, Middle and Late Iron Age, and early Romano-British sites in south-east England. Only sites with NISP of over 300 (ie, cattle+sheep+pig) have been included (see Appendix A). Site data after Albarella and Pirnie (2008) and Hambleton (1999 and 2009)

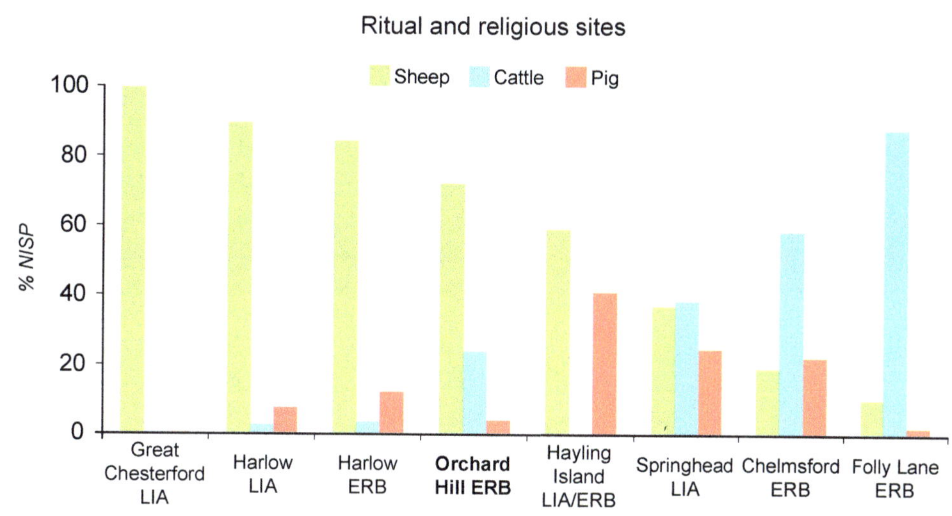

Figure 3.12 Relative frequency of livestock from selected Iron Age and Romano-British ritual and religious sites. Only sites with NISP of over 300 (ie, cattle+sheep+pig) have been included (see Appendix A). Site data after Albarella and Pirnie (2008) and Hambleton (1999 and 2009)

which is based on a much larger sample of data, shows three peaks of slaughter at MWS C (6–12 months), E (2–3 years) and G (4–6 years), and a minor peak at D (1–2 years). Those in the 6–12 month age group are likely to represent animals that did not survive their first winter or were culled as a deliberate measure to maintain flock size at the optimum capacity for the adequate provision of winter fodder. The older sheep aged 4–6 years might also be part of a deliberate policy to reduce flock size before winter by removing less productive older animals from the flock. As both of these age groups are likely to suffer a loss of condition over the winter months (see Jewell *et al.* 1974) a selective culling policy at the end of autumn would result in greater returns and ease the pressure on pasture and fodder supplies. This strategy complements extensive arable cultivation (Hambleton 1999, 70).

Using the mean values suggested by a large-scale study of tooth eruption and wear in live sheep of different breeds (see Jones 2006) it is possible to estimate more precisely when the slaughter of yearlings took place. The mean birth dates provided by the survey (*ibid.*, 156–7) fall between 31 March and 17 April (and range between 11 March and 22 May), therefore the season when 6–12 month old lambs were slaughtered falls between September/October, and the following March/April. As part of this study, Jones proposed a more refined method of estimating the age of sheep by sub-dividing Payne's original wear stages (Jones 2006, 177). This method was applied to early Romano-British sheep mandibles (Fig. 3.14) in an attempt to clarify seasonal slaughter patterns. The analysis indicates that most yearlings were slaughtered between the ages of 8–12 months (MWS C6+ after Jones 2006), and this corresponds to between November/December and the following March/April, depending upon which mean birth date is used. Closer examination of the tooth wear data for this group of mandibles further indicates that the majority (63%) of yearlings are at the lower end of the age range (ie, m1s in wear stages 7A and 8A), which suggests a peak of slaughter during the late autumn or early winter rather than late winter or early spring. This evidence fits with the concept of a deliberate cull policy before the onset of winter, although it is noteworthy that slaughter patterns at many Romano-British temples (eg, Uley, Harlow, Great Chesterford, see King 2005) also indicate that autumn was the main season in which votive offerings were made in more formal religious settings.

The assemblage includes a number of loose deciduous forth premolars (or Dp4s) from young lambs. The lack of wear on these teeth indicates that they are likely to be from animals aged 0–1 month (Jones 2006, 160), and the majority are from deposit (3711) in pit 3174.

A total of 24 complete cattle mandibles were recovered from the site. The mortality profile (Fig. 3.14) shows that the main peaks of slaughter are amongst adult and senile animals (MWS G and I after Halstead 1985). It is likely that these animals represent dairy cows or draught oxen. The majority of the other cattle were slaughtered between the ages of 18–36 months (MWS D and E) and represent prime meat animals. Cattle were therefore managed for a range of products including prime beef, milk and traction.

Five complete pig mandibles were recovered from phased contexts. Two are from 2–7 month old piglets, one is from a 7–14-month old animal and a further two

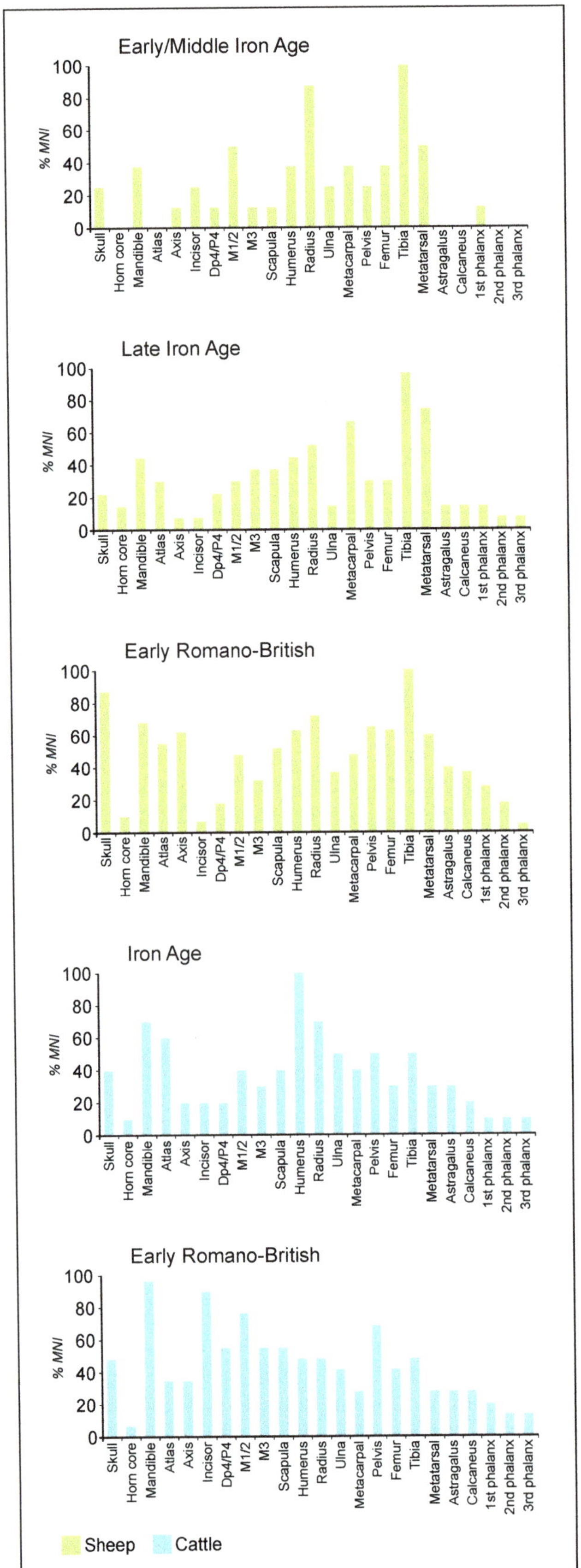

Figure 3.13 Sheep (top) and cattle (bottom) body part representation by phase expressed as a percentage of MNI in relation to the most common element

are from slightly older animals aged 14–21 months (MWS B–D after Hambleton 1999, 65). Pigs are usually slaughtered at a younger age than other livestock because they have large litters, reach full body weight quickly and provide no secondary products.

Epiphyseal fusion

The fusion data indicates that 13% of Iron Age sheep died or were slaughtered before the age of 10 months, and roughly 50% survived beyond 2 years of age. The mortality pattern for the early Romano-British period indicates a slightly lower mortality rate amongst the 10-month old age group and a gradual kill-off rate across all age classes, with 52% surviving beyond 2 years. The mortality profile is very similar to the Iron Age mortality profile, and if anything shows a slightly less intensive slaughter pattern.

There is an obvious discrepancy between mortality patterns suggested by the two ageing methods with regard to the kill-off rate of yearlings during the early Romano-British period (see Fig. 3.14). The fusion data suggest that this is relatively low (10%), while mandibles suggest that it is more like one third. However, it is generally accepted that tooth eruption/wear is a more accurate method than epiphyseal fusion. Overall the fusion data indicates that the majority of sheep were culled as prime meat animals and that there is likely to have been a policy of reducing flock size before winter.

The mortality profiles for cattle indicate some slight differences between phases, notably a more intense kill-off rate amongst younger animals during the Iron Age, when 19% of cattle were slaughtered before the age of 12–18 months, compared to just 8% in the early Romano-British period. The proportion of cattle surviving beyond 3½–4 years is roughly equal in both periods, with over half of cattle surviving to maturity. This pattern fits well with the mortality pattern suggested by the small group of mandibles and confirms that cattle were managed for secondary products and possibly traction. Unfortunately, there is an inadequate amount of biometric data to establish if the sex ratio of the cattle herd supports this theory.

The epiphyseal fusion information for pig is extremely limited but does at least confirm that they were killed at a younger age than other livestock, and this occurred within the first 2 years of life.

Butchery

Butchery marks are evident on only a small fraction of bones. The paucity of evidence indicates that carcasses were not extensively butchered, but this is unsurprising given that the assemblage includes a large number of ABGs. Cut marks are the most common type of butchery evidence in all three main phases. Knives were primarily used to disarticulate carcasses by cutting through the muscle attachments at major joints. Cut marks indicative of skinning and filleting were also noted. The use of heavy chopping tools appears to have been quite limited and was mainly restricted to use on dismembering larger carcasses. Saws were use in craft-activities, such as horn-working, for which there was a limited amount of evidence.

Biometry

The total quantity of biometric data from each phase is relatively small and this precludes detailed analysis to look for any chronological changes in the size and conformation of livestock at the intra-site level. Detailed examination of this data was restricted to the calculation of withers (or shoulder) height estimates and log ratio analysis.

Withers height estimates indicate that there was little overall change in the stature of sheep between the Late Iron Age and early Romano-British period. Withers height estimates for early Romano-British cattle suggest a range of 0.96 m to 1.25 m (mean 1.04 m), which is well within the expected range for this period.

The log ratio technique allows intra-site comparison between small samples of biometric data, providing a chance to identify changes in the size and conformation of livestock. In all cases the standard measurements used are the mean values from the preceding period; for example, Early/Middle Iron Age means were used to calculate Late Iron Age log ratios and so on. The results of the log ratio analysis are summarised below.

Analysis of sheep tooth widths suggests a slight increase in size during the Late Iron Age and greater variation in the size of early Romano-British sheep. Similar changes have been noted at other sites in the south-east region and it has been suggested that these result from genetic diversification and/or improvements in husbandry brought about by Romanising influences on the management of livestock (Albarella 2007; Albarella *et al.* 2008).

The same analysis was undertaken for sheep post-cranial bones. The results indicate that there was no significant change in the size or confirmation of sheep between the Late Iron Age and the early Romano-British periods. However, it is worth noting that some of the early Romano-British sheep have more robust limbs than Late Iron Age sheep, a change that could be due to greater genetic diversity and/or general improvements in husbandry.

The same analysis was undertaken for cattle teeth and post-cranial bones, and indicate that cattle teeth decrease in size between the Late Iron Age and early Romano-British periods; the reasons for this change are likely to be similar to those outlined above. Cattle post-cranial bones on the other hand show considerable variation, particularly in relation to width measurements, and this suggests that early Romano-British cattle have shorter and more robust limbs than Late Iron Age cattle. However, some of this variation could be partly due to sexual dimorphism.

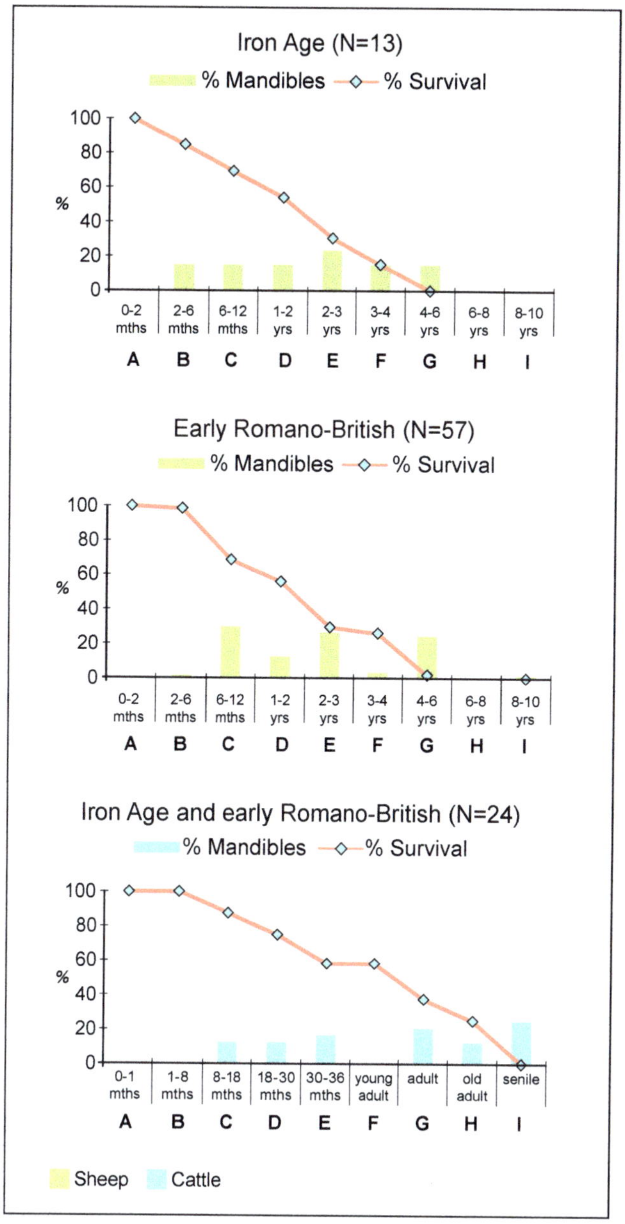

Figure 3.14 Sheep (top) and cattle (bottom) mortality profiles based on mandibles retaining 2+ teeth with recordable wear. Mandibular wear stages (or MWS) after Payne (1973) (sheep), and Halstead (1985) (cattle)

Other mammals

Goat

Two goat skeletal elements were distinguished from amongst the caprine remains; this is compared to 63 positively identified sheep bones. They include a horn core from Late Iron Age pit 3027, which is associated with a cattle ABG, and a skull fragment from early Romano-British pit 3596.

Horse

Horse bones account for 4% of the total NISP and were recovered from all three phases. The remains include eight ABGs, and a quantity of disarticulated bones scattered between a number of pits and the various phases of the enclosure ditch. Middle/Late Iron Age pit 3341 is noteworthy since it contained the disarticulated remains from a single animal.

Most of the horse bones are from adult animals, although juvenile bones (ABG 13) were recovered from Late Iron Age pit 3053, and prenatal bones (ABG 209) were recovered from early Romano-British pit 3174. The presence of these young animals indicates that horses were being bred and raised on site. The lack of similar evidence in the Early/Middle Iron Age could indicate that there was a different strategy in operation, for example horses may have been rounded up from free-ranging populations (Harcourt 1979, 158; Grant 1984, 521) or traded (Bendrey *et al.* 2009). However, given the importance of horses during the Iron Age it seems unlikely that their breeding was left to chance.

Butchery marks were recorded on a small number of horse bones. Iron Age horse bones show evidence for filleting, disarticulation, and skinning, but only skinning evidence was noted on early Romano-British horse bones. Evidence for the consumption of horseflesh has been recorded at a number of Iron Age sites in Britain (Maltby 1996, 23; Bendrey 2010, 12) but it is unlikely that it formed a regular part of the diet. Evidence for similar practices during the Romano-British period is scarce and classical sources indicate that in most parts of the Roman Empire, horsemeat was only eaten out of necessity during times of hardship (Tacitus Annals II, 24 and Histories IV, 60: quoted in Luff 1982).

Withers (or shoulder) height estimates for Late Iron Age horses range from 11 to 14.3 hands (mean 12.3 hands). An estimate of 11.2 hands was obtained for a single metacarpal from the early Romano-British assemblage. The horses at this site are all pony-sized animals.

Of particular note amongst the equid bones is a fragment of right distal radius from fill 3263 of Middle/Late Iron Age pit 3341. The bone is from a small animal with slender limbs, and has a mid-shaft diameter of just 26.7 mm and a distal breadth of 54.8 mm. The palmar side of the shaft is noticeably concave in the mid-shaft region, and the crista transversa forms a deep sulcus at the epiphyseal junction (Peters 1998; Johnstone 2004, 173–4). These two traits coupled with the small size of the bone, suggest that it belongs to an equid hydrid, most probably a donkey rather than a mule (see Johnstone 2006, 184). Donkeys are rare in the archaeological record but this is undoubtedly because they are so difficult to identify. Multivariate biometric methods (Johnstone 2004; 2006; 2008; 2010) have proved helpful but require a suite of measurements from complete bones, a situation that is rarely possible when dealing with archaeological material. The application of these methods has however led to the reclassification of some equid bones, including two donkey bones from a Middle Iron Age context at Danebury in Hampshire (Johnstone 2010, 22, tab. 2). The possible donkey bone from the present site has been radiocarbon dated to *100 cal BC–10 cal AD (SUERC-38342, 2055±30 BP at 95% probability)*.

Dog

The assemblage includes a large number of dog bones (23% of the total NISP), the vast majority (98%) of which are from 18 complete and partial skeletons (Table 3.12). There is a general trend toward the burial of dogs within pits from the Late Iron Age onwards, with the number of dog ABGs increasing from six to 12 in the early Romano-British period. This fits with general observations made by Morris (2008, 85; 2010, 15; 2011, 130) in his detailed study of ABGs from sites in southern England. The presence of articulated dogs in pits, wells and shafts is a common theme on many Iron Age and Romano-British sites and has been taken as a significant factor in the identification of ritual deposits (Ross 1968; Wait 1985; for local examples see Cotton 2001; Hastings 1965; Philp 1984; Philp *et al.* 1991).

Most of the dog ABGs and disarticulated bones are from adult animals, the rest are from juvenile and sub-adult animals, or foetuses. The demographics indicate that there was a local breeding population of dogs throughout the sequence of occupation, and while some of these animals might have been culled in an attempt to control population numbers (Hambleton 2006, 47), it is clear that others were sacrificed (as chthonic symbols – relating to the underworld) and placed within pits as part of complex structured deposits, which in some instances involved burnt animal remains (eg, deposit 3839 associated with ABG 115 in pit 3535), and the remnants from large social events (eg, deposit 3711 associated with ABG 131 in pit 3174).

Late Iron Age dogs were between 0.54–0.58 m at the shoulder (mean 0.56 m), while early Romano-British dogs range between 0.23–0.54 m (mean 0.45 m). The ranges are within those established for the Iron Age and Romano-British period and illustrate the diversity of dog sizes in the early Romano-British period, which is matched by variations in conformation (Harcourt 1974, 163–6; Clark 1995; 2000; Cram 2000, 171–2).

Two distinct skull morphologies were recognised; the most common is a terrier-type, which is here defined as being well proportioned with a sagittal crest. Dogs with this type of skull morphology have been identified in all three main phase, and they fall within the middle to upper size range defined above.

The second skull type is shorter and broader, with a rounded cranium and no sagittal crest. This type of skull morphology, generally referred to as bracycephalic, is most obvious amongst smaller dogs that generally retain paedomorphic (ie, juvenile) characteristic such as large eyes, well-spaced within a domed head (Clark 2000, 165). A small dog (ABG 131) from early Romano-British pit 3174 has this type of skull morphology. Two other early Romano-British dogs (ABG 92 and 115) with these characteristics were also noted, but because they are juvenile they cannot confidently be ascribed to this category (Harcourt 1974, 166). It is noteworthy, however, that both are small, gracile individuals with long straight limbs similar to ABG 131, and that all three animals are associated with complex structured pit deposits.

Lapdogs were first bred in Italy during the early Roman period (Mazzorin and Tagliacozzo 2000) and exported to other areas of the Empire including Britain. Two main forms have been identified: chrondrodystrophic dwarf hounds and toy or midget dogs. The former has shortened and thickened limb bones that are often bowed and splayed at the ends, while the latter have crania with a juvenile appearance (or paedomorphic) and straight slender limb bones. These are often referred to as the Maltese type or *Melitaei* of Pliny and other Roman authors. Both types are rare from early Romano-British contexts (Harcourt 1974, 163–6; Clark 2000) but become more common later on.

The dog from pit 3174 at Orchard Hill is similar to the Maltese type and representations of these dogs have been recorded on statues, grave stones and mosaics from sites in the Mediterranean part of the Roman Empire. Jenkins (1957, pl. 7) and Toynbee (1962, pl. 76) cite examples of statues showing lapdogs held by women from Roman Britain however to date there has been little research in this area and no attempt to classify or compare the evidence with dog skeletal remains (Cram 2000, 174).

Deer

Three red deer bones were recovered from the Late Iron Age features. These include a metacarpal from the ditch of Enclosure 1 (4229), a fragment of antler from pit 3025 and a metatarsal from pit 3852. Cut and shave marks on the antler indicate that it is an off-cut that has been systematically reduced to provide raw material for object manufacture (MacGregor 1985, 68, fig. 42). Two fragments of roe deer pelvis were recorded from Early/Middle Iron Age pits 3011 and 3940.

Fox

The assemblage includes a small number of disarticulated fox bones and a complete skeleton (ABG 91). The latter is from early Romano-British pit 3535, and was found in association with several other complete and partial skeletons. It is one of only a few wild species included as part of a complex pit deposit.

Cat

The partial remains of a neonatal cat (ABG 251) were recovered from Late Iron Age pit 4313. Although cat ABGs are comparatively rare in the archaeological record the remains of neonatal fatalities are more commonly recorded than adult remains (Morris 2011, 41–2).

Hare

A single hare radius was recovered from early Romano-British pit 3921 together with a modest amount of butchery waste from the processing of sheep carcasses.

Small mammals and amphibians

Most of the small mammal and amphibian bones are from Middle/Late Iron Age pit 3341 and early Romano-British pit 3535, both of which contain ABGs. This evidence suggests that some pits were left open for a period with the contents visible, and similar evidence has been noted at a range of other Iron Age and Romano-British sites (Hambleton and Maltby 2008, 87; Higbee 2008, 50; 2011, 76; Cotton 2001, 8).

Birds

The bird bone assemblage comprises domestic fowl and corvids. All of the domestic fowl bones are from early Romano-British pits, and include a single humerus from 3289 and the remains of two individuals (ABG 255) from 3174.

Both large (ie, raven) and small (ie, crow/rook) corvids are present in the assemblage. The former is represented by two complete skeletons, one from Middle/Late Iron Age pit 3341 (ABG 98) and the other from early Romano-British pit 3174 (ABG 200), and the latter by four leg bones from 3174. Corvids are common scavengers around settlement sites, but as they were also important in Iron Age and Roman ritual and religious practices as chthonic symbols (relating to the underworld) their presence in the pit assemblages is almost certainly deliberate (Hambleton and Maltby 2008, 87; Serjeantson and Morris 2011, 103; Serjeantson 1991, 481; Serjeantson 2009, 360).

Associated bone groups (ABGs)

A number of pits contain structured deposits of animal bone and other finds, the most significant of which were from pits 3341, 3535, 4376 and recut 3174.

Early/Middle Iron Age
The partial, semi-articulated remains of a neonatal lamb (ABG 113) were placed on the base of pit 3846, and were found in association with a small number of disarticulated horse bones.

Late Iron Age
Pits 2061 and 3223 both contained single horse ABGs (238 and 57), while pits 2047, 3027, 3220 and 3386 all contained two ABGs each. The last two of these features contained the partial remains of a neonatal lamb and pig, which suggests that these features were backfilled during the spring.

Pits 3053 and 4313 contained three ABGs each. The ABGs from pit 3053 include two articulating horse legs (ABGs 13 and 226), and a complete dog skeleton (ABG 144). The latter is a mature adult with worn teeth and signs of degenerative osteoarthritis on some of the thoracic vertebrae. All of the ABGs from pit 4313 are from young animals, and include the foetus of a pig, the partial remains of a neonatal lamb and the hind leg bones of a neonatal cat (ABGs 250–2).

Pit 3231
Pit 3231, which is dated to the Middle Iron Age, contained five ABGs including the partial remains of an adult sheep (ABG 244: *180–50 cal BC, SUERC-38154, 2115±35 BP at 95% probability*) and an articulated section of cattle vertebrae (ABG 80) from the primary fill. The sheep bones are all from the right side of the carcass this is highly suggestive of ritual practices in which propitiatory offerings were made of certain carcass parts (Davis 2008). The pit was then partially backfilled and then left for a period, accumulating a few pitfall victims and a thin layer of silt. The partial remains of two pigs (ABG 71 and 232) were then deposited, followed by the near complete remains of a horse (ABG 70). The animal had been skinned and its forequarters removed.

Pit 3341
A total of eight ABGs were recovered from pit 3341, which is dated to the Middle to Late Iron Age. Most are from the lower half of the pit; these include in order of deposition, a dog foetus (ABG 245), a raven (ABG 98: *130–10 cal BC, SUERC-38159, 2085±35 BP at 95% probability*), a neonatal sheep (ABG 234), a second dog foetus (ABG 69), and two neonatal pigs (ABG 67 and 64). Rodent and amphibian bones were found with the ABGs from three of the lower fills, which suggests that the pit was left open for short periods of time. The presence of newborn livestock further indicates that the lower fills are likely to have been deposited during the spring. Two adult dogs (ABGs 61 and 62) were then deposited near the top of the feature, one of which was radiocarbon dated to *60 cal BC–cal AD 60 (SUERC-38144, 2030±35 BP at 95% probability)*. The dogs are similar in stature (0.55–0.56 m) and appear to have been positioned as if in the act of mating (Pl. 2.4), although this could just be fortuitous. The pit also contained a small but significant number of disarticulated bones, including the possible donkey radius.

Early Romano-British
Several ABGs were identified from the early Romano-British enclosure ditches. The remains consist of an articulated section of cattle vertebral column (ABG 1) from Enclosure 2c (ditch 2071), and the partial remains of a lamb foetus and a neonatal sheep and the foetus of dog (ABGs 227–9) from Enclosure 5 (ditch 4378). These deposits are similar in character to those recovered from pits, although they are rare components of the ditch assemblage which largely consists of disarticulated mixed bone waste from the processing of cattle and horse carcasses.

Single ABGs were recovered from pits 3183, 3311 (cut into the upper fill of early Romano-British pit 3229, below) and 3921. The remains include a neonatal lamb (ABG 230), the complete skeleton of an adult dog (ABG 68), and the articulated axial skeleton from a sub-adult cattle (ABG 249). The terrier-type dog from pit 3311 has an estimated shoulder height of 0.52 m. These pits also include relatively large amounts of disarticulated sheep and cattle bones, some of which appear to be from one or more different animals. This evidence suggests that only a short time lagged between the butchery and consumption of animal carcasses, and the disposal of waste into pits. Secondary deposition via surface accumulations (eg, middens) would result in obvious differences in preservation condition within contexts (see for example Garrow 2006, 110), fewer associated bones, and a more arbitrary collection of material. Also of note is the complete skeleton of an adult terrier-type dog (ABG 2) from pit 2047, which was associated with an articulated section of cattle vertebrae, sacrum and pelvis (ABG 3) (see back cover, middle).

Pit 3870
Two ABGs were recovered from pit 3870; these have been identified as the skull, mandibles and cervical vertebrae from an adult horse (ABG 114) and the remains of an adult male dog (ABG 137) with an estimated shoulder height of 0.48 m. This feature also includes a reasonable amount of disarticulated material and appears to represent 'normal' waste discarded directly into the pit.

Pit 3229
The three ABGs from pit 3229 are all sheep and were recovered from the upper fill (3230). They include the near complete skeleton of an immature animal (ABG 58), the spinal column and pelvic girdle from an adult (ABG 59) and the lumbar vertebrae, pelvic girdle and hindquarters from a sub-adult (ABG 60).

Pit 3419

Three ABGs were recovered from pit 3419. The lower fill includes a cattle forelimb from the right-side (ABG 77), which was radiocarbon dated to *90 cal BC–cal AD 50 (SUERC-38150, 2045±35 BP at 95% probability)*. The other two ABGs are from the secondary fill and include partial skeletons from an adult and a neonatal sheep (ABGs 72 and 237).

Pit 4052

Pit 4052 also contained three ABGs, these include the partial remains of two sheep and a dog from the upper fill. One of the sheep is an adult animal and is represented by a section of spinal column (ABG 246), and the other is a neonate (ABG 247). The presence of the neonate suggests that the final in-filling of the pit occurred sometime in spring. The dog skull, mandibles and forelimbs (ABG 248) are those from an adult animal with an estimated shoulder height of 0.54 m.

Pit 3535

Pit 3535 contained a sequence of deliberate and structured deposits comprising of 16 ABGs and a deposit of burnt animal bone. The primary deposit 3890 included the burial (ABG 115) of a small dog, around one year old, with a shoulder height of 0.39 m, and a smashed cordoned jar (ON 118) that contained an ashy deposit and the burnt remains of at least two lambs (Fig. 2.11). A radiocarbon date of *50 cal BC–cal AD 70 (SUERC-38160, 1985±35 BP at 95% probability)* was obtained for dog ABG 115. The presence of small mammal pitfall victims from this level indicates that the pit was left open for a period after the dog burial and jar/burnt remains had been deposited. It is likely therefore that the contents were intended to be viewed (Hambleton and Maltby 2008, 87; Higbee 2011, 76 and 2008, 50; Wilson 1999, 302).

At some later point the pit was partially backfilled and 15 ABGs were deposited. Most of the ABGs are complete skeletons and these were densely packed into the pit, with no obvious positioning or arrangement. They include the complete and partial remains of five cattle, four sheep, four dogs, a fox and a horse skull. The five cattle ABGs include the complete skeleton of an adult animal minus the skull and mandibles (ABG 100), the axial skeleton (ie, skull, mandibles, vertebral column and ribs) of a senile animal (ABG 101, MWS I), the right (ABG 108) and left (ABG 242) forequarters of a third adult, and the right forequarter from a calf (ABG 243). Skinning marks were evident on the skull and/or phalanges of all three adult animals, however there is no evidence that they were processed for meat. The deposit also includes four complete sheep skeletons, one adult aged 4–6 years (ABG 239), one sub-adult aged 2–3 years (ABG 83) and two neonates (ABG 240), as well as the right fore- and hindquarters from a second adult (ABG 244). The presence of the neonatal sheep suggests that the animal carcasses were deposited during the spring and despite the lack of butchery evidence it is likely that the carcasses of the adult animals had been processed for meat after only minimal disarticulation.

The dog ABGs included three complete skeletons, two adults (ABG 90 and 109), a sub-adult (ABG 92) and the partial remains of a foetus (ABG 241). The skull of one of the adult animals (ABG 109) is absent and the skull of the other (ABG 90: *30 cal BC–cal AD 90, SUERC-38153, 1955±35 BP at 94.9% probability*) shows signs of blunt force trauma. The severity of the damage suggests that this was the means used to dispatch, or at least stun the animal. None of the other dog skulls from the site show signs of injury or trauma, however, most of the skulls are heavily fragmented and could not be reconstructed to establish if anymore dogs had been dispatched using this method. One of the dogs (ABG 92) is a small, gracile animal with a shoulder height of only 0.23 m, it is too small to have served any useful purpose, and would undoubtedly have struggled to survive as a scavenger, indeed it is unlikely to have survived at all without human shelter and protection (Harcourt 1974, 172). Small dogs of this type are quite rare in Britain during the early Romano-British period and are likely to have been highly prized (Cram 2000, 171–2). Its death, therefore, particularly if a deliberate act, is likely to represent a considerable sacrifice on the part of its owner.

The other ABGs from 3535 include a horse skull (ABG 107) and the complete skeleton of a fox (ABG 91). Cut mark evidence indicates that the animal had been stripped of its pelt. The remains of wild animals such as foxes are rare in structured pit deposits and the majority are from the Late Romano-British period (Morris 2011, 40–1).

Pit 4376/3174

The largest and most complex pit deposits on the site are from Late Iron Age/early Romano-British pit 4376, and early Romano-British recut 3174. Deposited near the base of 4376 were the partial remains of at least two neonatal lambs (ABG 201) and these were radiocarbon dated to *100 cal BC–cal AD 60 (SUERC-38161, 1990±35 BP at 95% probability)*. Two further ABGs were then deposited, including the partial remains of a 2–3-year-old sheep (ABG 205) and the left hindquarter from a cattle carcass (ABG 206).

The initial deposit 3711 into the recut 3174, included large numbers of articulated sheep carcass parts (ABGs 170–196, 198–9, 207–8, 215, 217–222, 224–5, 253–4 and 256–265). The ABGs are from a minimum of 14 foetal/neonatal lambs, and 42 juvenile/adult sheep. It is clear from the range of body parts (Fig. 3.15) and the correlation between left and right elements (Fig. 3.16) that whole, disarticulated carcasses are represented. The carcasses were divided into large units comprising complete limbs, parts of the axial skeleton (ie, ribs, thoracic/lumbar vertebrae and pelvic girdle), and the skull and cervical (ie, neck) vertebrae. Butchery evidence is scarce but indicates that primary dismemberment was carried out using a sharp knife to cut through the muscle mass at major joints, and that meat was filleted off the bone. The degree of articulation

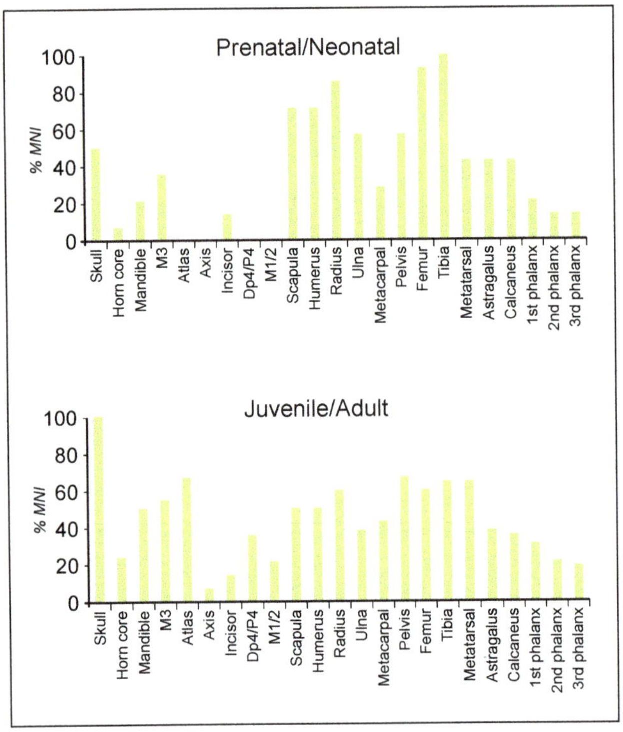

Figure 3.15 Early Romano-British pit 3174 fill (3711): sheep body part representation expressed as a percentage of MNI in relation to the most common element. Prenatal/neonatal bones shown separately from juvenile/adult bone

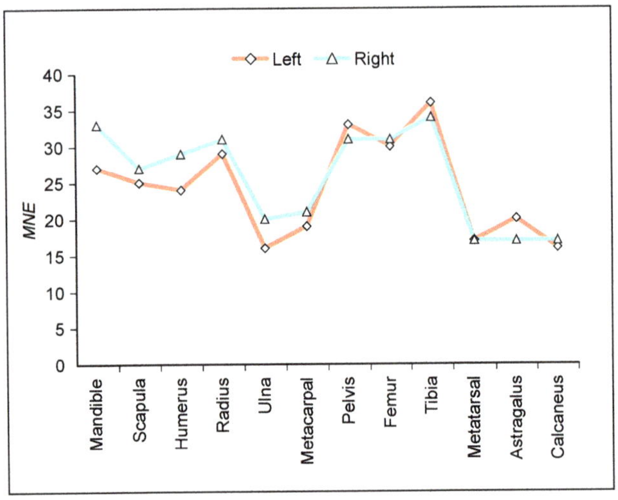

Figure 3.16 Number of left and right sheep bones from early Romano-British pit 3174

strongly suggests that the carcass parts were discarded directly into the pit soon after the meat had been consumed.

Mandibular wear stage data indicates two main peaks of slaughter, one at 6–12 months (MWS C) and another at 4–6 years (MWS G), with a minor peak at 2–3 years (MWS E). As indicated above (see Mortality Profiles – Mandibles), yearlings were principally slaughtered in late autumn/early winter, which given the articulated condition of the sheep bones implies that this is also the time of year when the butchered carcass parts were deposited. However, the presence of foetal and neonatal lambs contradicts this seasonal time estimate, and suggests that the deposit formed over a longer period which extended into the spring lambing season. The presence of small mammals and amphibians further indicates that the deposit was exposed at the bottom of the recut for at least a short period of time, so it is at least possible that deposit 3711 formed as a result of several depositional episodes; a rapid event during the autumn following the slaughter and consumption of significant numbers of yearlings and older sheep, and a more gradual accumulation during the spring when foetal and neonatal mortalities were deposited.

A small number of cattle ABGs were dispersed throughout deposit 3711. The general character of which is similar to the sheep ABGs, and includes the articulated right foot, and lumbar vertebrae and sacrum of an adult (ABG 210 and 214), and several articulated units from at least two juveniles (ABGs 211, 213–6, and 223).

Overlying the sheep bone deposit, within the top 0.2–0.3 m, were the remains of three dogs (ABGs 116, 131 and 197), two domestic fowl (ABG 255), a raven (ABG 200), and a horse foetus (ABG 209). The latter was only recognised in post-excavation therefore its location within the deposit is unknown. However, given the complex and structured nature of the deposit it is unlikely to be incidental, particularly given the investment involved in breeding and rearing horses, and the prestige associated with their ownership.

The adult dogs from deposit 3711 are different sizes and have distinctly different skull morphologies. The larger dog (ABG 116), which has a shoulder height of 0.44 m, has a well-proportioned skull with a pronounced sagittal crest. The smaller dog (ABG 131), with a shoulder height of only 0.37 m, has thin slender limbs, a rounded (bracycephalic) skull and over-crowed teeth due to the small size of its jaw. As previously indicated in relation to the small lapdog from pit 3535, dogs with this type of skull morphology are comparatively rare in the early Romano-British period, and this one has been radiocarbon dated to *cal AD 10–110 (SUERC-38158, 1900±35 BP at 95% probability)*. This animal is likely to have been highly prized and cosseted by its owner since it is unlikely to have been able to fend for itself (Baxter 2006, 19; Cram 2000, 171–2).

These ABGs appear to mark the end of the primary deposit in recut 3174, although it is clear from subsequent deposits that the pit was revisited several times to incorporate other ABGs and two infant burials. The ABGs include the skull, mandibles, cervical vertebrae and left scapula from an 8–18-month old calf (ABG 203, *cal AD 20–130, SUERC-38143, 1865±35 BP at 95% probability*), the cervical vertebrae and right forequarter from an adult cattle (ABG 204), which was found in association with infant burial 3654, and a pair of cattle mandibles (ABG 202: *cal AD 50–170, SUERC-38141, 1880±35 BP at 95% probability*).

Discussion

The assemblage is dominated by sheep and this is a general reflection of their importance to the pastoral economy of the region during the Iron Age and early Romano-British period. Bones from foetal and neonatal lambs were recovered from a number of pits, and while natural mortalities such as these are to be expected, it is likely that these losses were a cause of concern, particularly since the spring lambing season is when self-sufficient communities start to plan and focus on the new agricultural year after the lean, dark winter months. Perhaps therefore by 'giving' early losses to the earth by placing them in pits recently cleared of stored grain, the people of the site hoped to have better success in the year ahead.

Raven burials, like the ones from pits 3341 and 3174, have been recorded from a number of Iron Age and Romano-British sites in Britain and are frequently deposited in association with dogs (Serjeantson and Morris 2011, 96). Their general characteristics (ie, black, glossy carrion-eaters) single them out as symbols of death and darkness (Green 1992, 174), and consequently their remains are usually deposited into features that penetrate deep into the earth. As such they are thought to represent propitiatory offerings intended to ensure a favourable outcome to some future event (Serjeantson and Morris 2011, 102).

Domestic fowl are also known to have been widely used in religious activities (Toynbee 1996, 257) and were associated with the Roman deity Mercury, as for example at Uley shrine in Gloucestershire (Levitan 1993; King 2005, 332–4), which was connected to prosperity, success and general well-being (Green 1992, 150). The two domestic fowl from pit 3174, which were deposited at the same level as the raven mentioned above, and several dogs, are likely therefore to have held greater significance beyond that of mere food offerings.

Complete and partial dog burials in pits are another common feature of the assemblage. The evidence suggests that these animals were deliberately killed but it cannot be established with certainty that they were sacrificed for their chthonic symbolism, or simply to control population size (Hambleton 2006, 47). However, given the structured nature of some of the pit deposits, and the inclusion of small lapdogs, which were rare in Britain during the early Romano-British period and therefore highly prized (Cram 2000, 171–2), it seems likely that dogs were deliberately killed for ritual purposes.

In Iron Age and Roman religion dogs were associated with healing, death and hunting, and were often used as symbols to convey opposing concepts (King 2005, 352; Green 1992, 83, 87–8). The primary deposit from pit 3535, which comprises a dog (ie, chthonic symbol) buried with the burnt remains of two 10 month old lambs suggests an emphasis on dualistic themes possibly inspired by the end of winter and the coming of spring (ie, dark and light, life and death). Burnt offerings of sheep carcass parts are common at Romano-British religious sites, for example Wanborough in Surrey (King 2005, 341–2; Nicolaysen 1994, 162), but they are also found on settlement sites, for example at Reigate Road in Ewell, Surrey, where a cordoned jar containing the burnt remains of a sheep/goat were deposited into a pit (Nicolaysen 2001, 25).

The largest and most significant deposit of animal bone recorded from the site is from pit 4376 and its subsequent recut 3174. The characteristics of the sheep bone deposit from the recut pit – ie, large concentration of bones, a predominance of one species, joints in articulation and minimal dismemberment of carcasses prior to cooking, fits with criteria used to identify feasting deposits (Serjeantson 2006b; 2011, 72), and the mortality profile of the sheep suggests that these animals were slaughtered and consumed before the onset of winter. This is in keeping with a selective culling policy designed to ease pressure on grazing land and winter fodder supplies by removing excess lambs and old unproductive sheep.

It is significant that the remnants of the feast were collected up and deposited together in the recut of an earlier pit. Perhaps the intention was to memorialise the social gathering and reinforce links to past events. Similar connections have been noted in the spatial association between features of different dates at other sites, for example at the rural religious complex at Marcham/Frilford in Oxfordshire where a *favissa*-like pit was intentionally sited in the same area as a large group of Iron Age pits (Kamash *et al.* 2010, 100). The same theme can be seen in the associations between Roman religious practise and earlier monuments (Williams 1998); the Bronze Age barrow at Stanwick, for example, became the focus for ritual deposition in the Romano-British period, and an entire shrine complex at Snow's Farm, Haddenham in Cambridgeshire, was positioned on the edge of an earlier round barrow (Lawrence and Smith 2009, 325). Further examples include the Romano-Celtic temple built over the pyre mound in the mortuary enclosure at Folly Lane, St Albans (Nibblett 1999), and the Romano-British feasting deposit overlying the Middle Iron Age chariot burial at Ferrybridge (Boyle 2004).

In many respects the large sheep bone deposit from pit 3174 is similar to that recovered from pit A12 at Baldock in Hertfordshire (Chaplin and McCormick, 1986, 411), which contained the remains of 98 sheep, five cattle, nine pigs and 12 domestic fowl. The sheep had been slaughtered during the winter, and their carcasses stripped of meat but not otherwise jointed or dispersed. The deposit dates to AD 50–70 and the authors suggest that it might be associated with a Roman military unit provisioning itself with meat at the time of the Boudiccan rebellion. However, in summarising the site, Stead and Rigby (1986, 85–6) acknowledge that the deposit could equally represent the remains of a feast related to a fair or a religious gathering.

Conclusions

The assemblage includes a number of unusual pit deposits. These have been interpreted as propitiatory offerings intended to appease the forces responsible for productivity and continued success of the society. They share similarities with the types of deposits recorded at some shrine and temple sites in Britain (ie, a predominance of sheep slaughtered during the autumn/winter), but here the context is informal and appears to be related to concepts and themes associated with the agricultural cycle of events, specifically the end of winter and the coming of spring.

The same themes are evident in the later prehistoric period as represented by special deposits of items associated with the production and storage of food at settlement sites, and suggest a growing concern with fertility (Bradley 2000, 152–3). The Late Bronze Age/Early Iron Age pit deposits at Westcroft Road in Carshalton are a local example of this phenomenon and have been interpreted as an 'integral part of the everyday agricultural cycle of the community, and not a separate and exclusive sacred activity' (Proctor 2002, 98–9). The fact that this theme also runs throughout the sequence of occupation at the site is significant, but unsurprising if we consider that the primary concerns of a self-sufficient farming community are likely to have been a successful harvest and healthy livestock in order to ensure continued prosperity and food security.

Egg Shell

by L. Higbee

Eighty-one fragments of egg shell were recovered from fill 3711 in early Romano-British pit 4376/3174. The fragments were found together and appear to be from a single egg, although it could not be established if the egg was deposited whole or broken, or indeed if it had hatched. The thickness of the larger fragments was measured using a micrometre and compared to thickness ranges of selected domestic and wild species (after Keepax 1977, 1981; Sidell 1993). The fragments varied in thickness from 230 μm to 310 μm which corresponds with the thickness range for domestic fowl (or chicken) eggs.

This fits with the bone evidence – domestic fowl being one of only three bird species identified in the entire assemblage, the other two species are members of the corvid family (see Table 3.11). Indeed, two domestic fowl (ABG 255), a raven and several dogs were deposited after the main feasting deposit, and although it is uncertain where exactly in the deposit the egg shell fragments were found, it is possible that the egg was included because it symbolises fertility and rebirth in its purest and most obvious form.

Whole eggs have been recorded from a variety of different contexts at other sites, but there was a tradition in the Roman world of placing eggs, and in particular hens' eggs, in graves as food offerings (Serjeantson 2009, 178–9).

Chapter 4
Environmental Remains

Charred Plant Remains

by Sarah F. Wyles

A total of 98 samples, from Early Iron Age to early Romano-British features, were processed for the recovery and assessment of charred plant remains. The assessment showed that material was well represented in most of the samples and 21 of the samples were chosen for further analysis. The samples were processed using standard flotation methods with the flot collected on a 0.5 mm mesh. For the analysed samples all identifiable charred plant macrofossils were extracted from the flots, together with the 2 mm and 1 mm residues. In two instances, sample 70 from enclosure ditch 2071 (3008) and sample 66 from pit 3174 (3177), the samples were so rich that only 10% of the 0.5 mm flot fraction was sorted. These counts were then multiplied by 10 to give estimates for those items identified within this fraction, added to the totals and signified with 'est.'. Identification follows the nomenclature of Stace (1997) for wild species and the traditional nomenclature as provided by Zohary and Hopf (2000, tables 3 and 5), for cereals. The results are presented in Tables 4.1 and 4.2.

Early and Middle Iron Age

The assemblage from pit 3940 was the richest of the four Early–Middle Iron Age pits sampled, with relatively few remains were recovered from the other two (2017 and 3820) (Table 4.1). However, the occurrence in all of them of hulled wheats, emmer or spelt (*Triticum dicoccum/spelta*), with smaller quantities of barley (*Hordeum vulgare*), is similar to that recorded from earlier work on the site (Bruce and Giorgi 1994).

It contrasts, however, with an earlier excavation within and around the Late Bronze Age ringwork, and an excavation at Westcroft Road, Carshalton, at both of which barley was predominant (Scaife 2002a; 2002b). The Westcroft Road site is located on the Thanet Sands, to the north of the chalk ridge, where barley may have been a more suitable crop for the local soils. Emmer, spelt and barley, with emmer and spelt often in similar proportions, are characteristic of Late Bronze Age to Early Iron Age sites in the region (Bruce and Giorgi 1994; Carruthers 2010; Stevens 2015).

The predominance of hulled wheat glumes in the sample from pit 3940 suggests that the material derives from the charring of dehusking waste, which is generated as quantities of grain, stored as spikelets, were routinely taken from storage and processed before milling. Two of the grains appeared to be germinated. The weed seeds within the samples are typical of arable, field margin, grass land and wasteland environments.

Late Iron Age

The eight samples (from seven pits) all produced high numbers of plant remains, the majority of them dominated by glumes and grains of hulled wheat, predominantly spelt, although the quantities of barley in some of the samples suggests that it was also an important crop. There are differences in the assemblages, however. Those from pits 3027, 3088, 3579 and 3513 are dominated by chaff fragments of both emmer and spelt, with almost equal numbers of emmer and spelt glumes and spikelet forks in pits 3027 and 3088, but with spelt being more numerous in pit 3513. The dominance of spelt by the Late Iron Age has been noted at other sites around London to the north-west (Carruthers 2010; Stevens 2015), and more widely in the region, such as St John's Vicarage, Old Malden (Hinton 2001), and Heathrow where emmer wheat was also well represented (Carruthers 2010). The assemblages from the Middle/Late Iron Age samples compare well with those recovered from a Middle Iron Age pit at Carshalton War Memorial Hospital (Archaeology South East 2009).

As in the Early Iron Age, the dominance of glume bases in five of the samples suggests the burning of dehusking waste, as the hulled wheat grain, generally stored as spikelets, was taken from storage and processed. However, the amount of processing undertaken before storage appears to have varied (Stevens 2003; Fuller and Stevens 2009), with some of the samples being less dominated by larger seeds and/or grain. The predominance of grain in pits 3088 and 3513 suggests that these assemblages may have been from slightly later stages of processing. Pit 2025 had more equal numbers of glumes and grain, but a much greater quantity of weed seeds, including a greater number of larger weed seeds; this sample also

Table 4.1 *Charred plant remains: Iron Age*

			Early–Middle Iron Age			Late Iron Age						
	Period											
	Phase	EIA	EIA	EIA	MIA	M/LIA	M/LIA	M/LIA	M/LIA	LIA	LIA	LIA
	Feature	Pit 2017	Pit 3820	Pit 3940	Pit 3231	Pit 2025	Pit 3513	Pit 3998	Pit 3998	Pit 3027	Pit 3088	Pit 3579
	Context	2020	3736	3941	3598	2029	3647	3999	4114	3046	3089	3609
	Sample	20	118	144	100	19	104	145	151	55	59	102
	Vol (l)	10	10	20	20	10	20	20	10	20	20	20
	Flot size (ml)	10	25	80	15	30	50	10	75	130	60	25
	% roots	60	10	5	5	10	60	5	5	5	70	35
Cereals												
Hordeum vulgare L. *sl* (grain)	barley	1	4	1	4	13	19	1	27	1	4	4
T. dicoccum (Schübl) (glume base)	emmer wheat	–	–	–	–	–	2	1	–	1	8	1
T. dicoccum (Schübl) (spikelet fork)	emmer wheat	cf. 1	–	–	–	–	1	–	–	1	cf. 1	
Triticum spelta L. (glume bases)	spelt wheat	1	3	17	12	3	10	2	cf.1	2	10	6
Triticum dicoccum/spelta (grain)	emmer/spelt wheat	1	11	15	7	14	21	5	4	5	5	3
T. dicoccum/spelta (germinated grain)	emmer/spelt wheat	–	–	2	–	–	–	–	–	–	–	–
T. dicoccum/spelta (spikelet fork)	emmer/spelt wheat	2	5	3	5	2	9	–	–	4	20	5
T. dicoccum/spelta (glume bases)	emmer/spelt wheat	7	11	62	42	17	72	14	3	18	134	168
T. dicoccum/spelta (rachis)	emmer/spelt wheat	–	–	–	–	–	–	–	1	–	–	–
T. dicoccum/spelta (basal rachis)	emmer/spelt wheat	–	–	1	–	–	–	–	–	–	–	–
Cereal indet. (grains)	cereal	3	32	48	15	4	57	4	14	6	32	17
Cereal frag. (est. whole grains)	cereal	14	41	51	17	17	82	9	11	5	49	28
Cereal frags (rachis frags)		–	–	–	–	–	–	–	–	–	2	–
Cereal frags (culm node)	cereal	–	–	7	–	–	–	–	5	1	–	–
Other species												
Ranunculus sp.	buttercup	–	–	–	–	–	1	–	–	–	–	–
Papaver rhoeas/dubium L.	common/long-headed poppy	–	–	17	–	–	–	–	–	–	–	–
Papaver rhoeas/dubium conglom.	common/long-headed poppy	–	–	3	–	–	–	–	–	–	–	–
Urtica urens L.	small neetle	–	–	–	–	2	1	–	–	1	1	–
Corylus avellana L. (fragments)	hazel	–	–	–	3	–	1	6	1	1	–	1
Chenopodiaceae	goosefoot family	–	–	–	–	–	8	15	–	3	–	–
Chenopodium sp.	goosefoot	2	1	6	–	9	–	66	6	–	–	–
Chenopodium album L.	fathen	–	–	20	5	–	8	–	–	1	5	–
Atriplex sp. L.	oraches	–	–	7	–	–	–	10	–	2	–	–
Stellaria sp. L.	stitchworts	6	1	–	–	21	–	1	1	–	–	1
Silene sp.L.	campions	2	–	3	–	3	–	3	–	–	–	–
Persicaria lapathifolia/maculosa (L.) Gray/Gray	redshank/pale persicaria	–	–	–	–	–	–	1	–	–	1	–
Polygonum aviculare L.	knotgrass	2	1	–	–	2	3	2	116	3	2	1
Fallopia convolvulus (L.) À. Löve	black bindweed	1	3	5	–		1	52	117	1		–
Rumex sp. L.	docks	24	12	6	2	37	19	37	83	11	2	1
Rumex acetosella group Raf.	sheeps sorrel	–	–	–	1	3	6	20	2	–	1	
Malva sp. L.	mallow	–	–	–	1	–	–	–	–	–	–	–
Brassica sp. L.	brassica	1	–	–	–	–	–	5	5	–	–	–
Potentilla sp. L.	cinquefoils	–	–	–	–	–	1	–	–	–	–	–
Prunus spinosa	sloe stone	–	–	–	–	–	–	–	1	–	–	–

Prunus spinosa/Crataegus monogyna (thorns)	hawthorn/sloe thorns	–	–	–	–	–	–	–	1	–	1	–
Vicia L./*Lathyrus* sp. L.	vetch/pea	6	4	18	3	11	8	4	5	2	3	–
Medicago/Trifolium sp. L.	clover/medick	–	–	–	–	–	5	1	–	–	–	–
Medicago sp. *L.*	medick	1	–	–	–		2	–	–	–	1	–
Trifolium sp. L	clover	–	–	–	–	–	–	–	–	5	2	–
Rhamnus cathartica L.	buckthorn	–	–	–	1	–	–	–	–	–	–	–
Scandix pectin-veneris L.	Shepherd's-needle	–	–	–	–	–	–	–	cf. 1	–	–	–
Aethusa cynapium L.	fool's parsley	–	–	–	–	–	–	–	2	–	–	–
Torilis sp. Adans	hedge-parsley	–	–	–	–	–	–	–	–	–	2	–
Myosotis L.	forget-me-nots	–	–	–	–	–	–	–	–	1	–	–
Plantago lanceolata L.	ribwort plantain	–	–	–	–	–	2	–	–	–	–	–
Odontites vernus	red bartisia	–	–	–	–	5	–	2		3	2	–
Sherardia arvensis L.	field madder	–	1	–	–	–	–	2	3	1	–	–
Galium sp. L.	bedstraw	–	–	–	–	–	5	–	–	2	–	1
Valerianella rimosa	broad-fruited cornsalad	–	–	–	–	–	–	cf.1	–	–	–	–
Valerianella dentata (L.) Pollich	narrow-fruited cornsalad	–	–	–	–	–	1	–	–	–	–	1
Cardus/Cirsium	thistle	–	1	–	–	–	–	–	–	–	–	–
Leucanthemum vulgare Lam.	oxeye daisy	1	–	–	–	51	–	–	–	–	–	–
Tripleurospermum inodorum (L.) Sch. Bip.	scentless mayweed	–	–	–	–	–	1	1	1	–	–	–
Poaceae basal culm node	grass	–	1	5	–	–	–	–	–	–	–	–
Poaceae culm node	grass	–	–	–	–	–	2	–	2	2	–	3
Poaceae internode frags	grass	–	5	12	3	–	10	–	8	–	–	1
Lolium/Festuca sp.	rye grass/fescue	–	–	2	–	–	1	10	5	–	–	–
Poa/Phleum sp. L.	meadow grass/cats'-tails	2	–	35	3	18	95	7	–	1	6	5
Arrhenatherum elatius Var. bulbosum (Willd)	false oat–grass	–	–	1	1	–	1	–	–	–	2	–
Avena sp. L. (grain)	oat grain	–	2	3	–	7	2	–	4	–	2	1
Avena sp. L. (awn)	oat awn	–	–	–	1	–	2	1	–	–	–	2
Avena L./*Bromus* L. sp.	oat/brome	2	17	35	2	98	2	–	–	5	29	2
Bromus sp. L.	brome grass	–	4	6	–	3	2	–	–	–	6	–
Small seed indet.		–	–	–	–	2	–	–	1	–	1	–
Bud		–	–	–	–	–	–	1	–	–	1	–
Parenchyma/dung/bread		–	1	–	–	–	–	–	–	16	–	–
Tuber		–	–	2	–	–	–	1	1	–	–	–
Birch tar frags >4 mm		–	–	–	–	–	–	–	5	–	–	–
Ergot		–	–	–	–	–	–	–	1	–	–	–

Table 4.2 *Charred plant remains: early Romano-British*

		Feature	Pit 3015	Pit 3058	Pit 3174	Pit 3183	Pit 3183	Pit 3870	Pit 3921	Ditch 2071	Ditch 2071	Ditch 4378
		Cut	3467	–	–	–	–	–		3006	2051	3068
		Context	3499	3059	3177	3197	3669	3871	3922	3008	2053	3066
		Sample	87	57	66	113	119	142	138	70	26	61
		Vol (L)	20	8	20	20	40	1.5	20	20	1.7	20
		Flot size	25	50	60	40	50	25	30	130	25	75
		%Roots	5	70	5	15	20	50	10	65	30	10
		% 0.5 mm fraction analysed	–	–	10	–	–	–	–	10	–	–
Cereals												
Hordeum vulgare L. *sl* (grain)	barley		9	5	37	8	10	7	34	1	–	2
Hordeum vulgare L. *sl* (grain) germinated	barley		–	–	–	–	–	–	1	–	–	–
Hordeum vulgare L. *sl* (rachiis frag)	barley		3	–	7	7	–	4	1	2	–	–
Hordeum vulgare L. *sl* (rachiis frag 6 row)	barley		–	–	2	–	–	–	–	–	–	–
T. dicoccum (Schübl) (glume base)	emmer wheat		3	1	4	4	cf. 4	3	3	4	–	3
T. dicoccum (Schübl) (spikelet fork)	emmer wheat		5		4	–	–	1	1	3	–	
Triticum spelta L. (glume bases)	spelt wheat		27	41	55	33	46	40	–	76	13	17
Triticum spelta L. (spikelet fork)	spelt wheat		–	–	3	–	1	1	–	29	–	–
Triticum dicoccum/spelta (grain)	emmer/spelt wheat		8	10	180	22	19	21	17	33	4	3
T. dicoccum/spelta (spikelet fork)	emmer/spelt wheat		14	16	est. 151	46	16	30	20	est. 81	5	10
T. dicoccum/spelta (glume bases)	emmer/spelt wheat		375	759	est. 2876	902	104	265	181	est. 2598	90	201
T. dicoccum/spelta (rachis)	emmer/spelt wheat		–	6	–	10	–	11	–	–	–	–
Triticum sp. (grain)	wheat		–	3	–	2	6	–	–	–	–	2
Cereal indet. (grains)	cereal		31	45	290	45	48	60	98	80	7	23
Cereal frag. (est. whole grains)	cereal		80	102	312	98	108	32	163	177	17	68
Cereal frags (rachis frags)			3	–	–	–	–	–	–	3	–	–
Cereal frags (culm node)	cereal		–	–	4	–	3	1	2	–	–	–
Cereal frags (basal culm node)	cereal		–	–	–	–	1	–	–	–	–	–
Other species												
Juniperus communis L.	common juniper		–	–	–	–	–	–	cf.1	–	–	–
Papaver rhoeas/dubium L.	common/long-headed poppy		–	–	–	–	–	–	1	–	–	–
Fumaria officinalis L.	common fumitory		–	–	–	–	–	–	–	1	–	–
Urtica urens L.	small neetle		1	–	–	–	–	1	1	–	–	–
Corylus avellana L. (fragments)	hazel		3	1	–	–	–	–	1	1	–	2
Chenopodiaceae	goosefoot family		–	–	–	–	–	–	4	–	–	–
Chenopodium sp.	goosefoot		–	–	–	1	–	–	–	1	–	–
Chenopodium ficifolium Sm	fig-leaved goosefoot		1	–	–	–	–	–	–	–	–	–
Chenopodium album L.	fathen		–	–	–	–	–	–	1	–	–	–
Atriplex sp. L.	oraches		2	–	–	2	–	5	3	–	–	1
Montia fontana subsp. *Chondrosperma* (Fenzl) Walters	blinks		–	–	–	–	–	–	1	1	1	–
Caryophyllaceae (cf. Agrostemma) *capsules*			1	–	–	–	–	–	–	–	–	–
Stellaria sp. L.	stitchworts		–	–	–	1	–	8	2	–	–	–
Silene sp.L.	campions		–	1	–	4	4	12	1	1	2	–
Polygonum aviculare L.	knotgrass		–	–	2	2	4	–	2	–	1	–

Fallopia convolvulus (L.) À. Löve	black bindweed	1	–	2	1	2	–	1	–	–	–
Rumex sp. L.	docks	7	2	est. 14	6	5	9	9	2	2	1
Rumex acetosella group Raf.	sheeps sorrel	–	–		8	2	6	6	–	–	–
Malva sp. L.	mallow	–	–	–	–	2	–	–	–	–	–
Vicia L./*Lathyrus* sp. L.	vetch/pea	8	2	est. 73	41	33	17	20	48	9	1
Lathyrus cf. *nissolia* L.	grass vetchling	–	–	1	2	–	2	–	1	–	–
Medicago/*Trifolium* sp. L.	clover/medick	4	–	est. 23	4	5	12	11	1	–	–
Medicago sp *L.*	medick	–	–	–	8	5	–	5	–	–	–
Trifolium sp. L	clover	–	–	–	9	–	–	1	–	1	–
Aethusa cynapium L.	Fool's parsley	–	–	–	–	–	–	1	–	–	–
Torilis sp. Adans	hedge-parsley	–	–	–	1	–	–	5	1	–	–
Lithospermum arvense L.	corn gromwell	–	–	1	6	26	3	–	–	–	–
Prunella vulgaris L.	selfheal	–	–	–	–	–	1	–	–	–	–
Plantago lanceolata L.	ribwort plantain	–	–	–	–	2	1	–	–	–	–
Odontites vernus	red bartisia	–	–	est. 20	4	–	7	12	–	1	–
Sherardia arvensis L.	field madder	–	–	2	1	1		5	–	1	–
Galium sp. L.	bedstraw	1	–	4	–	4	1	1	–	–	–
Valerianella dentata (L.) Pollich	narrow-fruited cornsalad	–	–	–	1	–	–	1	–	–	–
Scabiosa columbaria L.	small scabious	–	–	–	–	–	1	1	3	–	–
Centaurea cyanus L/	cornflower	–	–	–	–	–	–	–	cf. 1	–	–
Tripleurospermum inodorum (L.) Sch. Bip.	scentless mayweed	–	–	–	7	–	12	1	–	–	–
Eleocharis cf. *palustris* (L.) Roem. & Schult.	common spike-rush	–	–	–	–	2	–	–	–	–	–
Carex sp. L. triganous	sedge trigonous seed	–	–	–	–	–	–	–	–	1	–
Poaceae basal culm node	grass	–	–	–	–	1	–	–	2	–	–
Poaceae culm node	grass	–	–	2	–	3	2	8	–	–	–
Poaceae internode frags	grass	–	–	–	4	2	9	8	2	–	–
Poaceae rachis frag	grass	–	–	–	–	–	1	–	–	–	–
Poaceae basal rachis frag	grass	–	–	–	–	–	2	–	–	–	–
Lolium/*Festuca* sp.	rye grass/fescue	2	–	1	3	1	3	–	–	–	–
Poa/*Phleum* sp. L.	meadow grass/cats'-tails	4	–	–	7	–	3	4	1	1	–
Arrhenatherum elatius Var. bulbosum (Willd)	false oat-grass	–	–	–	–	3	1	–	–	–	–
Avena sp. L. (grain)	oat grain	2	–	3	3	6	6	11	2	–	1
Avena sp. L. (awn)	oat awn	7	1	est. 79	15	1	18	22	4	–	–
Avena L./*Bromus* L. sp.	oat/brome	9	2	4	14	26	15	19	12	–	1
Bromus sp. L.	brome grass	1	–	3	3	6	5	4	2	2	–
Small seed indet.		–	–	–	–	–	–	–	1	–	–
Bud		1	–	–	–	1	–	–	–	–	–
Parenchyma/dung/bread		–	–	–	–	–	1	–	–	–	–
Large tuber with morphology	?dandelion/burdock/?carrot	–	–	–	–	1	–	–	–	–	–
Tuber/fruit		1	–	–	–	–	–	–	–	–	–
Pieces highly silicaceous stem masses ?stabling		–	–	–	–	–	5	–	–	–	–

had slightly more barley, possibly indicating hand sorting with a small amount of fine-sieving.

While grain was more dominant than weed seeds in the assemblage from pit 3579, smaller weed seeds were generally represented in a similar proportion to large weed seeds. This might indicate that fine sieving had not been fully completed and that the spikelets were not fully cleaned prior to storage, as large grain-sized weed seeds would be expected to be predominant in that instance. The samples also had a number of interculm nodes of grasses and some grass tubers, which tend to be removed in earlier stages of crop processing; again this suggests that crops may have been stored in a slightly less processed state.

The material from pit 3998 was unusual in that the two samples (from contexts 3999 and 4114) showed some distinct differences. The latter was dominated by seeds of several larger seeded species, and as such would appear to represent waste from hand-sorting, in which grain/spikelet sized weed seeds are removed by hand. However, hulled cereal remains are very poorly represented in this deposit, although a number barley grains were recorded; the presence of birch tar lumps may indicate that this was an unusual deposit. The sample from context 3999, although also having fewer cereal remains and many of seeds from larger-seeded species, also had many smaller weed seeds, especially those of the goosefoot family (Chenopodiaceae), perhaps indicating that the waste was from an earlier stage crop processing.

The weed seeds are again mainly typical of arable, field margin, grass land and wasteland environments. The presence of field madder (*Sherardia arvensis*) and narrow-fruited cornsalad (*Valerianella dentata*) indicates that dry calcareous soils were under cultivation. The possible exploitation of acid sandy soil is hinted by the presence of sheeps sorrel (*Rumex acetosella* group), although this is also common on drier patches of circum-neutral soils overlying gravels. The presence of seeds of free-standing weeds, such as fat-hen, would suggest harvesting by sickle, while the presence of seeds of low growing species, in particular clover (*Trifolium* sp.), would indicate a low-harvesting height (Hillman 1981). This is typically the case for this period (Wilkinson and Stevens 2003).

Other charred plant remains within these samples included a few fragments of hazelnut (*Corylus avellana*) shell, a fragment of sloe (*Prunus spinosa*) stone and a few hawthorn/sloe thorns (*Crataegus monogyna/Prunus spinosa*). There were also several tubers of false oat-grass (*Arrhenatherum elatius* var. *bulbosum*) and a number of basal culm nodes and internode fragments of grasses (Poaceae), possibly derived from material brought in for use as fuel or tinder, or from the creation of a fire break, which also might account for the predominance of smaller seeds and grasses. However, such tubers are frequently uprooted during the harvesting of the crop, even when using a sickle, and therefore might have entered the assemblage through this means (see Stevens 2006). A number of dung-like parenchyma fragments were retrieved from pit 3027. An unusual item observed from context 4114 has been identified as possible ergot, possibly infecting a grain of oats.

It is noteworthy that a number of birch tar lumps with impressions of stems/twisted fibres were recovered from pit 3998. Birch tar can have a number of uses, including the repair of pottery (see Seager Smith *et al.* 2011), as evident on some of the early Romano-British pottery in pit 3503 (see Seager Smith, Chapter 3). It is possible that the fibres (possibly nettle), were used as a binding during such repairs; alternatively, they could have formed part of a basketwork container.

Early Romano-British

Ten samples were analysed from early Romano-British features; seven were from (six) pits, and three were from the enclosure ditches – two from Enclosure 2c, and one from Enclosure 5.

All the pit samples produced large assemblages, in particular those from pit 3174 and from context 3197 in pit 3183. They were all dominated by glumes of hulled wheat, with spelt greatly outnumbering emmer among the identifiable fragments. Barley grains were also present in all the pits, as were awns of oats. This is similar to the assemblages from St John's Vicarage (Hinton 2001), and to the north-west at Staines (Clapham 2004), RMC Land Harlington (Stevens 2015) and also Heathrow Terminal 5 (Carruthers 2010), although the latter again has a much better representation of emmer wheat within several of the samples than seen on the other sites of this period. Also it might be noted that the sites to the north-west all produced evidence for rye in the Romano-British period which was absent at this site.

The samples had much higher numbers of hulled wheat glume bases than grains (more so than in the previous periods), suggesting again that the material was the burnt waste from the dehusking process. Larger weed seeds were dominant in all but one sample, as were grains in comparison to weed seeds (again to a much greater extent than in the earlier samples). This pattern is typical of the processing of crops for storage. In the case of spelt (after being threshed, winnowed, coarse and fine-sieved) it is more or less clean of spikelets, or, in the case of barley, as almost clean grain. The assemblages, therefore, represent the final dehusking and hand-sorting stages, involving the removal of glumes in the case of spelt, or the paleas/lemmas in the case of barley, by dehusking and sieving/winnowing, and the removal of the larger weed seeds by hand. Corn gromwell, which was recovered only from samples of this period, is a large seed with a very tough coating, which had to be removed by hand before the grain was milled.

Once again the weed seeds were mainly typical of arable, field margin, grass land and wasteland environments. Their range, however, suggests cultivation of a range of environments, with common spike-rush (*Eleocharis* cf. *palustris*), blinks (*Montia fontana* subsp. *chondrosperma*), sedge (*Carex* sp.) and mallow (*Malva* sp.) typical of wetter environments, sheeps sorrel typical of acid sandy soils or circum-natural soils overlying gravels, and corn gromwell (*Lithospermum arvense*), field madder, small scabious (*Scabiosa columbaria*) and narrow-fruited cornsalad being characteristic of calcareous soils. The absence of stinking mayweed (*Anthemis cotula*), a species of heavier clay soils, should be noted, as it has been recorded at several other sites in the region, most notably in occasional samples at RMC Land Harlington (Stevens 2015) and Heathrow Terminal 5 (Carruthers 2010); it was largely absent at Staines (Clapham 2004). As with the earlier samples there are occasional tubers of false oat grass, either collected for tinder or uprooted during harvesting. The presence of low growing, free-standing weeds would indicate that such harvesting was conducted low on the culm, probably by sickle rather than scythe.

Conglomerated burnt masses of siliceous stems, possibly straw, from a dump of burnt material (context 3871) in pit 3870, may represent stabling waste in the form of animal dung mixed with straw. However, this layer also contained a dog skeleton and horse bones, suggesting it was a special deposit; it is worth noting that potentially structured pit deposits from other sites have sometimes contained such midden material (Carruthers 2008).

Conclusion

Most of the remains represent the burnt waste from the processing and cleaning of crops stored either as spikelets (hulled wheats) or grain (hulled barley). With the exception of the birch tar lumps from the Middle/Late Iron Age pit 3998, and the possible midden/stabling material in early Romano-British pit 3870, there is no clear relationship between the charred material and the special placed deposits found in several of the pits. Much of the material probably represents domestic waste either dumped in the pits or becoming incorporated in their fills by chance.

The samples are generally consistent in composition from the Early Iron Age through to the early Romano-British period, with the predominance of hulled wheat, in particular spelt but with some emmer, and barley generally present in low levels, which seems to be the typical pattern for rural settlements in the region. The presence of seeds of low growing, free-standing weeds indicate that crops were harvested low on the culm, probably by sickle as is typical for the period.

However, there are some indications the stage at which the crop was put into storage changed over time. By the early Romano-British period, the harvested crops would have been threshed, winnowed, coarse and fine-sieved, perhaps in the field or upon a specially prepared threshing-floor in the settlement, prior to being put into storage as semi-clean spikelets. Quantities would then have been taken from storage, as and when needed, through the year, and the larger grain-sized weeds removed by hand, and the barley then dehusked or dehulled. The waste may have been used as tinder for hearths, or simply disposed of by burning. In contrast, in the Late Iron Age, the crops may have been slightly less clean when stored, although in few of the samples were small weed seeds present in large enough quantities to suggest that the crops had been stored more or less unprocessed, as is seen at some other sites (Stevens 2003; Fuller and Stevens 2009). More probably it was just the fine-sieving stage that had been omitted prior to storage.

The site is located on the Chalk, close to where it meets the Thanet Sands and London and Lambeth Clays, with head deposits of sand, silt and gravels also nearby, and there are indications, in the later periods, of cultivation not only of calcareous soils characteristic of the Chalk, but also of wetter soils and circum-neutral to more acidic sandy soils, the latter associated with the Thanet Sands.

Wood Charcoal

by Catherine Barnett

Four samples were chosen for charcoal analysis, three from pits (Middle/Late Iron Age pits 3998 and 3027, and early Romano-British pit 3174) and one from a possible posthole (3301) cutting the upper fill of the first phase enclosure ditch 4242 (alternatively, this may have been a small dump of charcoal-rich material in the ditch). The fragments were prepared for identification according to the standard methodology of Leney and Casteel (1975, see also Gale and Cutler 2000). Identification was undertaken according to the anatomical characteristics described by Schweingruber (1990) and Butterfield and Meylan (1980) to the highest taxonomic level possible, usually that of genus, with nomenclature according to Stace (1997).

A minimum of seven woody species were represented (Table 4.3). Even though only four assemblages were examined, the relatively short list of

Table 4.3 Wood charcoal

	Phase	M/LIA	LIA	ERB	?LIA or later
	Feature	Pit 3998	Pit 3027	Pit 3174	? Posthole 3301
	Context	4114	3046	3659	3300
	Sample	151	55	116	81
	Size (l)	10	20	20	15
	Flot size (ml)	75	130	1100	400
	Charcoal 4/2 mm	15/10 ml	20/20 ml	300/350 ml	30/100 ml
Alnus glutinosa	alder	–	6	–	–
Corylus avellana	hazel	5, 1 twd	3	–	–
Fraxinus excelsior	ash	11	–	–	–
Pomoideae	apple/whitebeam/hawthorn	1	1	–	–
Quercus sp.	oak	46	70, 19 rwd	98, 2 rwd	45, 55 rwd*
Salix/Populus sp.	willow/aspen	1	–	–	–
Viburnum sp.	guelder rose/wayfaring-tree	–	1	–	–
Unidentified		–	–	–	–
Total no. frags used		65	100	100	100
Comments		a	b	c	d

Key: twd: twigwood; rwd: roundwood
Comments:
a. Small assemblage but good condition
b. Large assemblage, clean fresh pieces; scan of remainder of sample indicates most if not all other pieces are also oak; some pieces seemingly display obliquely cut ends
c. Small but fresh assemblage; occasionally vitrified
d. Thin flaky pieces; * too fragmented to judge age of cutting but likely <15 years

taxa may be due to a concentration on the exploitation of oak at the site. The wood charcoal from the possible posthole was solely of young oak (*Quercus* sp.) wood, raising the possibility that this was a roundwood post burnt *in situ*. The assemblages from the pits were also dominated by oak (including oak roundwood) at 70–100%. The sample from pit 3174 contained a large charcoal assemblage, comprising solely oak, mainly mature, several pieces of which appeared to display obliquely cut ends. The smaller assemblages from pits 3027 and 3998 contained lesser quantities of alder (*Alnus glutinosa*), hazel (*Corylus avellana*), Pomoideae, guelder rose/wayfaring-tree (*Viburnum* sp.) and willow/poplar (*Salix/Populus* sp.), and, in the case of pit 3998, 17% ash (*Fraxinus excelsior*).

From the few features analysed, therefore, it appears there was a reliance on oak for fuel as well as for structural timbers, with a small number of other common deciduous types used to a lesser degree. Most of the taxa inhabit a variety of well-drained soils as open woodland or hedgerows, but ash and *Viburnum* tend to favour base-rich conditions such as those found on the upland Chalk to the south of Carshalton (BGS Sheet 270), suggesting collection at a distance from the site. The presence of alder and willow/poplar indicates the exploitation of wetland fringe habitats, such as those edging the nearby River Wandle.

The size and type of the charcoal assemblage from pit 3174 is consistent with fuel derived from an industrial activity, such as the ironworking indicated by the 2.5 kg of slag from the same context. Large oak timbers would have provided the hot, steady and prolonged burn required for this activity, as oak is a dense wood of high calorific value. A similar reliance on oak (along with lesser amounts of hazel), was noted at the late Romano-British pottery production sites at Alice Holt and Frith End, Hampshire (Birbeck *et al.* 2008; Barnett 2012), where it was proposed that large-scale management of local oak stands and hazel coppice had occurred in order to fuel the kilns. It is unclear, given the scale of analysis here, whether similar local management was undertaken but it is certainly possible.

Radiocarbon Dating

by Alistair J. Barclay

Introduction

Eighteen samples were submitted to the Scottish Universities Environmental Research Centre (SUERC) from selected Iron Age and Romano-British features (Table 4.4) to try and address a number of research aims regarding the site. Fifteen dates are on samples of animal bone, mostly articulated, and three are on samples of human bone from inhumation burials. In the absence of articulated or articulating bone care was taken to select animal bone in fresh condition (ie, from freshly killed animals).

Results and calibration

The radiocarbon results (Table 4.4) are quoted in accordance with the international standard known as the Trondheim convention (Stuiver and Kra 1986).

Table 4.4 Radiocarbon dates obtained for selected samples. Calibrated using OxCal v4.2.3 and Intcal13. Calibrated ranges have been rounded out to the nearest 10 years. The posterior density estimates derive from the model shown in Figure 4.1

Lab reference	*Feature*	*Context*	*Material*	*Date BP*	$\delta^{13}C$	$\delta^{15}N$	*C:N*	*Calibrated date range (95% confidence)*	Posterior density estimate (95% probability)
SUERC-38149	1st phase ditch 4242 (cut 3303)	3302	horse 1st phalanx with slight but clear cut marks	2060±35	-21.8‰	5.4	3.2	180 cal BC–30 cal AD	*170–60 cal BC*
SUERC-38151	1st phase ditch 4242 (cut 3493)	3490	pig metacarpal	2005±35	-20.6‰	8.5	3.2	100 cal BC–80 cal AD	*100 cal BC– 80 cal AD*
SUERC-38152	2nd phase ditch 4237 (cut 3498)	3496	pig right mandible retaining all teeth apart from m3	2095±35	-21.9‰	7.5	3.2	210–30 cal BC	*130–1 cal BC*
SUERC-38159	Pit 3341	3728	raven synsacrum, from complete skeleton (ABG 98)	2085±35	-20.2‰	13.7	3.2	200–1 cal BC	*130–10 cal BC*
SUERC-38342	Pit 3341	3263	?donkey right radius, single bone in good condition	2055±30	-22.3‰	7.0	3.2	170 cal BC–20 cal AD	*100 cal BC–10 cal AD*
SUERC-38144	Pit 3341	3249	dog left pelvis, from whole skeleton (ABG 61)	2030±35	-20.6‰	8.5	3.2	170 cal BC–60 cal AD	*60 cal BC–60 cal AD*
SUERC-38150	Pit 3419	3479	cattle right humerus, from an articulated leg (ABG 77)	2045±35	-20.9‰	5.7	3.2	170 cal BC–50 cal AD	*90 cal BC–50 cal AD*
SUERC-38160	Pit 3535	3890	dog left pelvis, from whole skeleton (ABG 115)	1985±35	-19.9‰	8.5	3.2	50 cal BC–130 cal AD	*50 cal BC–70 cal AD*
SUERC-38153	Pit 3535	3537	dog left pelvis selected from whole skeleton (ABG 90)	1955±35	-19.6‰	9.4	3.2	60 cal BC–90 cal AD	*30 cal BC–90 cal AD (94.9%)*
SUERC-38154	Pit 3231	3598	sheep/goat right metatarsal, from whole skeleton (ABG 244)	2115±35	-21.1‰	5.5	3.2	350–40 cal BC	*180–50 cal BC*
SUERC-38142	Pit 3231	3232	horse rib, from partial skeleton (front legs missing)	2100±35	-22.2‰	5.6	3.2	210–40 cal BC	*150 cal BC–10 cal AD*
SUERC-38161	Pit 3174	4183	sheep/goat left tibia, from partial lamb skeleton recovered from sample 153	1990±35	-20.9‰	7.1	3.2	60 cal BC–80 cal AD	*100 cal BC–60 cal AD*
SUERC-38158	Pit 3174	3711	dog right radius, from whole skeleton (ABG 131)	1900±35	-20.1‰	7.9	3.1	20–220 cal AD	*10–110 cal AD*
SUERC-38143	Pit 3174	3247	cattle left mandible, from a deposit that includes the cranium and cervical vertebra; all teeth retained suggesting freshly killed; juvenile (ABG 203)	1865±35	-20.6‰	5.1	3.2	60–240 cal AD	*20–130 cal AD*
SUERC-38141	Pit 3174	3177	cattle left mandible, one of a matching pair from an adult; all teeth retained suggesting freshly killed (ABG 202)	1880±35	-21.0‰	4.7	3.1	50–240 cal AD	*50–170 cal AD*
SUERC-39061	1st phase ditch 4242 (cut 3580)	3466	human left femur	2055±30	-19.5‰	10.1	3.1	170 cal BC–20 cal AD	*120 cal BC–30 cal AD*
SUERC-39062	Pit 3901	3809	human right tibia	1955±30	-19.3‰	12.2	3.0	40 cal BC–130 cal AD	*40 cal BC –90 cal AD (93.2%)*
SUERC-39063	Grave 3651	3652	human left femur	1975±30	-19.3‰	10.8	3.0	50 cal BC–90 cal AD	*50 cal BC–80 cal AD*

They are conventional radiocarbon ages (Stuiver and Polach 1977) that have been calculated using the calibration curve of Reimer *et al.* (2013) and the computer program OxCal (v4.2) (Bronk Ramsey 1995; 1998; 2001; 2009). The calibrated date ranges cited in the text are those for 95% confidence. They are quoted in the form recommended by Mook (1986), with the end points rounded outwards to 10 years for errors >25 years. The ranges in plain type in Table 4.4 have been calculated according to the maximum intercept method (Stuiver and Reimer 1986). All other ranges are derived from the probability method (Stuiver and Reimer 1993).

A Bayesian approach has been adopted for the interpretation of the chronology from this site (Bayliss *et al.* 2007). Although the simple calibrated dates are accurate estimates of the dates of the samples, it is the dates of the archaeological events, which are represented by those samples, which are of interest. In the case of Orchard Hill, it is the chronology of the enclosures, pits, burials and other associated activity that is under consideration, not the dates of individual samples. The dates of this activity can be estimated not only using the absolute dating information from the radiocarbon measurements, but also by using the stratigraphic relationships between samples. The OxCal program provides the methodology to combine these different types of information explicitly, to produce realistic estimates of the dates of interest. However, the *posterior density estimates* produced by this modelling are not absolute. They are interpretative *estimates*, which can and will change as further data become available and as other researchers choose to model the existing data from different perspectives.

Details of the algorithms employed by this program are available from the on-line manual or in Bronk Ramsey (1995; 1998; 2001; 2009). The algorithm used in the model described below can be derived from the structures shown in Figures 4.1–4.

Aims

The radiocarbon dating programme was designed to answer the following questions:

- At what date were the enclosure ditches constructed, and over what period of time?
- Were any of the selected pits and discrete burials of a similar or later date to the cutting of the enclosure ditches? Is the overall age span of the dated pits similar or different to the enclosure ditches?
- What is the date of construction and age span of pit 3174? Is it pre- or post-Conquest? When did the substantial animal bone deposit in layer 3711 happen – before or after the Conquest? What is the overall duration of the pit filling? What date is the lapdog burial and is this early post-Conquest as suggested?
- Can the overall radiocarbon chronology be used to refine the pottery form and fabric series? Can it be used to identify any distinct groups of later Middle Iron Age (2nd and early 1st century BC) pottery?

Site Sequence

The site sequence used in the following models is summarised below and in Figure 4.1. All of the radiocarbon dates are listed in Table 4.4 and their calibrated ranges are quoted at 95% confidence and at 95% probability according to standard methodology (see above). The radiocarbon model incorporated the following key features and stratigraphic information. All of the bone is from articulated skeletons unless stated otherwise.

Enclosure ditches

Two samples of animal bone were associated with the first phase (Middle Iron Age) ditch: a horse 1st phalanx with slight gnawing but clear cut marks (SUERC-38149) from fill 3302 of ditch 3303 and a pig metacarpal (SUERC-38151) from fill 3490 of ditch 3493. This ditch was cut by burial 3652 (SUERC-39063) and by pit 3341 (SUERC-38144, 38159 and 38342) (see below), and the later phase ditches in the central area of the site.

Pits that cut enclosure ditches

Two pits cut enclosure ditches. Pit 3341 cut the silted up first phase ditch and pit 3419 cut the silted up second phase (Late Iron Age) ditch.

Pit 3341 contained a series of animal bone deposits from which the following were radiocarbon dated. Near the pit base was a raven skeleton (SUERC-38159), the middle fill contained a possible donkey radius (SUERC-38342) and in the upper fill contained a dog burial (SUERC-38144). The possible donkey bone was dated to test whether it was intrusive and also to provide a precise date for this species (see Higbee, above).

Pit 3419 contained an articulated cattle limb near its base (SUERC-38150).

Discrete pits

Three pits (3231, 3535 and 3174) with notable animal bone deposits were selected for radiocarbon dating.

Pit 3231

This pit contained a series of animal bone deposits in its lower fills. A single date (SUERC-38154) was obtained from a sheep/goat burial placed within the

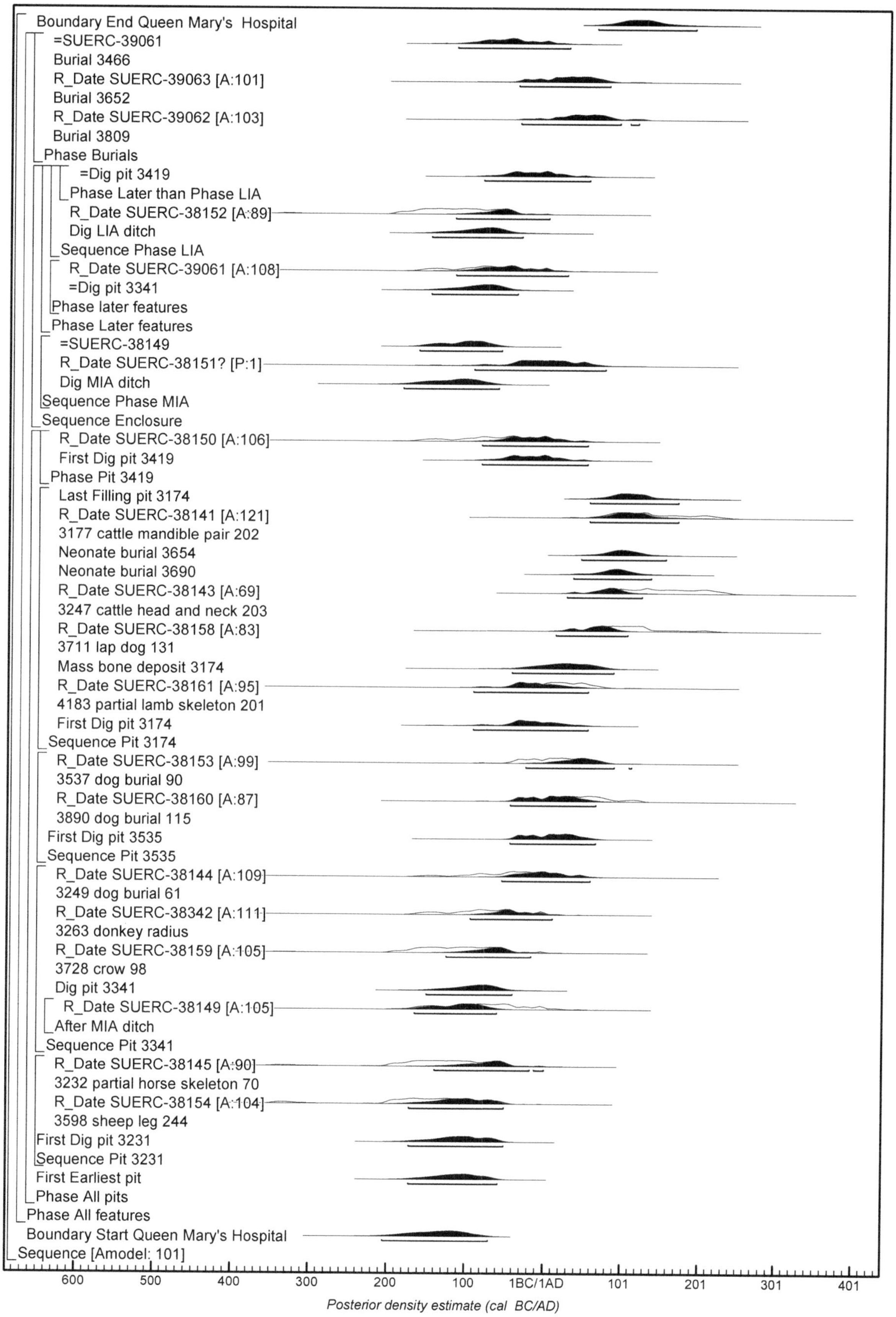

Figure 4.1 Probability distributions of dates relating to Orchard Hill based on the outlined model. The structure and key words are shown on the left. For each date two distributions are plotted: one in outline, which is the simple radiocarbon distribution, and a solid one, based on the modelled data. Other distributions refer to aspects of the model

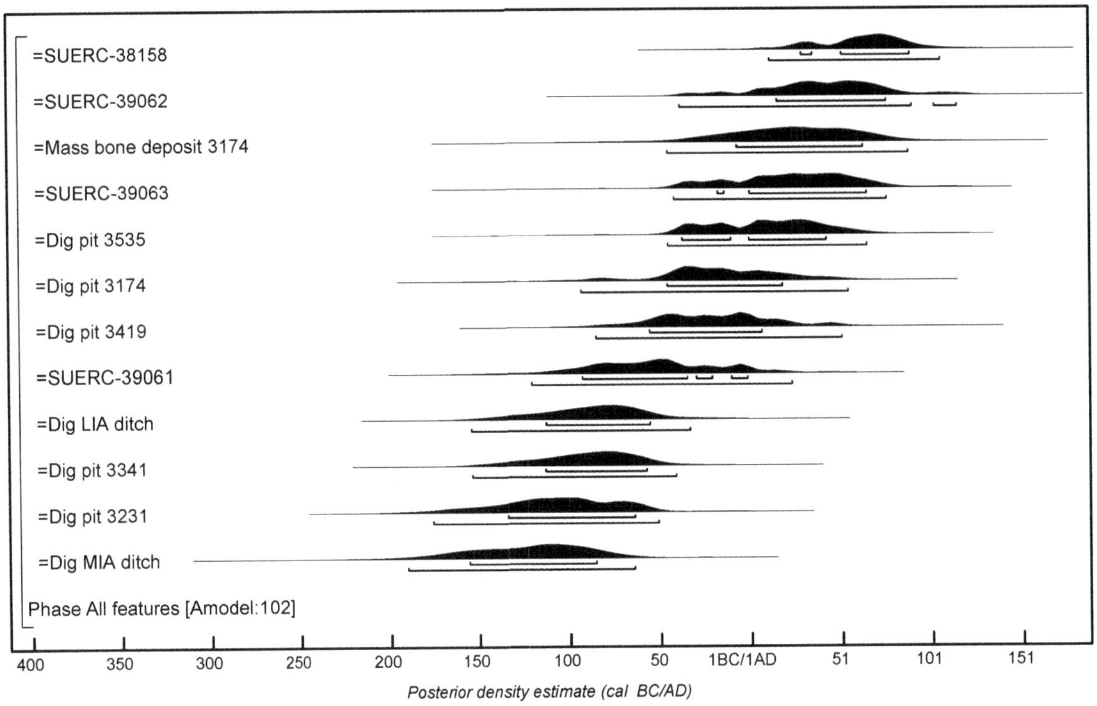

Figure 4.2 Probability distributions for selected events (digging of features), significant deposits and burials. The data derive from the model shown in Figure 4.1

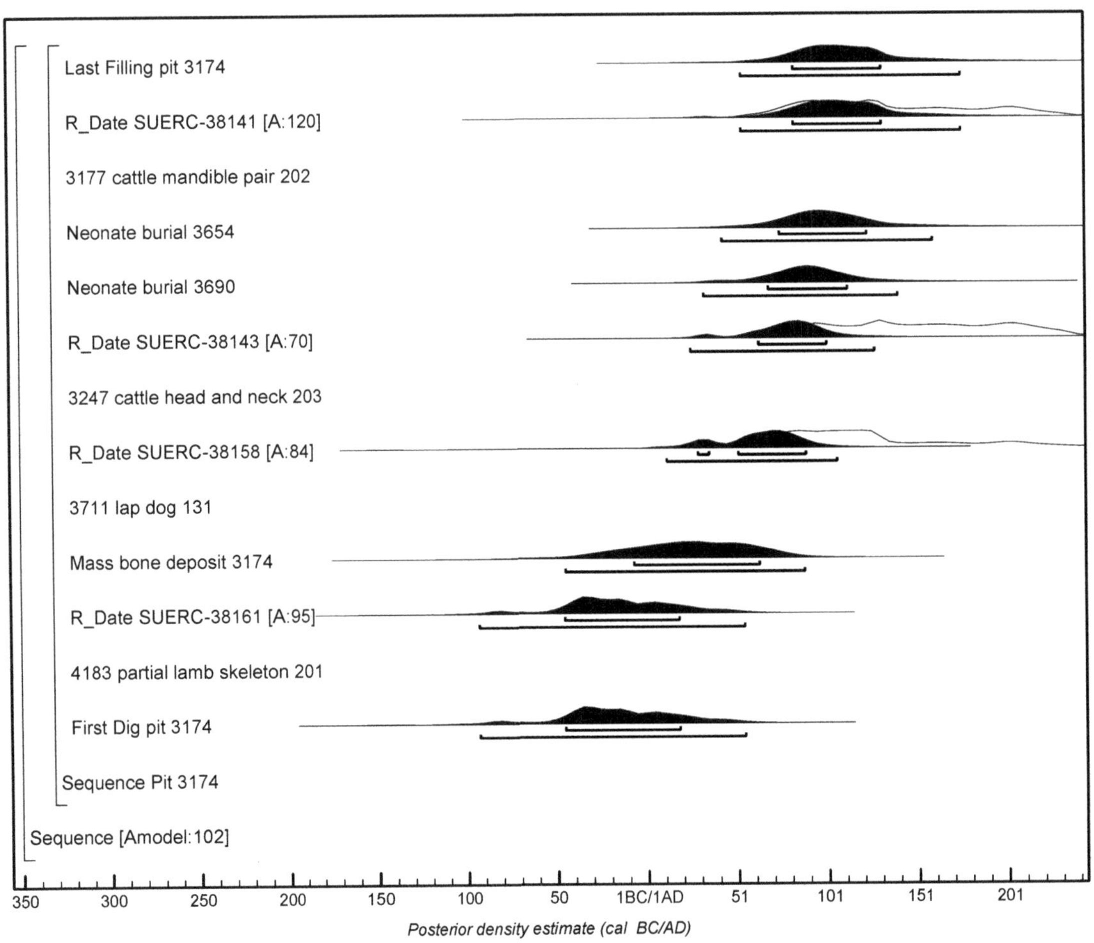

Figure 4.3 Probability distributions for pit 3174. The data derive from the model shown in Figure 4.1

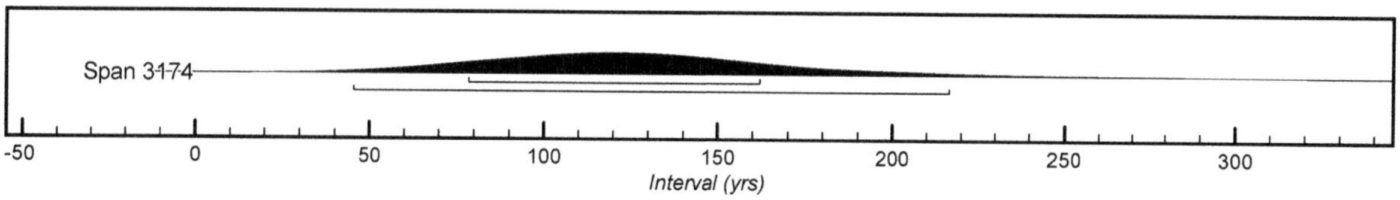

Figure 4.4 Probability distribution of the number of years (modelled as 'Span 3174') during which deposits were made and formed within pit 3174

primary fill 3598 and a partial horse burial from the central fill 3232 was dated by SUERC-38142. The two measurements are statistically consistent X^2 test T'=0.1; ν=1; T'(5%)=3.8) indicating that they belong to the same phase of activity.

Pit 3535
This pit contained a complex series of animal bone deposits. A dog burial, part of a complex deposit near the pit base (primary fill 3890), was dated by SUERC-38160. Central fill 3537 contained a series of animal deposits. A dog burial near the top of the fill was dated by SUERC-38153. The two measurements are statistically consistent (X^2 test T'=0.4; ν=1; T'(5%)=3.8) indicating that they belong to the same phase of activity.

Pit 3174
This pit contained a complex sequence of animal deposits. A partial lamb burial (SUERC-38161) was recovered from fill 4183, an upper deposit within the lowest pit fills. Despite been recovered from a soil sample these bones are likely to represent an *in situ* burial. Fill 4183 seals the primary basal fills 4184–88. Fill 4183 is overlain by deposit 3740 which in turn is covered by the substantial deposit 3711 that contained the carcasses of 25–30 animals. One of these, a lapdog, was directly dated by SUERC-38158. Part of a cattle mandible was dated from central fill 3247. This deposit was overlain by fill 3710 that contained human burial 3690, by fill 3659, and by the more substantial fill 3246 that contained human burial 3654.

The four measurements are statistically consistent (X^2 test T'=7.7; ν=3; T'(5%)=7.8) indicating that they belong to the same phase of activity.

Inhumation burials
Three human burials were selected for radiocarbon dating. Burial 3466 cut the first phase enclosure ditch (4242), while the other two burials (3809 and 3652) were in discrete grave cuts. A further two burials (3654 and 3690) were within a pit sequence 3174 (see above) and although samples from these skeletons were not directly measured, their dates have been estimated using the OxCal program.

Overall Model

The stratigraphic matrix used as a basis for the model reflects the interpretation of the site that is given above in Chapter 2. The stratigraphy also has good concordance with the pottery analysis (see Seager Smith, Chapter 3). Figure 4.1 is made up of the following stratigraphic strands of information: intercutting enclosure ditches and later features (including pit 3341 and burial 3466), discrete graves 3809 and 3652, and discrete pits 3231, 3535 and 3174. The model has good overall agreement (Amodel: 101) is SUERC-38151 is treated as an outlier (intrusive).

Results and Interpretation

Pits
Date estimates for the digging of the five pits (3231, 3341, 3419, 3535 and 3174) have been calculated using the site model (Fig. 4.1) and the OxCal parameter '*First*' (summarised in Table 4.5). All of which are placed in sequence using the OxCal probability *Order* function (see Table 4.5 and Fig. 4.2). The earliest pits are 3231 (*135–60 cal BC at 68% probability*) and 3341 (*115–55 cal BC at 68% probability*), both of which post-date the first enclosure ditch, although all three features were created at the end of the Middle Iron Age during the late 2nd century or at the start of the 1st century

Table 4.5 Modelled radiocarbon dates for the digging event ('First') of selected individual pits (see Figures 4.1–2)

Pit	*68%*	*95%*	*Comment*
3231	*135–60 cal BC*	*175–50 cal BC*	consistent with the MIA pottery
3341	*115–55 cal BC*	*155–40 cal BC*	consistent with the MIA/LIA pottery
3419	*60 cal BC–10 cal AD*	*85 cal BC–55 cal AD*	–
3535	*40 cal BC–45 cal AD*	*50 cal BC–65 cal AD*	slightly earlier than the suggest date of the pottery jar
3174	*50 cal BC–20 cal AD*	*95 cal BC–55 cal AD*	consistent with the LIA/ER pottery

Table 4.6 Modelled dates for the construction event of each enclosure ditch phase

Ditch phase	*68%*	*95%*	*Comment*
MIA	*160–80 cal BC*	*200–65 cal BC*	consistent with the MIA/LIA pottery
LIA	*120–50 cal BC*	*160–30 cal BC*	consistent with the MIA/LIA pottery

cal BC. Three other pits, all stratigraphically discrete, were dug after the LIA enclosure ditch. The earliest of these pits was 3419 (*60 cal BC–10 cal AD at 68% probability*), followed by 3174 (*50 cal BC–20 cal AD at 68% probability*) and the latest was 3535 (*40 cal BC–45 cal AD at 68% probability*).

Pit 3174

The pit was probably constructed in one year during *50 cal BC to cal AD 20 (at 68%) (or during 95 cal BC to 55 cal AD at 95% probability)*. The significant bone deposit which may have been deposited quite rapidly (see Higbee, above) happened only after the pit had been back-filled and then mostly cleaned out. This bone deposit (*'Mass bone deposit 3174'*) formed at some point between *10 cal BC to cal AD 70 cal AD (68%) or 50 cal BC to cal AD 90 (95% probability)* (Fig. 4.3). Whilst the pit may have been dug decades before the Conquest the bone deposit could have been made in the decades immediately before or after this event. In contrast, the lapdog (ABG131 SUERC-38158), thought to be a Roman introduction after the Conquest appears to have been buried between *cal AD 50 to cal AD 90 (62.3%) (at 68% or 10 to 110 cal AD at 95% probability)*.

Enclosure ditches

The modelled results (Figs 4.1–2; Table 4.6) indicate that the earliest enclosure ditch (phase MIA) was constructed at some point between *160–80 cal BC (68%) and/or 200–65 cal BC (95% probability)*, and the later phase enclosure ditch was constructed between *120–50 cal BC or160–50 cal BC (95% probability)*. At least some pits were earlier than the MIA ditch, including pit 3306 which was cut by the ditch. Pit 3341 cut the MIA ditch and was probably earlier than or close in date to the construction of the LIA ditch (51% probability). Pits 3419, 3174 and 3535 are certainly or probably later than the LIA ditch.

Burials

Three human burials were directly dated by radiocarbon and the dates of two further burial events within pit 3174 (3690 and 3654) were estimated using the OxCal '*Date*' function. The earliest of the burials is 3466 (SUERC-39061), which was made at some point during *170 cal BC to cal AD 20*. As the burial was cut into the silted up MIA enclosure ditch it could belong with the LIA enclosure. Using the OxCal *Order* function (see Table 4.7), the construction of the LIA ditch is probably (81%) earlier than the placing of burial 3466. This burial is earlier than the two other directly dated burials, 3809

Table 4.7 Probability (%) order of radiocarbon dates for selected events. The table should be read from the left hand column across each row. The stated value (%) is the probability that the radiocarbon date or estimate listed in the left hand column is older than each date in the row

	Dig MIA ditch	*Dig pit 3231*	*Dig pit 3341*	*Dig LIA ditch*	*SUERC-39061 (burial 3466)*	*Dig pit 3419*	*Dig pit 3174*	*Dig pit 3535*	*SUERC-39063 (burial 3652)*	*Mass bone deposit 3174*	*SUERC-39062 (burial 3809)*	*SUERC 38158*
Dig MIA ditch	0	73	1	1	1	1	99	1	1	1	1	1
Dig pit 3231	27	0	75	76	92	99	97	1	1	1	1	1
Dig pit 3341	0	25	0	53	84	98	95	99	1	99	1	1
Dig LIA ditch	0	24	47	0	81	1	94	99	99	99	1	1
SUERC-39061 (burial 3466)	0	8	16	19	0	75	77	90	93	93	97	99
Dig pit 3419	0	1	2	0	25	0	54	74	82	82	90	98
Dig pit 3174	1	3	5	6	23	46	0	71	80	1	89	1
Dig pit 3535	0	0	1	1	10	26	29	0	62	63	77	92
SUERC-39063 (burial 3652)	0	0	0	1	7	18	20	38	0	50	65	84
Mass bone deposit 3174	0	0	1	1	7	18	0	37	50	0	65	1
SUERC-39062 (burial 3809)	0	0	0	0	3	10	11	23	35	35	0	71
SUERC-38158 (dog burial ABG131)	0	0	0	0	1	2	0	8	16	0	29	0

(SUERC-39062) and 3652 (SUERC-39063). Both burials are likely to belong to the first half of the 1st century AD (SUERC-39062, *cal AD 20–80 at 68%*, and SUERC-39063, *cal AD 1–70 at 65.9%*). However, burial 3809 is likely to be later than all these events but is probably earlier than the burial of the lapdog in pit 3174 (Table 4.7). The two burials in the upper fills of 3174 both belong to the later part of the 1st century AD or the early decades of the 2nd century AD (estimated using '*Date*': 3690 *cal AD 60–120 68%*, and 3654 *cal AD 70–130 68% probability*). This supports the suggestion (see Egging Dinwiddy, above) that the practice of burying neonates continues from the Late Iron Age and throughout the Romano-British period.

Pottery

One of the aims of the radiocarbon programme was to try and define a more precise chronology for the pottery or at least provide a more precise framework for the later prehistoric pottery chronology. At the assessment stage the pottery assemblage had been considered to be mainly Late Iron Age and Early Roman. However, the results of the radiocarbon dating suggested a longer chronology for the enclosure ditches and pits with origins in the later Middle Iron Age. A potential mismatch between the radiocarbon dating and pottery chronology led to a comprehensive reassessment of the pottery by Seager Smith (see above). This found that the pottery assemblage did indeed contain a Middle Iron Age component. The following section discusses the association between the radiocarbon dating and the key features.

Summary Sequence

The overall radiocarbon sequence is presented in Figure 4.1, which gives in its structure (shown on the left side) the stratigraphic relationships between the selected features. Figure 4.2 illustrates selected features and events (eg, the digging of an enclosure ditch or a pit) in date order (see also Table 4.7). As noted above at least two pits, and probably more, pre-date the MIA enclosure ditch. The construction date for the ditch falls within the later part of the 2nd century BC and the early half of the 1st century BC (*160–80 BC at 68% or 200–65 BC at 95% probability*). The construction of the LIA ditch occurred at some point during the final quarter of the 2nd century BC or the first half of the 1st century BC (*120–50 cal BC 68%*) or possibly the early half of the 2nd and 1st centuries BC (*160–30 cal BC at 95%*). The two enclosures layouts were probably constructed between one or two generations apart (estimated at up to 29 years (at 68%) or 65 years (at 95%): calculated using the OxCal *difference* function). The construction of the final phase enclosure could not be calculated due to insufficient samples to date. However, the ditch was known to cut the MIA and LIA ditches (see above). Pits 3419, 3174 and 3535 were all dug after the LIA Probably all within the second half of the 1st century BC or the early decades of the 1st century AD (see Table 4.5).

Pit 3174 had a long period of use from the Latest Iron Age into the early Romano-British period. In use over a number of decades, its fills and associated animal bone deposits and human burials span between 79 to 162 years (at 68%) or 46 to 217 years (at 95% probability with a median of 124 years: modelled as '*Span 3174*') (Figs 4.3–4). This pit was possibly excavated a decade or more before the Conquest, with the large animal bone deposit accumulating at some point between 10 BC to 70 AD (at 68% probability: '*Date Mass bone deposit 3174*': Fig. 4.3). At the top of this deposit was placed the burial of a lapdog (ABG 131), thought to be a post-Conquest introduction. This burial was made at some point between *AD 50 to AD 90 (at 68% probability or AD 10 to AD 110 at 95% probability)*. The two inhumation burials in layers 3710 and 3246 within the middle section of the pit were probably both made in the later decades of the 1st century AD or the start of the 2nd century AD. The stratigraphically latest and highest radiocarbon dated animal bone deposit within the pit was ABG 202 (SUERC-38141) in layer 3177. The date of this deposit appears later than the Conquest (*cal AD 80–140 at 68% probability*).

Assuming that the early pits radiocarbon dated represent the true date of Middle Iron Age activity and that deposit ABG 202 in the upper part of pit 3174 represents the latest activity then this phase of the site's use (Middle Iron Age to the early Romano-British period) lasted for *190 to 305 years (at 68%) or 140 to 390 years (at 95% probability: 'Span all' activity)*.

Chapter 5
Discussion

Despite the proximity to the site of the Late Bronze Age ringwork, no features or pottery of comparable date were identified during the excavation; 15 sherds (109 g) of Late Bronze Age pottery were recovered during the watching brief, but these came from a pit (5010) observed in a pipe trench to the east of the enclosure. Conversely, despite the fact that no Iron Age or Romano-British pottery was recovered from the (admittedly very limited) excavation of the enclosure ditch, as re-analysed by Adkins and Needham (1985, 32), the present excavation indicated nearby occupation and settlement extending largely unbroken through the Iron Age and into the early Romano-British period.

Robarts concluded that the enclosure ditch must have silted up at an early date (Robarts 1905, 388; 1910, 147), and this appeared to be confirmed by Lowther's excavation; he suggested that little trace of the earthwork can have existed by the Roman period (Lowther 1944–5, 56). It is likely, however, that the enclosure would still have been a significant feature in the landscape when the Early Iron Age open settlement was established just downslope from it. It is possible that the absence of Iron Age and Romano-British finds from the ditch reflects some deliberate avoidance of the earlier monument, or that it was used for activities, perhaps as a stock enclosure, which resulted in no significant deposition of domestic waste.

The extent of the settlement through the Iron Age and early Romano-British period is not known. The single Early/Middle Iron Age roundhouse was the only recognisable domestic structure recorded on the site, even though large quantities of settlement waste were recovered from the arrays of pits and from the ditches of the contemporary enclosures. The recovery from Romano-British contexts of a piece of a saw blade, as well as iron nails and possible fittings likely to have been used in timber construction, provide indirect evidence for building activity, but the absence of direct evidence for structures may be largely a consequence of the heavy truncation which parts of the site had suffered. While it is possible that the sequence of Iron Age and Romano-British enclosures which take up most of the site had predominantly agricultural functions, perhaps as animal pens, with settlement structures arranged outside them (and so beyond the excavated area), the presence of storage and other pits within the enclosures would argue against this.

The site, therefore, appears to represent part of a small but well-established farming settlement, which continued in occupation apparently little changed until the early 2nd century AD, through the period rapid but largely peaceful transition which saw the wider region being brought under Roman control (Poulton 2004, 60). The changing organisation of the agricultural economy, leading to the abandonment of the site may be represented in part by the establishment of a possible villa near the spring-line to the north, at West Street, Carshalton (GLAAS 2002).

There was evidence, from all phases, for a mixed agricultural economy typical for the region, and in many respects a continuation of the Late Bronze Age economy (Bruce and Giorgi 1994, 177). This involved the cultivation of hulled wheat and barley, with many of the arable weeds recovered being typical of the dry calcareous soils which are found locally. There were, however, some developments over time in the manner of the harvesting, storage and processing of these crops. There was possible evidence for above-ground storage only in the Early/Middle Iron Age, in the form of the square 'granary' structure beside the roundhouse, at a time when there were few pits of a form and depth suitable for storage. As time progressed, the size and number of storage pits increased, this enlargement of the settlement's storage capacity probably reflecting greater productivity in its arable cultivation, or possibly the extension of arable land. Fragments of Greensand and lava quernstones were found in Early Iron Age and early Romano-British contexts, respectively.

The animal bone assemblage, however, indicates that a significant part of the landscape must have been devoted to the pastoral economy, dominated by sheep. It appears that many of the excess lambs and old unproductive sheep were slaughtered before the winter to ease pressure on grazing land and winter fodder supplies. Other farm animals included cattle, pig, goat and horse, and domestic fowl were also kept. In addition to meat, the animals would have contributed many other secondary products and resources (milk, leather, hides, wool, bone, manure, traction and transport etc); some vessels with perforations, for example, were possibly used for making cheese. Dogs were also important animals within these communities, having a variety of uses, such as for hunting and protecting and controlling livestock, as guard dogs, as lapdogs/companion animals, and even, according to classical writers, possibly as food (Diodorus Siculus V, 28, 4). In fact, there was little evidence either for hunting – a few bones of red deer and hare were present in the bone assemblage – or for the exploitation of wild plant foods – there were a few fragments of hazelnut shell among the charred plant remains.

There was also limited evidence for identifiable craft activities undertaken on the site, although the recovery of chalk spindlewhorls in Late Iron Age and early Romano-British pits indicates the production of yarns and textiles – unsurprising given the importance of sheep. Weaving may also be indicated by the presence of perforated triangular fired clay objects of a form frequently interpreted as loomweights, although these objects have also been interpreted as some form of oven furniture (see Seager Smith, Chapter 3). Such objects were found, for example, along with burnt flint, in a possible oven (3317) with evidence of burning on the base and stakeholes possibly supporting some superstructure, but there were no other identifiable hearths, ovens or kilns. The oven is comparable to similar features, also with stakeholes, interpreted as ovens used for a range of crop-processing and other related activities, recorded at Theobalds Road, Wivelsfield, East Sussex (Powell 2015).

Relatively large quantities of burnt flint were recovered from a number of Early Iron Age pits, some of which also contained the fired clay objects, but what purpose they fulfilled is unknown. Although no evidence was found for pottery production, the tempers used were locally available and it is likely that much of the Iron Age pottery was made on a small scale, fired in bonfires or clamp kilns within or close to settlements.

The lumps of birch tar with impressions of twisted vegetable fibres (recovered from Iron Age pit 3998 with its distinctive deposit of pottery and metal objects) could have had a wide range of possible uses, such as for making composite tools or undertaking repairs, such as the repaired Iron Age pottery in pits 3341, 3513 and 4313, and early Romano-British pottery in pit 3503; the fibres themselves may have been used as some form of binding, or for making basketry containers.

Among the metal objects in pit 3998 was an iron forger's set hammer, and while an offcut from a square-sectioned iron rod, possibly an ingot, was recovered from another Iron Age pit (3852), there was no evidence of actual metalworking on the site until the Romano-British period. Most of this later evidence, comprising slag, hearth bottoms and hammerscale, came from pit 3174 (perhaps significantly the same pit, and context (3711), which also contained the large deposit of animal carcasses). This suggests that metalworking may have been very localised on the site, and short-lived; natural iron deposits were recorded in another Romano-British pit (3458). Iron Age weaponry is represented by the the decorated spearhead, although it may have been an ensign or standard, rather than an effective weapon. There are also few indications of the personal or individual among the finds – four brooches, and two groups of hobnails possibly from a single boot.

While the evidence for mixed farming and craft activities indicates a settlement that would have been potentially largely self-sufficient, it is likely that it would also have been tied into networks of local and regional trade and exchange, circulating primary and secondary agricultural products, and other materials, seen for example in the presence of regionally traded pottery wares, of amphora sherds probably from vessels traded as containers, and of pieces of briquetage from salt production zones in the lower Thames estuary or on the south coast.

Apart from a single redeposited human bone from an adult (from an enclosure ditch), all the human remains were of neonates. Seven burials were identified, but only two were from features which could be clearly classed as graves (3052 and 3651), the others being from contexts within pits and ditches; the remaining neonate bones were redeposited (again recovered from pits and ditches). While the occurrence of the neonate burials in pits, many of which also contained dumps of domestic waste, might indicate a low level of regard for the deceased, the significance of such burials should be viewed in the context of the much more complex deposits, of selected objects and whole or partial animal carcases, made in many of these pits, some of which were of neonate animals – sheep, pigs, dogs and a cat.

The deposition of cultural material in pits, including complete or partial animal remains, is a practice that appears to have endured from the Neolithic many millennia before, presumably reflecting some long-standing ideas about its ritual efficacy; locally, Late Bronze Age ritual deposits in pits were found at Westcroft Road, Carshalton (Proctor 2002). Deposition in Iron Age pits is a subject that has received much consideration (eg, Cunliffe 1995; Hill 1995), the apparent formality with which many of such deposits were made indicating that they had some ritual context. However, this was ritual behaviour that was firmly rooted within everyday social and economic life, undertaken within the settlements as opposed to at some separate ritual or religious structure, although shrines and other religious structures are also known from the Iron Age.

The character of such deposition on this site varies considerably – in its contexts, its formality, its materials, its associations, and probably also, therefore, in its meanings and purpose. It covers, for example the careful selection and arrangement of objects in pits apparently dug deliberately for them, such as the large flint nodule and pottery in Late Iron Age pit 3088. Of particular note is the small hoard, or *pars pro toto* deposit of objects – the set hammer, spearhead, nave hoop, birch tar/fibre lumps and large pieces from a single jar – found in Late Iron Age pit 3998, the grave-like shape of which may indicate something of its meaning. The association between the objects selected, a number of which were deliberately broken, is far from clear, although while each had a practical function they also had potential symbolic meanings; the decorated spearhead, for example, may have been used as a standard or ensign (see Fitzpatrick, Chapter 3), while the wheel (represented by the nave hoop) was a symbol frequently used in Iron Age religion, as well as being a feature of chariot burials (Green 1984).

Many of the deposits, however, particularly those containing significant animal remains, were made in reused storage pits. The often apparently careful arrangement of these remains shows that they were not simply dumped (Wait 1985, 151). These pits were the facilities where the grain, upon which the survival and agricultural productivity of the community depended, had been stored, and it would not be surprising if the storage process was accompanied, both before and after, by ceremonies of offering and sacrifice to appease and give thanks to the relevant (possibly underworld) deities (*ibid.* 153; Green 2002, 103), so investing the pits with symbolic significance relating to ideas of life and death, decay, regeneration and fertility. The practice of animal sacrifice by the Celts is well documented by Roman writers, and it is clear that these persisted into the Romano-British period (Fulford 2001).

While the subsequent deposition in the emptied pits may have been in part acts of post-storage gratitude and closure, the deposition of animal remains may have involved some of the same symbolism expressed in the storage of the grain, intended to ensure the continued productivity of the community's livestock; it is notable that it was the remains of only domestic animals, not of wild, hunted animals, which were deposited. The community's livestock would have had much more than simple economic value; it was also an important indicator of wealth and social status, as expressed on occasion through feasting, exchange and conspicuous consumption. Examples include the extraordinary deposit, in pit 3174, of butchered carcasses of up to 30 animals (mostly sheep/goat, but also cattle and horse), as well as the remains of dog (including lapdog), domestic fowl and raven; this deposit was associated not only with iron-working debris but also with materials which, under other circumstances, would be classified simply as domestic waste, but which here may well have been treated as principally symbolic in nature, representing some aspect of life within a more complex ritualised practice.

Given the implied symbolism of such storage pits, it may be that all acts of deposition in them should be viewed as being symbolic to some degree. Although much of the material in the pits appears to comprise informal dumps of domestic and hearth waste, or even just backfilled soil, there may be no clear distinction between what we should classify as ritual and non-ritual deposits. The fill sequences and rates of deposition varied considerably between contemporary pits, but the apparent levelling of some deposits, as indicated by their flat upper surfaces revealed in section (not the profile one would expect from unstructured dumping and backfilling), may indicate the infilling of many of the pits was sometimes undertaken with some care.

There are no clear associations at this site between different species either in pits or in individual contexts, although the number of pits containing animal bone groups of the different species gives a rough indication as to their relative ritual significance – sheep bone groups were found in 15 pits, cattle in 10 pits, followed by dog in eight and horse in seven; bone groups of all four species were found together in only two pits (3174 and 3535). The occurrence in some of these deposits of foetuses and neonates, both human and animals, is likely to represent an additional dimension to their symbolic complexity. The individual occurrences of fox and cat, and of two ravens, are also noteworthy additions. Pits with similar deposits of animal bone and other materials are common in the Iron Age, including other sites on the North Downs, such as Reigate Road, Ewell (Cotton 2001), Hawk's Hill, Leatherhead (Hastings 1965), Lower Warbank, Keston (Philp *et al.* 1991), Farningham Hill (Philp 1984).

Notable among the animal deposits are those of dogs. Dog burials are a relatively frequent occurrence on Iron Age and Romano-British sites (Black 1983) – a dog skeleton was found on the base of a Late Iron Age/early Romano-British storage pit at Ewell (Cotton 2001, 8), and two dogs were buried in a wooden box, with 2nd-century AD pottery, at Elephant and Castle, Southwark (Green 1976, 230). The occurrence in both periods of multiple dog burials makes it more likely that these were ritual in character (Wait 1985, 150; Merrifield 1987, 46–7); 16 dogs were found were found at the base of a well at Staines, Middlesex (Chapman and Smith 1988).

As scavengers and carrion-eaters, dogs came to be associated with death in both the Celtic and classical religious traditions (Green 2002, 197–8). Dog sacrifice is linked to a number of Roman agricultural rituals, such as the festival of *Robigalia* held in April to protect crops against disease (De Grossi Mazzorin and Minniti 2006, 65), although such beliefs may be unrelated to these deposits.

Because of the potentially close relationships between dogs and people it is possible that particular care was taken in their deposition. The burial of two adult dogs arranged in a position suggesting that they were mating (the same pit, perhaps significantly, containing two dog foetuses) was clearly powerfully symbolic, but one for which there are few other parallels – and those being from rare artistic representations on portable Roman objects. At Silchester, for example, the burial of two dogs and a puppy was accompanied by a knife with an ivory handle depicting two dogs mating (http://www.reading.ac.uk/silchester/ discoveries-at-silchester/sil-discoveries.aspx), while a similar image is depicted on a red jasper ringstone (1st century BC/AD), of unknown provenance, in the Classical Art Research Centre's Danicourt Collection (https://www.beazley.ox.ac.uk/gems/danicourt/animals.htm). The burials of dogs in 'life positions' have been suggested elsewhere, with one dog 'urinating' and another in the 'curled up' position at Silchester, while others have been found extended, as if running, and in an attitude to reflect sitting on their haunches (Mike Fulford, Kate Clark pers. comm.).

The burial of the young dog on the base of pit 3535 is of comparable symbolic potency; a jar containing the burnt remains of at least two lambs (and a fragment of saw blade) appears to have been deliberately broken as part of the 'burial' rite, and its contents spread out (perhaps 'served up') in front of the dog, partly covering its head. While burials of dogs with meat bones are not unknown, such as the adult terrier-type dog in pit 2047 (back cover, middle), and at Gravelly Guy, Oxon (Lambrick 1985, 108), burials with vessels are very rare. A comparison may be drawn, however, with the burial of a medium-sized adult dog at Bury Close, Fawler, Oxon, which was accompanied by a 1st century AD wine flagon placed upright next to its head (Allen 1988). Given the special nature of the burial in pit 3535, it is quite possible that the overlying bone-rich deposit, which contained three further dogs (one headless), four sheep (including two further lambs), a fox, a horse skeleton, a near complete cattle skeleton and other cattle bones, was deliberately associated with it.

Fitzpatrick (Chapter 3) has suggested that the objects in pit 3998, either deliberately broken or selected from a necessarily larger set, form a *pars pro toto* deposit, the items deposited to represent the complete whole. A similar principle could apply equally to many of the other deposits. Many of the animal bone groups, for example, were of partial carcasses, with some animals partly eaten, with the rest, or whole animals possibly offered in sacrifice; even a whole sheep carcass could be viewed as representative of the larger flock. This may also apply to less apparently structured deposits; while we tend to characterise these as dumps of domestic waste, they could be samples of midden material selected for their symbolic value, and deposited in pits for essentially similar reasons.

Conclusion

The excavation at the Queen Mary's Hospital site has uncovered significant features, and raised important questions about the nature of Iron Age settlement and economy in the London region. Its elevated position, with its access to extensive agricultural land, both arable and pasture, as well as to the resources of the Wandle valley to the north and the Weald to the south, may have made this site a natural choice for the establishment of a small farming community. However, its location next to a substantial defended enclosure, constructed, occupied and abandoned in the preceding Late Bronze Age, would clearly have been a significant factor, not least in highlighting the significant changes taking place at the start of the Iron Age.

The abandonment of the ringwork enclosure, which must have been a site of regional importance (Needham and Burgess 1980), reflects the start of an apparent hiatus in settlement patterns seen more widely within the region, in which the Early and Middle Iron Age are poorly represented in the archaeological record (Wait and Cotton 2000). The extensive, centrally organised field systems of the later Bronze Age were abandoned, and there was no comparable system of the landscape division until the Late Iron Age and Romano-British period. Instead there appears to have developed a pattern of small-scale autonomous farming settlements. This may reflect climatic change, with increased rainfall, suggested by increased evidence for alluviation and peat formation, leading to a reduction in agricultural productivity. It might also reflect social changes resulting from the introduction of ironworking and the consequent undermining of economic structures based on the production, consumption and deposition of bronzes.

Comparable Late Bronze Age ringwork enclosures, such as at Mucking and Springfield Lyons in Essex (Jones and Bond 1980; Brown and Medlycott 2013), have strong associations with metalworking, and a number of hoards of Late

Bronze Age metalwork have been found in the Carshalton area (Adkins and Needham 1985, fig. 17). By contrast, only a single piece of metalwork from this site, a La Tène I brooch, can be assigned an Early–Middle Iron Age date.

Whatever its causes, this hiatus in occupation is a feature found widely across the region in the Early Iron Age, as on the gravel terraces of the Middle Thames Valley to the west and the Lea Valley to the east (Greenwood 1997; Wait and Cotton 2000; Framework Archaeology 2010; Powell 2012; Powell *et al.* 2015). At this site too, therefore, the contrast between the Late Bronze Age ringwork and the subsequent open Iron Age settlement is marked.

The evidence for the establishment of that settlement in the Early Iron Age, and the apparent continuity it displays through the rest of the Iron Age and into the Romano-British period, throws important light on what has previously been poorly defined and understood. While the excavation revealed the localised enclosure of small areas of land from the end of the Middle Iron Age, it provided no evidence as to the wider division and organisation of the landscape. From the Middle Iron Age, the settlement's wealth appears to be based increasingly on its production of, and trade in agricultural resources, reaching a peak in the centuries spanning the Roman Conquest. A similar pattern was evident at nearby Reigate Road, Ewell (Cotton 2001, 36–8), and it is likely that similar unenclosed Late Iron Age settlements were widely distributed across a range of soil types.

Despite the market created by the Roman occupation, there appears to have been no substantial change, either in the organisation of agricultural production or in the ritual practices which were seen to underpin it, in the early Romano-British period. Only with a reorganisation of agricultural production, probably associated with the development of villas, such as at Beddington, and perhaps West Street, Carshalton, did the occupation of this long-settled farmstead, with its enduring economic and religious concerns, come to an end.

Appendix 1
Summary of pits

Pit	*Period*	*Width (m)*	*Depth (m)*	*No. fills*	*Pot*	*FCl*	*AB*	*Fl*	*BFl*	*Slag*	*St*	*Objects, ABGs and burials*	*Other*
2006	LIA/ERB	1.7	>1.2	3	✓	✓	✓	✓	✓	–	–	–	–
2017	EIA	1.4	0.4	3	✓	–	–	✓	✓	–	–	–	–
2021	ERB	1.7	1.4	4	✓	✓	✓	✓	✓	–	–	ON 10: iron loop	–
2025	M/LIA	2.1	0.8	4	✓	–	✓	✓	✓	–	–	–	–
2047	LIA/ERB	1.4	0.3	1	✓	–	✓	✓	✓	–	–	ABGs 2–3	–
2061	LIA	1.5	0.5	3	✓	–	✓	✓	✓	–	–	ABG 238	–
3011	EIA	1.5	1.0	3	✓	✓	✓	✓	✓	–	–	ON 160: perforated fired clay object	–
3015/ 4199	ERB	2.4	1.6	6	✓	✓	✓	✓	✓	–	–	ON 76: iron shank ON 154: perforated fired clay object	–
3017	?	0.9	0.2	1	–	–	–	–	–	–	–	–	–
3018	E/MIA	1.8	0.4	1	✓	–	✓	–	✓	–	–	–	–
3025	M/LIA	1.1	0.3	1	✓	–	✓	✓	✓	–	–	ON 50: iron object ON 53: nail	–
3027	LIA	2.9	1.4	10	✓	✓	✓	✓	✓	–	–	ABGs 51–2	–
3053	LIA	1.8	1.1	3	✓	✓	✓	–	✓	–	–	ABGs 13, 144, 226	–
3058	ERB	0.7	0.2	1	✓	–	✓	–	✓	–	–	–	–
3079	EIA	1.0	0.5	6	✓	–	✓	✓	✓	–	–	–	–
3088	LIA	0.7	0.3	2	✓	✓	✓	✓	✓	✓	–	–	–
3133	?	3.1	0.4	1	–	–	✓	✓	✓	–	–	–	–
3135	LIA	1.4	0.9	3	✓	–	✓	–	–	–	–	–	–
3142	LIA	1.2	0.4	2	✓	✓	✓	✓	✓	–	–	–	–
3163	?	3.0	0.7	2	–	✓	✓	–	–	–	–	–	–
3178	EIA	2.2	1.3	12	✓	–	✓	✓	✓	–	–	ON 153: perforated fired clay object	–
3183	ERB	1.9	2.0	21	✓	✓	✓	✓	✓	✓	✓	ON 89: copper alloy Colchester brooch ON 94: iron chain ONs 97, 104: hobnail groups ONs 155, 163–6: perforated fired clay objects ABG 230	Iron
3219	EIA	2.3	0.8	4	✓	✓	✓	✓	✓	–	–	ON 145: perforated fired clay object	–
3220	LIA	1.8	0.5	6	✓	–	✓	✓	✓	–	–	ABGs 231, 233	Human bone
3223	M/LIA	1.2	0.5	3	✓	–	✓	✓	✓	–	✓	ABG 57	–
3225	LIA	>2.1	3.0	18	✓	✓	✓	✓	✓	–	–	–	–
3229	LIA/ERB	2.3	1.8	24	✓	–	✓	✓	✓	–	–	ON 65: iron nail ON 66: iron staple ABG 58–60	–
3231	MIA	1.7	1.4	4	✓	✓	✓	✓	✓	–	–	ABGs 70–1, 80, 232, 244	Glass
3234	LIA/ERB	1.1	0.1	1	✓	–	–	–	✓	–	–	–	–
3250	LIA	1.5	0.7	4	✓	✓	✓	✓	✓	✓	–	–	–
3280	M/LIA	1.8	0.4	2	✓	–	✓	–	✓	–	–	–	–
3286	?	1.7	0.7	3	–	–	–	–	–	–	–	–	–
3289	ERB	2.2	1.2	6	✓	✓	✓	✓	✓	–	–	–	–
3306	EIA	2.4	0.7	2	✓	✓	✓	–	–	–	–	–	–
3311	ERB	1.4	0.7	1	–	–	✓	–	–	–	–	ABG 68	–
3331	LIA	1.7	0.2	1	–	–	–	–	–	–	–	–	–
3341	M/LIA	2.0	1.4	17	✓	✓	✓	✓	✓	–	–	ONs 93, 95: chalk spindlewhorls 3 ABGs 61–2, 64, 67, 69, 98, 234, 245	–
3344	LIA	2.4	1.2	17	✓	✓	✓	✓	✓	✓	–	ON 146: perforated fired clay object	–
3386	LIA	1.6	1.4	11	✓	✓	✓	✓	✓	–	–	ABGs 235–6	–
3399	LIA/ERB	1.8	1.3	10	✓	✓	✓	–	✓	–	–	ON 75: perforated fired clay object	–
3419	ERB	1.2	1.2	4	✓	✓	✓	–	–	–	–	ABGs 72, 77, 237	–
3423	?	>0.6	0.8	3	–	–	–	–	–	–	–	–	–

Summary of pits continued

Pit	*Period*	*Width (m)*	*Depth (m)*	*No. fills*	*Pot*	*FCl*	*AB*	*Fl*	*BFl*	*Slag*	*St*	*Objects, ABGs and burials*	*Other*
3430	?ERB	>1.6	1.2	3	✓	–	–	✓	✓	–	–	–	–
3434	?	>0.8	>1.0	>1	–	–	–	–	–	–	–	–	–
3436	?	1.5	1.15	15	–	–	✓	✓	✓	✓	–	–	–
3458	ERB	2.7	1.8	>10	✓	–	✓	–	✓	–	✓	–	–
3482	ERB	>1.0	0.4	3	✓	✓	✓	✓	✓	–	–	Inhumation 3483 ON 73: iron ferrule	–
3501	?	1.5	0.3	1	–	–	✓	–	–	–	–	–	–
3503	ERB	2.3	1.9	14	✓	✓	✓	✓	✓	–	–	–	–
3513	M/LIA	>1.7	1	9	✓	–	✓	✓	✓	–	✓	ONs 85, 86: pottery vessels	–
3533	ERB	1.1	?	1	✓	–	✓	–	–	–	–	–	–
3535	ERB	2.0	1.9	5	✓	✓	✓	✓	✓	–	–	ON 122: iron saw ON 118: pottery vessel ABGs 83, 90–2, 100–1, 107–9, 115, 239–43	–
3553	?	2.0	0.7	3	–	–	✓	✓	–	–	–	–	–
3579	LIA	2.4	1.2	10	✓	✓	✓	✓	✓	–	–	ON 81: pottery vessel	–
3596	ERB	1.9	0.6	5	✓	–	✓	✓	–	–	–	ON 79: iron nail	–
3599	M/LIA	1.0	0.4	2	✓	–	✓	✓	✓	–	–	Fragment of worked bone with incised ring-and-dot decoration	
3635	ERB	1.9	1.2	6	✓	✓	✓	✓	✓	✓	–	–	–
3676	?	2.5	3.7	>6	–	–	–	–	–	–	–	–	–
3683	ERB	>4.5	1.7	7	✓		✓	✓	✓	–	–	ON 78: copper alloy Nauheim-derivative brooch	CBM
3737	LIA	1.5	>2.2	>10	✓	✓	✓	✓	✓	–	–	–	Iron
3759	EIA	1.3	0.4	1	✓	✓	✓	✓	✓	–	–	–	–
3761	EIA	0.8	0.5	2	✓	✓	✓	–	–	–	–	–	–
3790	ERB	1.2	0.2	2	✓	✓	✓	–	✓	–	–	–	–
3820	EIA	1.8	0.4	5	✓	✓	✓	–	✓	–	✓	ONs 103, 105, 110: perforated fired clay object	–
3825	EIA	1.7	0.5	6	✓	✓	✓	✓	✓	–	–	–	–
3835	?	1.4	0.5	1	–	–	✓	–	–	–	–	–	–
3837	?	1.0	0.4	2	–	–	✓	–	✓	–	–	–	–
3846	EIA	1.8	0.7	4	✓	–	✓	–	–	–	–	ABG 113	–
3852	LIA	1.4	0.8	4	✓	–	✓	✓	✓	–	–	ON 117: iron bar	–
3853	ERB	1.7	0.7	3	✓	–	✓	–	–	–	–	–	–
3856	LIA	1.3	0.2	1	✓	–	✓	–	✓	–	–	–	–
3870	ERB	2.8	2.0	25	✓	✓	✓	✓	✓	–	–	ON 150, 156: perforated fired clay object ABGs 114, 137 Stabling waste	–
3874	LIA	0.9	0.3	1	✓	✓	–	–	–	–	–	–	–
3878	?	1.0	0.9	2	–	–	✓	–	–	–	–	–	–
3879	EIA	2.5	1.0	7	✓	✓	✓	✓	✓	–	–	–	–
3901	?	1.0	0.2	1	–	–	✓	✓	–	–	–	–	–
3903	?	1.0	0.2	1	–	–	✓	–	✓	–	–	–	–
3907	EIA	1.0	1.2	7	✓	–	✓	✓	✓	–	–	–	–
3918	MIA	3.2	0.7	9	✓	–	✓	✓	✓	–	–	–	–
3920	LIA/ERB	1.0	0.6	1	✓	✓	✓	–	–	–	–	–	–
3921	ERB	1.1	0.9	15	✓	✓	✓	✓	✓	–	–	ON 119–20: iron nails ON 148: perforated fired clay object ABG 249	–
3932	EIA	2.0	0.5	2	✓	–	✓	–	–	–	–	–	–
3934	?	1.0	0.4	1	–	–	✓	✓	–	–	–	–	–
3940	EIA	2.4	1.3	7	✓	✓	✓	–	✓	–	–	ONs 121, 123–4, 128–9, 149: perforated fired clay objects	–
3985	ERB	2.9	1.6	12	✓	✓	✓	✓	✓	–	–	ON 126 pottery vessel	–
3994	?	1.7	0.3	3	–	–	–	–	–	–	–	–	–

Summary of pits continued

Pit	*Period*	*Width (m)*	*Depth (m)*	*No. fills*	*Pot*	*FCl*	*AB*	*Fl*	*BFl*	*Slag*	*St*	*Objects, ABGs and burials*	*Other*
3998	M/LIA	1.7	0.4	3	✓	✓	✓	✓	✓	–	–	ON 132: iron socketed spearhead ON 133: iron nave hoop ON 135: iron set hammer	Birch tar, vegetable fibres
4002	ERB	>1.7	0.8	5	✓	–	✓	–	✓	–	–	ON 125: copper alloy brooch	–
4007	ERB	1.7	1.2	4	✓	–	✓	✓	–	–	–	–	–
4045	LIA/ERB	1.9	0.8	6	✓	–	✓	–	✓	–	–	–	–
4052	ERB	2.5	1.8	14	✓	✓	✓	–	✓	–	–	ABGs 246–8	–
4066	EIA	1.7	0.9	5	✓	–	–	–	–	–	–	ON 134: iron La Tène 1 brooch	–
4079	?	1.7	0.6	7	–	–	–	–	–	–	–	–	–
4131	EIA	1.0	0.6	3	✓	✓	✓	✓	✓	–	–	–	–
4135	LIA	1.6	0.6	5	✓	✓	✓	–	✓	–	–	ON 151: perforated fired clay object	–
4182	?	1.5	0.7	2	–	–	–	–	–	–	–	–	–
4313	LIA	1.9	>1.2	2	✓	✓	✓	✓	✓	–	–	ABGs 250–2	–
4315	MIA	2.0	1.6	9	✓	✓	✓	✓	✓	–	–	–	–
4322	LIA	2.0	0.4	1	✓	✓	✓	–	✓	–	–	–	–
4324	E/MIA	1.0	0.2	2	✓	–	–	–	✓	–	–	–	–
4327	?	1.4	0.5	3	–	–	✓	✓	✓	–	–	–	–
4333	EIA	2.4	0.4	5	✓	✓	✓	✓	✓	–	–	–	–
4341	EIA	3.0	0.9	12	✓	–	✓	–	✓	–	–	–	–
4346	EIA	1.7	0.6	5	✓	–	✓	–	✓	–	–	–	–
4367	E/MIA	3.1	0.8	1	✓	✓	✓	–	✓	–	–	–	–
4372	EIA	0.8	0.1	1	✓	–	✓	✓	✓	–	–	–	–
4376/ 3174	ERB	2.0	2.8	24	✓	✓	✓	✓	✓	✓	–	ON 136: iron bar ONs 63, 106: RB pottery vessels ON 167: whetstone ON 168: chalk spindlewhorl ABGs 63, 116, 131, 170–225, 253–65	Shell

Key: Pot – pottery; FCl – fired clay; AB – animal bone; Fl – flint; BFl – burnt flint; St – stone

Appendix 2
Pottery fabric descriptions (all periods)

Fabric code	*Description*
BAET	Baetican amphora fabric (Dressel 20; Tomber and Dore 1998, 84–5, BAT AM)
BRIQ	Briquetage; fine-grained, slightly sandy fabric with sparse elongated (<4 mm) voids from lost organic (probably dung) inclusions; handmade; oxidised
F1	Hard; very common poorly-sorted calcined flint <2 mm across in a very slightly sandy matrix; predominantly dark fired; sometimes burnished
G1	Hard, fine-grained fabric; common rounded grog <1.5 mm (occasional <3 mm) and occasional calcined flint (<2 mm), quartz sand and/or ferrous particles; mostly dark fired; handmade
G100	Catch-all group for all latest Iron Age/Romano-British grog-tempered wares
G101	Sand and grog-tempered ware; moderate-common quartz sand <0.75 mm across with rare-sparse rounded grog <3 mm across
G2	Grog and shell-tempered ware; fine grained, well-sorted fabric containing sparse-moderate rounded grog <1 mm across (sometimes itself fine shell tempered) and sparse shell <1.5 mm across; dark fired; handmade
HWC	Highgate Wood fabric C (Davies *et al.* 1994, 82; Tomber and Dore 1998, 136, HGW RE C): *c.* AD 60–140/60, but most common *c.* AD 100–140
OXID	Catch-all group for all oxidised (white, orange, buff) wares; generally containing variable amounts of sand and/or mica, some white-slipped; unsourced
Q1	Sandy wares: fine-grained; naturally sandy matrix (abundant very fine quartz <0.125 mm across), variable quantities (generally fairly sparse) rounded quartz <1 mm; mostly dark-fired, sometimes partially oxidised surfaces; handmade
Q2	Sand and flint tempered: common/v common, poorly-sorted quartz sand, <0.5 mm, and variable quantities calcined flint <3 mm; occasional red/black ironstone particles <2 mm; mostly dark-fired, sometimes partially oxidised surfaces +/or red finished; handmade
Q3	Sand with distinctive iron pellets: moderately hard, predominantly dark fired fabrics containing soft, poorly-sorted, sub-angular, orange to red-brown inclusions, probably limonite, sometimes with occasional pieces of calcined flint, quartz sand and/or organic inclusions; handmade
Q4	Sand and organic tempered: very common/abundant quartz <0.5 mm with sparse elongated voids left by burnt-out organic material, probably animal dung; generally dark fired but sometimes oxidised; handmade
Q5	Glauconitic sand: moderately hard, generally dark fired and containing common rounded quartz and moderate sub-rounded glauconite, both <1 mm across; often burnished; handmade
S1	Shell: slightly sandy matrix, moderate-very common poorly-sorted crushed shell <4 mm; mostly dark-fired, but can be variably fired or oxidised; handmade
S2	Shell and grog: common–abundant, well sorted crushed shell <1.5 mm; occasional rounded limonite particles (or grog??) <2 mm and translucent quartz sand <0.75 mm
SAM CG	Central Gaulish samian (Tomber and Dore 1998, 32, LEZ SA 2)
SAM LG	South Gaulish samian (Tomber and Dore 1998, 28, LGF SA)
SAND	Catch-all group for all Romano-British greywares generally containing variable quantities of quartz sand; most are likely to be Alice Holt products but other, more local industries may be included
SHEL	Romano-British shell-tempered wares; generally hard-fired; sand and rarer shell inclusions
SUG	East Sussex Grog-tempered ware (Green 1980); fabric not clearly distinguishable from the general fabric G1; only identifiable by vessel form and/or decoration
TSK	Thameside, Kent greywares wares (Monaghan 1987, 245–9); includes 'BB2'
VRW	Verulamium-region white ware (Tomber and Dore 1998, 154, VER WH)

Appendix 3
Latest Iron Age and Romano-British vessel form codes

NB. Lon = Davies *et al.* 1994, 6–7

Form code	*Description*
form 18	Samian form 18 dish
form 24/25	Samian form 24/25 cup
form 30	Samian form 30 bowl
form 33	Samian form 33 cup
Lon HOF	Mortaria
Lon IB4	Ring-necked flagon with long, flaring neck; upper ring slightly more prominent than lower ones; first half of 2nd century AD
Lon IH	Wide-mouthed flagon or jug
Lon IIA	Bead rimmed jar
Lon IIB	Necked, globular-bodied jars with a thickened (beaded) or out-turned rim; no cordon or groove defining neck; later 1st century AD
Lon IIC	Necked jars with sharply carinated shoulders, with a cordon (less frequently, a groove) defining the base of the neck; Alice Holt early class 1; pre/early Flavian–early Antonine
Lon IIC or D	Necked jars with sharply carinated (Lon IIC) or rounded (Lon IID) shoulders, with a cordon (less frequently, a groove) defining the base of the neck; Alice Holt early class 1; pre/early Flavian–early Antonine; used for broken fragments where not enough of the shoulder survives to differentiate
Lon IID	Necked jars with rounded shoulders, a cordon (less frequently, a groove) defining the base of the neck; sometimes decorated; Alice Holt early class 1; pre/early Flavian–early Antonine
Lon IIF	Everted rim jars; later 2nd century AD onwards
Lon IIG	Necked jars
Lon IIH	Neckless jars, often lid-seated; 2nd century AD
Lon IIIA	Imitation butt beakers
Lon IIIC	Globular-bodied (sometimes slightly shouldered) jar/beaker with a short, sharply everted rim; 1st century AD
Lon IIIF	Poppy-head beaker
Lon IIIG	Carinated beaker with a flared rim; 1st or early 2nd century AD
Lon IIL	Necked storage jars; profiles vary
Lon IIN-Q	Necked, round-bodied jars/bowls with rounded shoulder and cordon at base of neck; indistinguishable from Lon II C or D if broken at/above neck/shoulder junction although the jar/bowl form generally has a larger diameter for size
Lon IVD	Bowl loosely based on samian form 29
Lon IVF	Rounded bowls with flat; hooked or folded over rims; AD 70–100 in grog and AD 100/130 in sandy fabrics
Lon IVH	Bowl/dish with straight sides and a triangular or rounded rim
Lon IVJ	Shallow, straight-sided, plain rimmed dish. 2nd century AD onwards
Lon IVK	Atrebatic or Surrey bowls; 1st–2nd century AD
Lon IXH	Strainer; sharply shouldered bowl with a short, flared, internally lid-seated rim; pre-firing perforations in base
M-K 12–14	Dressel 20 amphora rim; second half of 1st century AD (Martin-Kilcher 1983, types 12–14)
R100	Rim fragments too small for closer identification
R101	Narrow-necked jar (or possibly flagon) with a short, upright neck and an out turned rim; profiles variable: some are large, high-shouldered, probably fairly globular storage jar forms, others smaller
R102	Carinated bowl probably based on samian form 29 (Marsh 1978, 178, fig. 6.19 and 20, type 44)
R103	Small, round-shouldered necked jar with a cordon at base of neck and a girth groove
R104	Flagon or narrow-necked jar with a lid-seated, off-set rim, a slightly flaring neck with a central raised cordon; probably loosely based on Cam form 161
R105	Bead rim bowl; probably hemispherical (imitation form 37) or carinated, but insufficient survives to describe body shape
R106	Barrel-shaped jar or beaker with a small bead rim (Thompson 1982, class B5), sometimes decorated

Bibliography

Adkins, L. and Adkins, R., 1983. Excavations at Beddington 1982, *London Archaeol.* 4, 326–9

Adkins, L. and Needham, S., 1985. New research on a Late Bronze Age enclosure at Queen Mary's Hospital, Carshalton, *Surrey Archaeol. Collect.* 76, 11–49

Albarella, U., 2007. The end of the sheep age: people and animals in the Late Iron Age, in C. Haslegrove and T. Moore (eds), T*he Late Iron Age in Britain and Beyond,* 393–406. Oxford, Oxbow Books

Albarella, A., Johnstone, C. and Vickers, K., 2008. The development of animal husbandry from the Late Iron Age to the end of the Roman period: a case study from south-east Britain, *J. Archaeol. Sci.* 35, 1828–48

Allen, T. G., 1988. Excavations at Bury Close, Fawler, Oxon, *Oxoniensia* 53, 293–315

Archaeology South East (ASE), 2009. *An Archaeological Evaluation at Carshalton War Memorial Hospital, The Park, Carshalton, Sutton.* ASE unpubl. rep. 200900153

Barnett, C., 2012. Wood charcoal, in N. Cooke and A. B. Powell, *Prehistoric Settlement and a Romano-British Pottery Production Site at Groom's Farm, Frithend, Hampshire.* Salisbury, Wessex Archaeology online report 59794, 40–3. http://www.scribd.com/doc/115882793/Groom-s-Farm-Hampshire

Bass, W. M., 1987. *Human Osteology.* Columbia (MO), Missouri Archaeological Society

Baxter, I. L., 2006. A dwarf hound skeleton from a Romano-British grave at York Road, Leicester, in L.M. Snyder and E.A. Moore (eds), *Dogs and People in Social, Working, Economic or Symbolic Interaction,* 12–37. Oxford, Oxbow Books

Bayley, J. and Butcher, S., 2004. *Roman Brooches in Britain: a technological and typological study based on the Richborough Collection.* London, Society of Antiquaries

Bayliss, A., Bronk Ramsey, C., van der Plicht, J. and Whittle, A., 2007. Bradshaw and Bayes: towards a timetable for the Neolithic, *Cambridge Archaeol. J.* 17, 1–28

Beek, G. C. van 1983. *Dental Morphology: an illustrated guide.* Bristol, Wright

Bendrey, R., 2010. The horse, in T. O'Connor and N. Sykes (eds), *Extinctions and Invasions: a social history of British fauna,* 10–16. Oxford, Windgather Press

Bendrey, R., Hayes, T. E. and Palmer, M. R., 2009. Patterns of Iron Age supply: an analysis of strontium isotope ratios in teeth, *Archaeometry* 51, 140–50

Birbeck, V., Jones, G., Powell, A. B., Seager Smith, R.H., 2008. A Roman pottery kiln, kiln furniture and new vessel forms from Alice Holt Forest, Hampshire, *Proc. Hampshire Fld Club Archaeol. Soc.* 63, 110–28

Bird, D., 2004. *Roman Surrey.* Stroud, Tempus

Black, E., 1983. Ritual dog burials from Roman sites, *Kent Archaeol. Rev.* 71, 20–2

Boessneck, J., von den Driesch, A., Meyer-Lempennau, U. and Weschler-von Ohlen, E., 1971. *Das Tierknochenfunde aus dem Oppidum von Manching. Die Ausgrabungen in Manching* 6. Wiesbaden

Bond, J. M. and O'Connor, T. P., 1999. *Bones from Medieval Deposits at 16–22 Coppergate and Other Sites in York.* The Archaeology of York 15/5. York, CBA

Booth, P., 2006. The pottery and other ceramic finds, in J. Magilton, A Romano-Celtic temple and settlement at Grimstock Hill, Coleshill, Warwickshire, *Trans. Birmingham Warwickshire Archaeol Soc.* 110, 103–65

Bourdillon, J. and Coy, J. 1980. The animal bones, in P. Holdsworth, *Excavations at Melbourne Street, Southampton, 1971–76,* 79–121. London, CBA Res. Rep. 33

Boyle, A., 2004. Riding into history, *British Archaeol.* 76 (May), 22–7

Bradley, R., 2000. *An Archaeology of Natural Places.* London, Routledge

British Geological Survey online viewer. http://mapapps.bgs.ac.uk/geologyofbritain/home.html

Bronk Ramsey, C., 1995. Radiocarbon calibration and analysis of stratigraphy: the OxCal program, *Radiocarbon* 37, 425–30

Bronk Ramsey, C., 1998. Probability and dating, *Radiocarbon* 40, 461–74

Bronk Ramsey, C., 2001. Development of the radiocarbon calibration program OxCal, *Radiocarbon* 43, 355–63

Bronk Ramsey, C., 2009. Bayesian analysis of radiocarbon dates, *Radiocarbon* 51, 337–60

Bronk Ramsey, C., and Lee, S., 2013. Recent and planned developments of the Program OxCal, *Radiocarbon* 55 (2–3), 720–730

Brown, N. and Medlycott, M., 2013. *The Neolithic and Bronze Age Enclosures at Springfield Lyons, Essex: Excavations 1981–1991.* East Anglian Archaeology 149

Bruce, P. and Giorgi, J., 1994. Recent work at Orchard Hill, Queen Mary's Hospital, Carshalton, *London Archaeol.* 7(7), 171–7

Brunaux, J.-L. and Rapin, A., 1988. *Gournay II. Boucliers et lances, dépôts et trophées.* Paris, Errance & Revue Archéologique de Picardie

Buikstra, J. E. and Ubelaker, D. H., 1994. *Standards for Data Collection from Human Skeletal Remains.* Fayetteville (AR), Arkansas Archaeol. Surv. Res. Ser. 44

Butterfield, B. G. and Meylan, B. A., 1980. *Three-Dimensional Structure of Wood: an ultrastructural approach.* London and New York, Chapman & Hall

Callender, M. H., 1965. *Roman Amphorae.* Oxford, Oxford University Press

Carruthers, W. J., 2008. Mineralised plant remains in C. Ellis and A.B. Powell, *An Iron Age Settlement outside Battlesbury Hillfort, Warminster and Sites along the Southern Range Road,* 102–14. Salisbury, Wessex Archaeology Rep. 22

Carruthers, W. J., 2010. Charred and waterlogged plant remains, Framework Archaeology, *Landscape Evolution in the Middle Thames Valley: Heathrow Terminal 5 Excavations Vol. 2.* Oxford/Salisbury, Framework Archaeology Monogr. 3, CD-Rom, Section 14, 1–166

Chaplin, R. E. and McCormick, F., 1986. The animal bones, in I. M. Stead and V. Rigby, *Baldock: the excavation of a Roman and Pre-Roman settlement, 1968–72,* 396–415 London, Britannia Monogr. 7

Chapman, J., and Smith, S., 1988. Finds from a Roman well in Staines, *London Archaeol.* 6.1, 3–6

Charters, S., Evershed, R. P., Blinkhorn, P. W., and Denham, V., 1995. Evidence for the mixing of fats and waxes in archaeological ceramics, *Archaeometry* 37(1), 113–27

Clapham, A. J., 2004. Charred plant remains, in J. McKinley, Welcome to Pontibus... gateway to the west, *Surrey Archaeol. Collect.* 91, Supplement S1–S48. http://archaeologydataservice.ac.uk/archiveDS/archiveDownload?t=arch-379-1/dissemination/pdf/vol_91_sup/vol_91_supp.pdf (accessed 15-08-2012)

Clark, K., 1995. The later prehistoric and protohistoric dog: the emergence of canine diversity, *Archaeozoologia* 7(2), 9–32

Clark, K. M., 2000. Dogged persistence: the phenomenon of canine skeletal uniformity in British prehistory, in S. J. Crockford (ed.), *Dogs Through Time: an Archaeological Perspective,* 163–70. Brit. Archaeol. Rep. Int. Ser., 889

Clutton-Brock, J., 1982. The animal bone, in B. T. Perry, Excavations at Bramdean, Hampshire 1973 to 1977, Proc. *Hampshire Fld Club Archaeol. Soc.* 38, 57–74 and microfiche, 44–54

Cotton, J., 2001. Prehistoric and Roman Settlement in Reigate Road, Ewell: fieldwork conducted by Tom K. Walls 1945–52, *Surrey Archaeol. Collect.* 88, 1–42

Cram. L., 2000. Varieties of dog in Roman Britain, in S. J. Crockford, Dogs *Through Time: an archaeological perspective,* 171–80. Oxford, Brit. Archaeol. Rep. Int. Ser. 889

Cunliffe, B. W., 1991. *Iron Age Communities in Britain* (3rd edition). London, Routledge

Cunliffe, B., 1995. *Danebury: an Iron Age hillfort in Hampshire, vol. 6. A hillfort community in perspective.* York, CBA Res. Rep. 102

Cunliffe, B. and Poole C., 1991. *Danebury. An Iron Age hillfort in Hampshire, vol. 5: the Excavations 1979–1988: the finds.* London, CBA Res. Rep. 73

Darling, M., 1994. *Guidelines for the Archiving of Roman Pottery.* Study Group for Roman Pottery Guideline Advisory Document 1

Davies, B., Richardson, B., and Tomber, R., 1994. *A Dated Corpus of Early Roman Pottery from the City of London. Archaeology of Roman London Vol. 5.* York, CBA Res. Rep. 98

Davis, S. J. M, 2003. Animal bone, in C. Evans, Power and Island Communities: excavations at the Wardy Hill ringwork, Coveney, Ely. *East Anglian Archaeol.* 103, 122–31

Davis, S. J. M., 2008. 'Thou shalt take of the ram ... the right thigh; for it is a ram of consecration...': some zooarchaeological examples of body part preferences, in F. A'Andria, J. De Grossi Mazzorin and G. Fiorentino (eds), *Uomini, Piante E Animali Nella Dimensione Del Sacro,* 63–70. Bari, Edipuglia/Beni Archeologici – Conoscenza E Tecnologie 6

De Grossi Mazzorin, J. and Minniti, C., 2006. Dog sacrifice in the ancient world: a ritual passage? in L.M. Snyder and E.A. Moore (eds), *Dogs and People in Social, Working, Economic or Symbolic Interaction,* 62–6. Oxford, Oxbow Books

Dobney, K., Jaques, D., Barrett, J. and Johnstone, C., 2007. *Farmers, Monks and Aristocrats: the environmental archaeology of Anglo-Saxon Flixborough. Excavations at Flixborough volume 3.* Oxford, Oxbow Books

Dudd, S. N., and Evershed, R. P., 1999. Unusual triterpenoid fatty acyl ester components of archaeological birch bark tars, *Tetrahedron Letters* 40.2, 359–62

Duval, A., 1982. Note sur une pointe de lance provenant de Rebouseaux (Yonne), in P.-M. Duval and V. Kruta (eds), *L'Art celtique de la période de l'expansion IVe et IIIe siècles avant notre ère, Actes du colloque au Collège de France à Paris 1978, du 26 au 28 septembre 1978*, 137–47. Paris and Geneva: Libraire Droz

Egging Dinwiddy, K., 2011. Unburnt bone, in K. Egging Dinwiddy and P. Bradley, *Prehistoric Activity and a Romano-British Settlement at Poundbury Farm, Dorchester, Dorset*, 110–32. Salisbury, Wessex Archaeology Rep. 28

English, J., 2005. Two examples of Roman pottery repair in antiquity, *Surrey Archaeol. Collect.* 92, 263–5

Evans, C., 2006. Ritual structures, in Evans and Hodder 2006, 246–8

Evans, C., and Hodder, I. (eds), 2006. *Marshland Communities and Cultural Landscapes: the Haddenham Project Volume 2.* Cambridge, MacDonald Institute for Archaeology

Evans, J., 2007. Styles of pottery deposition at a Roman rural site in Hampshire, in R. Hingley and S. Willis (eds), *Roman Finds: context and theory*, 176–85. Oxford, Oxbow Books

Fell, C., 1998. Iron Age ferrous hammerheads from Britain, *Oxford J. Archaeol.* 17, 207–25

Fox, C., 1958. *Pattern and Purpose: a survey of Early Celtic Art in Britain.* Cardiff, National Museum of Wales

Framework Archaeology, 2010. *Landscape Evolution in the Middle Thames Valley: Heathrow Terminal 5 excavations.* Oxford/Salisbury: Framework Archaeology Monogr. 3

Freeman, S., Bishop, P., Bryant, C., Cook, G., Dougans, D., Ertunc, T., Fallick, A., Ganeshram, R., Maden, C., Naysmith, P., Schnabel, C., Scott, M., Summerfield, M. and Xu, S., 2007. The SUERC AMS laboratory after 3 years, *Nuclear Methods & Instruments in Physics B*, 259, 66–70

Fulford, M., 2001. Links with the past: pervasive 'ritual' behaviour in Roman Britain, *Britannia* 32, 199–218

Fulford, M., 2010. *Solent Thames Research Framework Resource Assessment: the Roman period.* http://thehumanjourney.net/pdf_store/sthames/phase3/Resource%20Assessments/Roman%20Resource%20Asessment.pdf

Fulford, M. G. and Timby, J., 2001. Timing devices, fermentation vessels, 'ritual' piercings? A consideration of deliberately 'holed' pots from Silchester and elsewhere, *Britannia* 32, 293–7

Fuller, D. and Stevens, C. J., 2009. Agriculture and the development of complex societies: an archaeobotanical agenda, in A. Fairbairn and E. Weiss (eds), *From Foragers to Farmer: papers in honour of Gordon Hillman*, 36–57. Oxford, Oxbow Books

Gale, R. and Cutler, D., 2000. *Plants in Archaeology.* London, Westbury and Royal Botanic Gardens Kew

Garrow, D., 2006. *Pits, Settlements and Deposition During the Neolithic and Early Bronze Age in East Anglia.* Oxford, Brit. Archaeol. Rep. 414

GLAAS (Greater London Archaeology Advisory Service), 2002. First Roman building discovered in Carshalton, *GLAAS Quarterly Review* March to May 2002

Grant, A., 1984. Animal husbandry, in B. Cunliffe (ed.), *Danebury: an Iron Age hillfort in Hampshire, vol. 2, the excavations, 1969–78: the finds*, 496–547. London, Coun. Brit. Archaeol. Res. Rep. 52

Green, C., 1980. Handmade pottery and society in late Iron Age and Roman East Sussex, *Sussex Archaeol. Collect.* 118, 69–86

Green, M. J., 1976. *A Corpus of Religious Material from the Civilian Areas of Roman Britain.* Oxford, Brit. Archaeol. Rep. 24

Green, M. J., 1984. *The Wheel as a Cult Symbol in the Romano-Celtic World.* Brussels, Latomus

Green, M. J., 1992. *Dictionary of Celtic Myth and Legend.* London, Thames & Hudson

Green, M. J., 2002. *Animals in Celtic Life and Myth* (2nd edition). London, Routledge

Greenwood, P., 1997. Iron Age London: some thoughts on Current Knowledge and Problems 20 years on, *London Archaeologist* 8(6), 153–61

Groves, J. and Lovell, J., 2002. Excavations within and close to the Late Bronze Age enclosure at the former Queen Mary's Hospital, Carshalton, *London Archaeologist* 10(1), 13–19

Guillaumet, J.-P., 1983. Le matériel du tumulus de Celles (Cantal), in J. Collis, A. Duval and R. *Pèrichon (eds), La deuxième âge du fer en Auvergne et en Forez et ses relations avec les regions voisines*, 189–211. Sheffield and St Etienne, University of Sheffield and Centre d'Etudes Foréziennes

Halstead, P., 1985. A study of mandibular teeth from Romano-British contexts at Maxey, in F. Pryor and C. French, *Archaeology and Environment in the Lower Welland Valley Vol. 1*, 219–24. East Anglian Archaeol. Rep. 27

Hambleton, E., 1999. *Animal Husbandry Regimes in Iron Age Britain: a comparative study of faunal assemblages from British archaeological sites.* Oxford, Brit. Archaeol. Rep. 282

Hambleton, E., 2006. Animal bone, 44–7 in J. Lovell, Excavation of a Romano-British farmstead at RNAS Yeovilton, *Proc. Somerset Archaeol. Nat. Hist. Soc.* 149, 7–70

Hambleton, E. and Maltby, M., 2008. Faunal remains, in C. Ellis and A. B. Powell, *An Iron Age Settlement Outside Battlesbury Hillfort, Warminster, and Sites along the Southern Range Road,* 84–93. Salisbury, Wessex Archaeology Rep. 22

Harcourt, R. A., 1974. The dog in prehistoric and early historic Britain, *J. Archaeol. Sci.* 1, 151–75

Harcourt, R. A., 1979. The animal bones, in G. J. Wainwright (ed.), *Gussage All Saints: an Iron Age settlement in Dorset,* 150–60. London, DoE Archaeol. Rep. 10

Harding, D. W., 1974. *The Iron Age in Lowland Britain.* London, Routledge & Kegan Paul

Hastings, F. A., 1965. Excavation of an Iron Age farmstead at Hawk's Hill, Leatherhead, *Surrey Archaeol. Collect.* 62, 1–43

Higbee, L., 2008. The vertebrate remains, 47–53 in D.E.Y. Young, Iron Age, medieval and recent activity at Whitegate Farm, Bleadon, North Somerset, *Proc. Somerset Archaeol. Nat. Hist. Soc.* 151, 31–81

Higbee, L., 2011. Animal bone, 70–9 in A. B. Powell, *An Iron Age Enclosure and Romano-British Features at High Post, near Salisbury.* Salisbury, Wessex Archaeology

Higbee, L., forthcoming. Animal bone, in M. Alexander, *Recreation Way, Mildenhall, Suffolk.* East Anglian Archaeol.

Hill, J. D., 1995. *Ritual and Rubbish in the Iron Age of Wessex: a study on the formation of a particular archaeological record.* Oxford, Brit. Archaeol. Rep. 242

Hillman, G. C., 1981. Reconstructing crop husbandry practices from charred remains of crops, in R. J. Mercer (ed.), *Farming Practice in British Prehistory,* 123–62. Edinburgh, University Press

Hinton, P., 2001. Charred plant remains, in P. Andrews, Excavations of a multi-period settlement site at the former St John's Vicarage, Old Malden, Kingston upon Thames, *Surrey Archaeol. Collect.* 88, 161–224

Howell, I., 2005. *Prehistoric Landscape to Roman Villa: excavations at Beddington, Surrey, 1981–7.* London, MoLAS

Hull, M. R. and Hawkes, C. F. C., 1987. *Corpus of Ancient Brooches in Britain: pre-Roman bow brooches.* Oxford, Brit. Archaeol. Rep. 168

Jackson, R., 2007. The surgical instruments, in P. Crummy, S. Benfield, N. Crummy, V. Rigby and D. Shimmin, *Stanway: an élite burial site at Camulodunum,* 236–52. London, Britannia Monogr. 24

Jay, M., Haselgrove, C., Hamilton, D., Hill, J. D. and Dent, J., 2012. Chariots and context: new radiocarbon dates and chronology of Iron Age burials and brooches in East Yorkshire, *Oxford J. Archaeol.* 31, 161–89

Jenkins, F., 1957. The role of the dog in Roman-British religion, *Latomas* 16, 60–76

Jewell, P. A., Milner, C. and Morton Boyd, J., 1974. *Island Survivers: the ecology of the Soay sheep of St Kilda.* London. Athlone Press

Johnstone, C. J., 2004. *A Biometric Study of Equids in the Roman World.* University of York, unpubl. PhD thesis

Johnstone, C.J., 2006. Those elusive mules: investigating osteometric methods for their identification, in M. Mashkour (ed.), *Equids in Time and Space: papers in honour of Véra Eisenmann,* 183–91. Oxford, Oxbow Books

Johnstone, C. J., 2008. Commodities or logistics? The role of equids in Roman supply networks, in S. Stallibrass and R. Thomas (eds), *Feeding the Roman Army: the archaeology of production and supply in NW Europe,* 128–45. Oxford, Oxbow Books

Johnstone, C. J., 2010. Donkeys and mules, in T. O'Connor and N. Sykes (eds), *Extinctions and Invasions: a social history of British fauna,* 17–25. Oxford, Windgather Press

Jones, G. G., 2006. Tooth eruption and wear observations in live sheep from Butser Hill, the Cotswold Farm Park and five farms in the Pentland Hills, UK, in D. Ruscillo (ed.), *Recent Advances in Ageing and Sexing Animal Bones,* 155–78. Oxford, Oxbow Books

Jones, G. P., 2009. Later Prehistoric and Roman pottery from the route of the Weatherlees–Margate–Broadstairs wastewater pipeline, on-line specialist report associated with P. Andrews, K. Egging Dinwiddy, C. Ellis, A. Hutcheson, C. *Philpotts, A.B. Powell and J. Schuster, Kentish Sites and Sites of Kent: a miscellany of four archaeological excavations.* Salisbury, Wessex Archaeology Rep. 24. http://www.wessexarch.co.uk/projects/kent/margate

Jones, G. P., 2011. Metalwork, in A. B. Powell, *An Iron Age Enclosure and Romano-British Features at High Post, near Salisbury,* 35–43. Salisbury, Wessex Archaeology

Jones, M. U. and Bond, D., 1980. Later Bronze Age settlement at Mucking, Essex, in J. C. Barrett and R. Bradley (eds) *Settlement and Society in the British Later Bronze Age,* 471–82. Oxford, Brit. Archaeol. Rep. 83

Jones, P., with Poulton, R., 2010. *The Roman and Medieval Town of Staines.* SpoilHeap Publications Monogr. 3

Jones, P., 2012. The pottery, in G. Hayman with R. Poulton, Archaeological excavation of Bronze Age, Iron Age and Roman field systems, enclosures and settlements at Thorpe Lea

Nurseries, Egham, Surrey, in G. Hayman, P. Jones and R. Poulton, *Settlement Sites and Sacred Offerings; prehistoric and later archaeology in the Thames valley, near Chertsey,* 117–57. SpoilHeap Publications Monogr. 4,

Jope, M. E., 2000. *Early Celtic Art in the British Isles.* Oxford, Clarendon

Kamash, Z., Gosden, C. and Lock, G., 2010. Continuity and religious practices in Roman Britain: the case of the rural religious complex at Marcham/Frilford, Oxfordshire, *Britannia* 41, 95–125

Keepax, C., 1977. *Identification of Avian Egg Shell from Archaeological Sites and the Potential Use of the Scanning Electron Microscope (SEM).* English Heritage, Ancient Monuments Laboratory Rep. 2415

Keepax, C., 1981. Avian egg-shell from archaeological sites, *J. Archaeol. Sci.*, 8, 315–35

Killock, D., 2012. An Iron Age and early Romano-British farmstead at the War Memorial Hospital, Carshalton, *London Archaeologist* 14(4), 102–8

King, A. C., 1988. A comment on the animal bones, 154–5 in T.W. Potter and S.D. Trow, *Puckeridge-Braughing, Hertfordshire: the Ermine Street excavations 1971–72. The Late Iron Age and Roman settlement.* St. Albans, Hertfordshire Archaeol. 10

King, A., 2005. Animal remains from temples in Roman Britain, *Britannia* 36, 329–69

King, A. and Soffe, G., 1998. Internal organisation and deposition at the Iron Age temple on Hayling Island, *Proc. Hampshire Fld Club Archaeol. Soc.* 53, 35–47

King, J., 1996. The animal bones, in D. F. Mackreth, *Orton Hall Farm: a Roman and Early Anglo-Saxon farmstead,* 216–18. East Anglian Archaeol. Rep. 76

Künzl, E., 1991. The tomb of the warrior and surgeon of München-Obermenzing and other archaeological evidence of Celtic medicine, in S. Moscate, O.-H. Frey, Kruta, V. Raftery, B. and Szabó, V. (eds), *The Celts,* 372–3. London, Thames & Hudson

Lambrick, G., 1985. Stanton Harcourt: Gravelly Guy, *South Midlands Archaeol.* 15, 107–10

Landry, C. and Blaizot, F., 2011. Une sépulture de guerrier celte à Chens-sur-Léman (Haute-Savoie), *Revue Archéologique de l'Est* 60, 147–71

Lawrence, S. and Smith, A., 2009. *Between Villa and Town: excavations of a Roman roadside settlement and shrine at Higham Ferrers, Northamptonshire.* Oxford Archaeology Monogr. 7

Leach, P., 1993. The pottery, in A. Woodward and P. Leach, *The Uley Shrines: excavation of a ritual complex on West Hill, Uley, Gloucestershire,* 1977–9, 219–49. London, English Heritage Archaeol. Rep. 17

Legge, A. J. and Dorrington, E., 1985. Harlow Temple: the animal bones, in F. R. Clark and I. K. Jones (eds), *The Romano-British Temple at Harlow, Essex,* 122–33. Gloucester, Alan Sutton

Leivers, M. with Every, R. and Mepham, L., 2010. Prehistoric pottery, specialist report in J. Lewis, M. Leivers, L. Brown, A. Smith, K. Cramp, L. Mepham and C. Phillpotts, *Landscape Evolution in the Middle Thames Valley: Heathrow Terminal 5 excavations, Volume 2,* Oxford/Salisbury: Framework Archaeology Monogr. 3 (CD-Rom)

Lejars, T., 2003. Les fourreaux d'épée laténiens. Supports et ornementations, in D. Vitaelli (ed.), *L'immagine tra mondo celtico e monde etrusco-italico. Aspetti della cultura figurativa nell'antichità,* 9–70. Bologna, Gedit

Leney, L. and Casteel, R. W., 1975. Simplified procedure for examining charcoal specimens for identification, *J. Archaeol. Sci.* 2, 153–9

Levitan, B., 1993. Vertebrate remains, in A. Woodward and P. Leach, *The Uley Shrines: excavation of a ritual complex on West Hill, Uley, Gloucestershire: 1977–9,* 257–301. English Heritage Archaeol. Rep. 17

Lewis M. E. and Roberts, C., 1997. Growing pains: the interpretation of stress indicators, *Int. J. Osteoarchaeol.* 7, 581–6

Lowther, A. W. G., 1935. An early Iron Age oven at St Martha's Hill, near Guildford, *Surrey Archaeol. Collect.* 43, 113–5

Lowther, A. W. G., 1944–5. Report on excavations on the site of the Early Iron Age camp in the grounds of Queen Mary's Hospital, Carshalton, Surrey, *Surrey Archaeol. Collect.* 49, 56–74

Luff, R. M., 1982. *A Zooarchaeological Study of the Roman North-Western Provinces.* Oxford, Brit. Archaeol. Rep. Int. Ser. 137

Lyne, M. A. B., and Jefferies, R. S., 1979. *The Alice Holt/Farnham Roman Pottery Industry.* London, CBA Res. Rep. 30

MacGregor, A., 1985. *Bone, Antler, Ivory and Horn: the technology of skeletal materials since the Roman period.* London, Croom Helm

Mackreth, D. F., 2011. *Brooches in Late Iron Age and Roman Britain.* Oxford, Oxbow Books

Macpherson-Grant, N., 2002. The Pottery, 75–85 in J. Proctor, Late Bronze Age/Early Iron Age placed deposits from Westcroft Road, Carshalton: their meaning and interpretation, *Surrey Archaeol. Collect.* 89, 65–103

Maltby, J. M., 1985. Assessing variations in Iron Age and Roman butchery practices: the need for quantification, in N. J. R. Fieller, D. D. Gilbertson and N. G. A. Ralph, *Palaeolbiological Investigations: research design, methods and data analysis*, 19–32. Oxford, Brit. Archaeol. Rep. Int. Ser. 266

Maltby, M., 1996. The exploitation of animals in the Iron Age: the archaeo-zoological evidence, in T. C. Champion and J. R. Collis (eds), *The Iron Age in Britain: recent trends*, 17–27. Sheffield, J. R. Collis Publications

Manning, W. H., 1985. *Catalogue of the Romano-British Iron Tools, Fittings and Weapons in the British Museum*. London, British Museum

Marsh, G., 1978. Early second century fine wares in the London area, in P. Arthur and G. Marsh (eds), *Early Fine Wares in Roman Britain*, 119–223. Oxford, Brit. Archaeol. Rep. 57

Marsh, G., and Tyers, P. A., 1978. The Roman pottery from Southwark, in J. Bird, A. H. Graham, H. Sheldon and P. Townend (eds), *Southwark Excavations 1972–74* (2 vols). London, London Middlesex Archaeol. Soc./Surrey Archaeol. Soc. Joint Publication No. 1, 533–82

Marter Brown, K., and Seager Smith, R. 2012. What did the apocrypha know? Glued pottery vessels from Springhead and other Romano-British sites in south and eastern England, in B. Jervis and A. Kyle, *Make-do and Mend: archaeologies of compromise, repair and reuse*, 5–11. Oxford, Brit. Archaeol. Rep. Int. Ser. 2408

Martin-Kilcher, S., 1983 Les amphores romaines a huile de Betique (Dressel 20 et 23) d'Augst (Colonia Augusta Rauricorum) et Kaiseraugst (Castrum Raurucense). Un Rapport preliminiaire, in J. M. Blazquez and J. Remesal (eds), *Prod. Y Com. Del Aceite en la Antiguedad*. II Congresso, Madrid, 337–47

Mazzorin, J. and Tagliacozza, A., 2000. Morpholoical and osteological changes in the dog from the Neolithic to the Roman period in Italy, 141–61 in S. J. Crockford (ed.), *Dogs Through Time: an archaeological perspective*. Brit. Archaeol. Rep. Int. Ser., 889

McKinley, J. I., 2004a. Welcome to Pontibus ... gateway to the west, *Surrey Archaeol. Collect.* 91, 1–70

McKinley, J. I., 2004b. Compiling a skeletal inventory: disarticulated and co-mingled remains, in M. Brickley and J. I. McKinley (eds), *Guidelines to the Standards for Recording Human Remains*, 13–16. Southampton and Reading, British Association for Biological Anthropology and Osteoarchaeology and Institute for Field Archaeology

McKinley, J. I., 2009. Human bone, in K. Egging Dinwiddy, *A Late Roman Cemetery at Little Keep, Dorchester, Dorset*, 11–35. Wessex Archaeology online publication: http://www.wessexarch.co.uk/reports/64913/little-keep-dorchester

Mepham, L., 2002. Finds, in Groves and Lovell 2002, 17–18

Merrifield, R., 1987. *The Archaeology of Ritual and Magic*. New York, New Amsterdam

MoLAS (Museum of London Archaeology Service), 1995. *The Former Queen Mary's Hospital Site, Carshalton, London Borough of Sutton: Stage One archaeological evaluation*. London, unpubl. MoLAS report QMA 95

Monaghan, J., 1987 *Upchurch and Thameside Roman Pottery; a ceramic typology for north Kent, first to third centuries AD*, Brit. Archaeol. Rep. Brit. Ser.173

Mook, W. G., 1986. Business Meeting: recommendations/resolutions adopted by the twelfth international radiocarbon conference, *Radiocarbon* 28, 799

Morris, E. L., 1994. *The Analysis of Pottery*. Salisbury, Wessex Archaeology Guideline 4

Morris, J., 2008. *Re-examining Associated Bone Groups from Southern England and Yorkshire*, c. *4000 BC to AD 1550*. Bournemouth University, unpubl. PhD Thesis

Morris, J., 2010. Associated bone groups; beyond the Iron Age, in J. Morris and M. Maltby (eds), *Integrating Social and Environmental Archaeologies: reconsidering deposition*, 12–23. Oxford, Brit. Archaeol. Rep. Int. Ser. 2077

Morris, J., 2011. *Investigating Animal Burials: ritual, mundane and beyond*. Oxford, Brit. Archaeol. Rep. Brit. Ser. 535

Navarro, J.-M., de, 1955. A Doctor's grave of the Middle La Tène period from Bavaria, *Proc. Prehist. Soc.* 21, 231–48

Needham, S. P. and Burgess, C., 1980. The Later Bronze Age in the Lower Thames Valley: the metalwork evidence, in J. C. Barrett and R. Bradley 1980 (eds), *Settlement and Society in the British Later Bronze Age*, 437–69. Oxford, Brit. Archaeol. Rep. 83

Neugebauer, J., 1992. *Die Kelten im osten Österreichs*, St Pölten-Vienna, Wissenschaftlicher Schriftenreihe Niederösterriech 92/93/94

Nibblett, R., 1999. *The Excavation of a Ceremonial Site at Folly Lane, Verulamium*. London, Britannia Monogr. 14

Nicolaysen, P., 1994. The animal remains, 161–4 in M. G. O'Connell and J. Bird, The Roman temple at Wanborough, excavations 1985–1986, *Surrey Archaeol. Collect.* 82, 1–168

Nicolaysen, P., 2001. Animal bone, in Cotton 2001, 24–5

Payne, S., 1973. Kill-off patterns in sheep and goats: the mandibles from Asvan Kale, *Anatolian Stud.* 23, 281–303

Peters, J., 1998. *Römische Tierhaltung und Tierzucht: eine Synthese aus archäozoologischer Untersuchung und schriftlich-bildlicher Überlieferung*. Passauer Universitätsschriften zu Archäologie Band 5. Rahden/Westfalen, Verlag Marie Leidorf

Philp, B., 1984. The Iron Age farmstead on Farningham Hill, in B. Philp, *Excavations in the Darent Valley, Kent,* 7–71. Dover, Kent Monogr. Ser. 4

Philp, B., Parfitt, K., Willson, J., Dutti, M. and Williams, W., 1991. *The Roman Villa Site at Keston, Kent: first report (excavations 1968–1978).* Dover Castle, Res. Rep. Kent Monogr. 6

Philpott, R., 1991. *Burial Practices in Roman Britain.* Oxford, Brit. Archaeol. Rep. 219

Piggott, S., 1962. Heads and hoofs, *Antiquity,* 36, 110–18

Piper, P. J. and O'Connor, T. P., 2001. Urban small vertebrate taphonomy: a case study from Anglo-Scandinavian York, *Int. J. Osteoarchaeol.* 11(5), 336–44

Pollard, R. J., 1988. *The Roman Pottery of Kent.* Maidstone, Kent Archaeol. Soc. Monogr. 5

Poole, C., 1984. The structural use of daub, clay and timber, in B. Cunliffe, *Danebury: an Iron Age Hillfort in Hampshire, vol. 1: the excavations 1969–1978: the site,* 110–23. London, CBA Res. Rep. 52

Poole, C., 1995. Loomweights versus oven bricks, in B. Cunliffe, *Danebury: an Iron Age hillfort in Hampshire, vol. 6,* 285–6. London, CBA Res. Rep. 102

Poulton, R., 2004. Iron Age Surrey, in Cotton, J., Crocker, G. and Graham, A. (eds), *Aspects of Archaeology and History in Surrey: towards a research framework for the county,* 51–64. Guildford, Surrey Archaeological Society

Powell, A. B., 2012. *By River, Fields and Factories: the making of the Lower Lea Valley. Archaeological and cultural heritage investigations on the site of the London 2012 Olympic and Paralympic Games.* Salisbury, Wessex Archaeology/Olympic Delivery Authority, Wessex Archaeology Rep 29

Powell, A. B., 2015. A Romano-British settlement with ovens and field system at Theobalds Road, Wivelsfield, East Sussex, *Sussex Archaeol. Collect.* 153, 47–61

Powell, A. B., Barclay, A. J., Mepham, L. and Stevens, C. J., 2015. *Imperial College Sports Ground and RMC Land, Harlington: the development of prehistoric and later communities in the Colne Valley and on the Heathrow Terraces.* Salisbury, Wessex Archaeology Report 33

Prehistoric Pottery Research Group (PCRG), 2010. *The Study of Prehistoric Pottery: general policies and guidelines for analysis and publication* (3rd edition). Prehistoric Pottery Research Group Occas. Pap. 1 and 2

Proctor, J., 2002. Late Bronze Age/Early Iron Age placed deposits from Westcroft Road, Carshalton: the meaning and interpretation, *Surrey Archaeol. Collect.* 89, 65–103

Regert, M., Vacher, S., Moulherat, C., and Decavallas, O., 2003. Adhesive production and pottery function during the Iron Age at the site of Grand Aunay (Sarthe, France), *Archaeometry* 45, 101–20

Reimer, P. J., Baillie, M. G. L., Bard, E., Bayliss, A., Beck, J. W., Bertrand, C., Blackwell, P. G., Buck, C. E., Burr, G., Cutler, K. B., Damon, P. E., Edwards, R. L., Fairbanks, R. G., Friedrich, M., Guilderson, T. P., Hughen, K. A., Kromer, B., McCormac, F. G., Manning, S., Bronk Ramsey, C., Reimer, R. W., Remmele, S., Southon, J. R., Stuiver, M., Talamo, S., Taylor, F. W., van der Plicht, J., and Weyhenmeyer, C. E., 2004. IntCal04 Terrestrial radiocarbon age calibration, 0–26 Cal Kyr BP, *Radiocarbon* 46,1029–58

Reimer, P. J., Bard, E., Bayliss, A., Beck, J. W., Blackwell, P. G., Bronk Ramsey, C., Buck, C. E, Cheng, H., Edwqards, L., Friedrich, Grootes, P M., Guilderson, T. P., Haflidason, H., Hajdas, I., Hatté, H., Heaton, T. J., Hoffmann, D. L., Hogg, A. G., Hughen, K. A., Kaiser, K. F., Kromer, B., Manning, S. W., Nui, M., Reimer, R. W., Richards, D. A., Scott, E. M., Southon, J. R., Staff, R. A., Turney, C. S. M., and van der Plicht, J., 2013. IntCal13 and Marine 13 Calibration Curves, 0–50,000 Years BP, *Radiocarbon,* 55 (4), 1869–1887

Robarts, N. F., 1905. Notes on a recently discovered British camp near Wallington, *J. Roy. Anthrop. Inst.,* new ser 8, 387–97

Robarts, N. F., 1909. Recent discoveries at Wallington, *Surrey Archaeol. J.* 22, 195–6

Robarts, N. F., 1910. The British town of Wallington in the first century BC, *Proc. Croydon Natur. Hist. Soc.* 6 (1905–6), 143–52

Ross, A., 1968. Shafts, pits, wells – sanctuaries of the Belgic Britons?, in J. M. Coles and D. D. A. Simpson (eds), *Studies in Ancient Europe,* 255–85. Leicester, University Press

Scaife, R., 2002a. Charred plant remains, in Groves and Lovell 2002, 18

Scaife, R., 2002b. The charred plant remains, 93–4 in J. Procter, Late Bronze Age/Early Iron Age placed deposits from Westcroft Road, Charlshalton: their meaning and interpretation, *Surrey Archaeol. Collect.* 89, 65–103

Scheuer, L. and Black, S., 2000. *Developmental Juvenile Osteology.* London, Academic Press

Schweingruber, F. H., 1990. *Microscopic Wood Anatomy* (3rd edition). Birmensdorf, Swiss

Federal Institute for Forest, Snow and Landscape Research

Scott, E., 1999. *The Archaeology of Infancy and Infant Death.* Oxford, Brit. Archaeol. Rep. Int. Ser. 819

Seager Smith, R., 2015. Later prehistoric and Romano-British pottery, in P. Andrews, P. Booth, A. P. Fitzpatrick and K. Welsh, *Digging at the Gateway: archaeological landscapes of South Thanet. The archaeology of the East Kent Access (Phase II), Volume 2, Finds, Environmental and Dating Reports.* Oxford, Oxford Wessex Archaeology Monogr. 8

Seager-Smith, R., Marter Brown, K. and Mills, J. M., 2011. The pottery from Springhead, in P. Andrews, E. Biddulph and A. Hardy, *Settling the Ebbsfleet Valley: CTRL excavations at Springhead and Northfleet, Kent – the late Iron Age, Roman, Saxon and medieval landscape, Volume 2, Late Iron Age–Roman Finds Reports,* 124–5. Oxford/ Salisbury, Oxford Wessex Archaeology

Sealey, P. R., 1999. Finds from the Cauldron Pit, in N.R. Brown, *The Archaeology of Ardleigh, Essex: excavations 1955–1980,* 117–24. East Anglian Archaeology Rep. 90

Sellwood, L., 1984. Objects of iron, in B. Cunliffe, *Danebury. An Iron Age hillfort in Hampshire, vol. 2: the excavations 1969–1978: the finds,* 346–71 & M9: B9–F14. London, CBA Res. Rep. 52

Serjeantson, D., 1991. The bird bones, in B. Cunliffe *and C. Poole (eds), Danebury: an Iron Age Hillfort in Hampshire, vol. 5: the excavations 1979–1988: the finds,* 479–481. London, CBA Res. Rep. 71

Serjeantson, D., 2006a. Animal remains, in C. Evans and I. Hodder (eds.), *Marshland Communities and Cultural Landscapes: The Haddenham Project Volume 2,* 213–48. Cambridge, McDonald Institute Monogr./English Heritage

Serjeantson, D., 2006b. Food or feast at Neolithic Runnymede? in D. Serjeantson and D. Field (eds), *Animals in the Neolithic of Britain and Europe,* 113–34. Oxford, Oxbow Books/Neolithic Studies Group Seminar Papers 7

Serjeantson, D., 2009. *Birds.* Cambridge, University Press

Serjeantson, D. 2011. *Review of Animal Remains from the Neolithic and Early Bronze Age of Southern Britain (4000 BC – 1500 BC).* Portsmouth, English Heritage Res. Dept. Rep. Ser. 29/2011

Serjeantson, D. and Morris, J., 2011. Ravens and crows in Iron Age and Roman Britain, *Oxford J. Archaeol.* 30(1), 85–107

Sidell, J., 1993. A methodology from the identification of avian eggshell from archaeological sites. *Archaeofauna. Archae-ornithology: birds and the archaeological record* 2, 45–51

Stace, C., 1997. *New Flora of the British Isles* (2nd edition). Cambridge, University Press

Stacey, R., 2004. Evidence for the use of birch bark tar from Iron Age Britain, *PAST* 47, 1–2

Stallibrass, S., 1982. Faunal remains, in T. W. Potter and C. F. Potter, *Romano-British Village at Grandford, March, Cambridgeshire,* 98–122. London, Brit. Mus. Occas. Pap. 35

Stead, I. M., 1979. *The Arras Culture.* York, Yorkshire Philosophical Society

Stead, I. M., 1991. *Iron Age Cemeteries in East Yorkshire: excavations at Burton Fleming, Rudston, Garton-on-the-Wold, and Kirkburn, London,* English Heritage Archaeological report 22.

Stead, I. M., 2006. *British Iron Age Swords and Scabbards.* London, British Museum

Stead, I. M., and Rigby, V., 1986. *Baldock: the excavation of a Roman and pre-Roman settlement, 1968–72.* London, Britannia Monogr. 7

Stenhouse, M. J. and Baxter, M. S., 1983. ^{14}C dating reproducibility: evidence from routine dating of archaeological samples, *PACT* 8, 147–61

Stevens, C. J., 2003. An investigation of agricultural consumption and production models for prehistoric and Roman Britain, *Environmental Archaeol.* 8, 61–76

Stevens, C. J., 2006. Charred plant remains, in M. G. Fulford, A. B. Powell, R. Entwistle and F. Raymond, *Iron Age and Romano-British Settlements and Landscapes of Salisbury Plain,* 152–8. Salisbury, Wessex Archaeology and University of Reading, Wessex Archaeology Rep. 20

Stevens, C. J., 2015. Charred and waterlogged plant remains, in Powell *et al.* 2015, 241–69

Stuiver, M. and Kra, R. S., 1986. Editorial comment, *Radiocarbon* 28(2B), ii

Stuiver, M. and Polach, H. A., 1977. Reporting of ^{14}C data, *Radiocarbon* 19, 355–63

Stuiver, M. and Reimer, P. J., 1986. A computer program for radiocarbon age calculation, *Radiocarbon* 28, 1022–30

Stuiver, M. and Reimer, P. J., 1993. Extended ^{14}C data base and revised CALIB 3.0 ^{14}C age calibration program, *Radiocarbon* 35, 215–30

Swan, V., 1984. *The Pottery Kilns of Roman Britain.* London, Roy. Comm. Hist. Monuments Engl. Suppl. Ser. 5

Thompson, I., 1982. *Grog-tempered 'Belgic' Pottery of South-eastern England.* Oxford, Brit. Archaeol. Rep. 108 (3 volumes)

Tomber, R., and Dore, J. 1998 *The National Roman Fabric Reference Collection: a Handbook,* MoLAS monograph 2, London

Toynbee, J. M. C., 1962. *Art in Britain under the Romans.* London, Phaidon Press

Toynbee, J. M. C., 1996. *Animals in Roman Life and Art*. Baltimore and London, John Hopkins University Press

Tucker, S., 1988. *Queen Mary's Hospital: an archaeological assessment*. London, unpubl. MoLAS archive report

Vandeputte, K., Moens, L. and Dams, R., 1996. Improved sealed-tube combustion of organic samples to CO_2 for stable isotope analysis, radiocarbon dating and percent carbon determinations, *Analytical Letters* 29, 2761–73

Van der Werff, J. H., 2003 The third and second lives of amphoras in Alphen aan den Rijn, The Netherlands, *J. Roman Pottery Stud.* 10, 109–16

Wait, G. A., 1985. *Ritual and Religion in Iron Age Britain*. Oxford, Brit. Archaeol. Rep. 149

Wait, G. and Cotton, J., 2000. The Iron Age, in Museum of London Archaeological Service, *The Archaeology of Greater London; an assessment of archaeological evidence for human presence in the area now covered by Greater London*, 101–17. London, Museum of London Archaeological Service

Ward-Perkins, J. B., 1939. Excavations on Oldbury Hill, Ightham, *Archaeol. Cantiana* 51, 137–81

Wessex Archaeology, 2008. *Former Queen Mary's Hospital, Carshalton, London: archaeological evaluation report*. Salisbury, unpubl. WA rep. 66940.03

Wessex Archaeology, 2009. *Orchard Hill, Carshalton, London Borough of Sutton: post-excavation assessment report*. Salisbury, unpubl. WA rep. 69944.01

Wessex Archaeology, 2011. *Orchard Hill, Carshalton, London Borough of Sutton, Greater London: post-excavation assessment report*. Salisbury, unpubl. WA rep. 69943.01

Wessex Archaeology, 2014. *Land at Cheesemans Green, Ashford, Kent; post-excavation assessment and updated project design*. Salisbury, unpubl. WA rep. 77711.03

Wicks, K. and Shillito, L-M., 2009. *Analysis of Residues on Romano-British Pottery by Fourier Transform Infrared Spectroscopy and Gas Chromatography Mass Spectrometry*. Archaeological, Forensic and Scientific Services, University of Reading, unpubl. rep. 38/07

Wild, J. P., 2002. The textile industries of Roman Britain, *Britannia* 33, 1–42

Wilkinson, K. and Stevens, C. J., 2003. Environmental Archaeology: approaches, techniques and applications. Stroud, Tempus

Williams, H. M. R., 1998. The ancient monument in Romano-British ritual practices, in C. Forcey, J. Hawthorne and R. Witcher (eds), *TRAC 97: Proceedings of the 7th Annual Theoretical Roman Archaeology Conference, Nottingham 1997*, 71–86. Oxford, Oxbow Books

Wilson, B., 1996. *Spatial Patterning among Animal Bones in Settlement Archaeology: an English regional exploration*. Oxford, Brit. Archaeol. Rep. 251

Wilson, B., 1999. Displayed or concealed? Cross cultural evidence for symbolic and ritual activity depositing Iron Age animal bones, *Oxford J. Archaeol.* 18(3), 297–305

Wymer, J. J. (ed.), 1977. *Gazetteer of Mesolithic Sites in England and Wales*. London, CBA Res. Rep. 20

Zohary, D. and Hopf, M., 2000. *Domestication of Plants in the Old World: the origin and spread of cultivated plants in West Asia, Europe, and the Nile Valley* (3rd edition). Oxford, Clarendon Press

Lightning Source UK Ltd.
Milton Keynes UK
UKOW07f1259220517
301732UK00007B/38/P